JOHN McC
POLICE
OFFICERS GUIDE

Copyright

All rights reserved. No part of this publication may reproduced, stored in a retrieval system, or transmitted, in any form or by any means, electronic, mechanical, photocopying, recording or otherwise, without the prior permission of the publishers.

Police Officers Guide

John McGrath

Copyright 2018 by John McGrath

ISBN-13: 978-1522739364

ISBN-10: 152273936X

CONTENTS

FOREWORD 4
UK LAW ENFORCEMENT AND ITS HISTORY 6
BECOMING A POLICE OFFICER 27
TRAINING 67
ON DUTY 80
LAW AND OFFENCES 127
ROAD TRAFFIC POLICING 188
DOMESTIC VIOLENCE 210
WITNESS STATEMENTS 221
CAREER DEVELOPMENT 230
Police Associations and Agencies 235
APPENDIX – Full List of Criminal Offences 237

FOREWORD

The past year has seen quite widespread recruitment, to make up for falling police officer numbers. This however has been followed by further saving police force have had to make, which will influence recruitment both in terms of police officers and police staff. Some forces are slowly recruiting and all forces want to increase their number of special constables. To provide support to regular colleges and offer more uniformed officers patrolling the streets or helping at events.

The number of police officers is now as low as the numbers in the 1980s. Current strength is 123,142 police officers, 23,550 less officers than in 2010. Special constables now amount to 13,503. The largest drop recently has been the special constabulary seeing a 15.6% drop in the last year. The need to investigate historic sex crimes and the rise of terrorist related investigations and incidents has seen demand rise. Violent crime is on the rise and Cyber Crime is still rising. The need for police forces to have specialist to deal with cyber security in the form of both open source investigation and digital forensics has seen more specialist training being rolled out to meet the 'digital' demand.

Many collaborative projects are underway from sharing armed response, traffic and police dogs to share IT systems with five forces all rolling out Niche RMS and integrated crime, intelligence and custody system. This could potentially lead to police forces merging in the longer term. As another potentially cost effective solution to reduced budgets.

Mobile and technology based solutions will be key to increasing productivity and enabling officers to stay more visible out on the streets. The use of body worn video cameras is increasing with more and more police forces rolling them out.

Being a Police officer is an extraordinary job, undertaken by extraordinary people. It is a job that never ends, not for Public Holidays or Christmas day. The job requires a group of people who can work around the clock and work shifts. The variety of roles is huge and is a career and a job for life for many. You may start as a Constable and end up as a Chief Constable. You may move out of uniform into CID or into one of the specialist branches such as firearms, traffic, dogs or mounted; the opportunities are wide and varied. The demands on police officers is ever increasing and special constables are expected to become more and more professional and stand shoulder to shoulder with their full time colleagues. Special constables are seen as a valuable resource that do make a real difference on the front line.

By going through some of the skills required and giving an in depth insight into what being a uniformed Police officer is all about. Be it a Special Constable or full-time regular officer. The book kicks off with the history of the police before moving on to, recruitment and training. A large section of the book is handed over to law and procedure that is known as core training, at the back of the book all offences have been listed in an appendix to act as a reference. One new introduction and one I think is quite excellent, has been derived from Israeli Special Forces as a way to gain intelligence by looking at something called 'Baseline', Baseline is what you would expect to see at a particular time in terms of the types of people and what they are doing in a specific location. For instance, if everyone in a station forecourt is travelling in one direction at speed in the early morning rush hour, what is the person doing with a bag going in the opposite way, stopping and constantly looking around. Do they deviate from the expected baseline of people making their way to work?

UK LAW ENFORCEMENT AND ITS HISTORY

Law enforcement in the United Kingdom is organised separately in each of the legal systems of the United Kingdom; England, Wales, Northern Ireland, and Scotland (administration of Police matters is not generally affected by the Government of Wales Act 2006). Geographical Police areas are arranged to match the boundaries of one or more local government areas. There are four general types of body, the first mostly concerned with policing the general public and their activities and the rest concerned with policing of other, usually localised, matters. There are 43 Police forces in England and Wales formed of 132,235 Police officers, 19,159 volunteer Special Constables and 14,400 Community Support Officers. Scotland has 17,496 Police officers and Northern Ireland has 10,330 Police officers. Recruitment for the Special Constabulary mainly due to the riots of 2011 saw a 50% increase in the number of application requests, which in real terms saw an increase of 10.4% or just over 5000 new Special Constables. However, the numbers have fallen slightly over the past year, and the retention rate is still around 40% with the average service being two years. The number of Police Officers in England and Wales is still falling to its lowest since 2002. The biggest change in 2012 for the 43 Police forces in England and Wales was the police and crime commissioners, being put in place. Police and crime commissioners will oversee how crime, it will be tackled in each force, less London where the Mayor is the PCC. Their aim will be to cut crime and to ensure the police force they oversee is effective. They will also bring more of a public voice to policing and meeting with the public they serve to help set community based policing and crime plans: Ensure the police budget is spent wisely and where it is needed the most. They also have the power to hire and fire underperforming Chief constables. The PCC is not there to run the police force, though, that will be left to the chief constable. Their power is far more wide ranging and will have influence in key decisions from street lighting to CCTV.

Territorial Police forces, who carry out the majority of policing, are the Police forces that cover a 'Police area' (a particular region) and have an independent Police Authority. The Police Act 1996, the Police (Scotland) act 1967 and the Police (Northern Ireland) act 2000, prescribe a number of issues such as the appointment of a Chief Constable, jurisdiction and responsibilities, for Police forces in England and Wales, Scotland and Northern Ireland respectively.

Special Police forces - which are national Police forces that have a specific, non-regional jurisdiction, such as the British Transport Police. The Serious Organised Crime and Police Act 2005 refers to these as 'Special Police forces'.

Non-Police law enforcement agencies, whose officers are not Police officers, but still enforce laws.

Miscellaneous forces that mostly having their foundations in older legislation or common law. These have a responsibility to Police specific local areas or activities, such as ports and parks and before the passing of recent legislation such as the Serious Organised Crime and Police Act 2005 were often referred to as 'Special Police forces,' care must therefore be taken in interpreting the historical use of that phrase. These constabularies are not within the scope of the legislation applicable to the previously-mentioned organisations, but can still be the subject of statutes applicable to e.g. docks, harbours or railways. Until the passing of Railways and Transport Safety act 2003, the British Transport Police was such a force.

In the United Kingdom, every person has limited powers of arrest if they see a crime being committed - these are called 'every person powers', commonly referred to as a 'citizen's arrest'. In England and Wales, the vast majority of attested constables enjoy full powers of arrest and search as granted by the Police and Criminal Evidence Act 1984. All Police officers are "constables" in law, irrespective of rank. Although Police officers have wide ranging powers, they are still civilians and subject to the same laws as members of the public. However, there are certain legal restrictions on Police officers such as the illegality of taking industrial action and the ban on taking part in active politics.

Territorial Police Constables

Most police officers are members of territorial police forces. Upon taking an oath for one of these forces, they have jurisdiction in one of the three distinct legal system, - England, Wales, Scotland or Northern Ireland. A police officer of one of the three legal systems has all the powers of a Constable throughout their own legal system, but limited powers in the other two legal systems. Certain exceptions where full Police powers cross the border with the officer are when officers are providing planned support to another force such as the G8

Conference in Scotland in 2005, officers of the Metropolitan Police who are on protection duties anywhere in the United Kingdom and when taking a person to or from a prison.

Special Constabulary

The Special Constabulary is the part-time volunteer section of a statutory Police force in the United Kingdom or Crown dependency. Its officers are known as Special Constables (all hold the office of Constable no matter what their rank) or informally as Specials, SC or SPC.

Every United Kingdom Territorial Police force has a Special Constabulary except the Police Service of Northern Ireland, where it is called the Reserve: however, the Royal Ulster Constabulary did have its own Ulster Special Constabulary, which was disbanded in 1970. The British Transport Police also has a Special Constabulary; in the Crown dependencies, the Isle of Man Constabulary and the States of Guernsey Police Service have Special constabularies, but the States of Jersey Police does not.

The strength of the Special Constabulary in England and Wales, as in 2015, was 16,101 with about a third of these being women and over 3% ethnic minorities. Special constables usually work for a minimum of four hours a week, although many do considerably more. Special constables might receive some expenses and allowances from the Police service, including a "recognition award" or "Bounty" of up to £1000 in Scotland. Some forces in England have this too, but the work is otherwise voluntary and unpaid.

Special constables have identical powers to their regular (full-time) colleagues and work alongside regular Police officers. Most special Constabularies in England and Wales have their own organisational structure and grading system. For example, some use section Officers as opposed to Special Sergeants and the structure does vary from force to force. Special Constabularies are headed by a Commandant or Chief Officer, who are themselves Special Constables. Within Scotland, and a number of forces in England and Wales, plus the British Transport Police, Special Constables have no separate administrative structure and no grading system.

Special constables generally wear uniforms identical to that of their full-time colleagues. In some constabularies, their shoulder. (or collar) number may be prefixed with a certain digit or they may have additional insignia on their epaulettes. This is usually a crown with the letters SC underneath it (although some forces just use the letters). Formerly, male Special Constables did not wear helmets while on foot patrol, but wore patrol caps instead, but in most forces, they now wear helmets of the same design as full-time officers. Some forces also issue Special Constables with a different hat badge from that of their regular counterparts although this is now extremely rare.

Historically, Special Constables were often seen as inferior and resented by regular officers, as they were sometimes seen as "hobby bobbies" and not proper Police officers. During the 1980's Specials were often considered to be preventing regular officers from earning overtime pay. Today, Specials and regulars have a much closer relationship (many regular officers having started their Police careers as Specials) and Specials are a supplement to any Police force. Some regulars and Specials work together as a team and of course, Specials are an important part of Neighbourhood Teams.

A sizeable proportion of regular officers have served as Special Constables before joining the regular force, and this is encouraged by recruitment departments. Allowing Special Constables to be paid for their work has been a contentious issue, with mixed comments from all sides. Some people think that as Specials are doing much the same job as regular officers they should be paid the same, but others think that this would attract the 'wrong' type of person (those motivated by monetary gain as opposed to those who are community minded).

This greater acceptance of Specials has led to them being found working in such areas as Public Order Units (PSU, or Police Support Unit) or Roads Policing, and some Specials have been response trained, which allows them to use blue lights and to pursue other vehicles.

Police Civilians

In England & Wales, the chief police officer of a territorial police force may designate any person who is employed by the Police authority maintaining that force, and is under the direction and control of that Chief Police Officer, as one or more of the following: Community Support Officer (commonly referred to as a Police Community Support Officer), Investigating Officer, Detention Officer, or Escort Officer.

They have a range of powers given by the Police Reform act 2002, and their chief police officer decides which of these powers they may use. Unlike a police constable, a police Community Support Officer (PCSO) only has powers when on duty and in uniform, and within the area policed by their respective force.

Until 1991, most parking enforcement was carried out by Police-employed Traffic Wardens. Since the passage of the Road Traffic Act 1991, decriminalised parking enforcement has meant that most local authorities have taken on this role and now only the Metropolitan Police employs Traffic Wardens, combining the role with PCSOs as, "Traffic Police Community Support Officers".

In Scotland, Police Custody and Security Officers have powers similar to those of detention officers and escort officers in England and Wales. Similar powers are available in Northern Ireland.

Accredited Persons

Chief Police officers of territorial Police forces (and the BTP) can also give limited powers to people not employed by the Police authority, under Community Safety Accreditation Schemes. A notable example is officers of the Vehicle and Operator services Agency, who have been given powers to stop vehicles. However, this practice has been criticised by the Police Federation who described it as 'half-baked'.

Members of the Armed Forces

In Northern Ireland, only, members of Her Majesty's Armed Forces have powers to stop people or vehicles, arrest and detain people for three hours and enter buildings to keep the peace or search for people who have been kidnapped. Additionally, commissioned officers may close roads. They may use reasonable force when exercising these powers. Under the Customs Management act 1979, members of Her Majesty's Armed Forces may detain people if they believe they have committed an offence under the Customs & Excise acts, and may seize goods if they believe they are liable to forfeiture under the same acts.

Other Civilians

Many employees of local authorities have powers of entry relating to inspection of businesses, such as under the Sunday Trading act 1994 and powers to give Fixed Penalty Notices for offences such as littering, graffiti or one of the wide-ranging offences in the Clean Neighbourhoods and Environment act 2005. Further, such powers may be given under local bylaws or local acts of Parliament. These are often street wardens or dog wardens.

When carrying out an investigation, staff of the Independent Police Complaints Commission has all the powers and privileges of constables throughout England and Wales and the territorial waters.

Employees of the Serious Organised Crime Agency can be designated, with the powers of a Constable, Revenue and Customs officer and immigration officer. These designations can be unconditional or conditional: time limited or limited to a specific operation.

Employees of the UK Border Agency may be Immigration Officers and/or customs officers. They hold certain powers of arrest, detention and search.

In England & Wales, water bailiffs employed by the Environment Agency have certain powers in relation to enforcement of fishing regulations. Scottish water bailiffs have similar powers. There are also seven types of court officer - two in Scotland and five in England & Wales, commonly referred to as 'bailiffs', who can enforce court orders and in some cases arrest people.

Traffic officers are employed by the Highways Agency and maintain traffic flows on trunk roads and some bridges and tunnels. There are different types of traffic officer, and they are appointed under separate acts. They have limited powers to direct traffic and place road signs.

Wildlife inspectors have certain powers of entry and inspection in relation to wildlife and licenses relating to wildlife.

Employees of public fire and rescue services have extensive powers in the event of an emergency, and more limited ones in certain other circumstances, such as investigations into fires.

Prison officers have all the powers, authority, protection and privileges of a Constable when acting as prison officers.

Other Constables

There are many constables who are not members of territorial Police forces. The most notable are members of the three forces referred to as 'Special Police forces': the British Transport Police, Ministry of Defence Police and Civil Nuclear Constabulary. These officers have the 'powers and privileges of a Constable' on land relating to their work and in matters relating to their work. BTP (British Transport Police) and MDP officers have additional jurisdiction where requested by a Constable of another force, in which case they take on that constable's jurisdiction. Upon request from the chief Police officer of a Police force, members of one of the above three forces can be give the full powers of constables in the Police area of the requesting force. This was used to supplement Police numbers in the areas surrounding the 2005 G8 summit at Gleneagles.

There are also many acts which allow companies or councils to employ constables for a specific purpose. Firstly, there are ten companies whose employees are sworn in as constables under section 79 of the Harbours, Docks, and Piers Clauses act 1847. As a result, they have the full powers of a Constable on any land owned by the harbour, dock, or port and at any place within one mile of any owned land. Secondly, there are also some forces created by specific legislation such as the Port of Tilbury Police (Port of London act 1968), Mersey Tunnels Police (County of Merseyside act 1989) and the Epping Forest Keepers (Epping Forest act 1878).

Thirdly, under Article 18 of the Ministry of Housing and Local Government Provisional Order Confirmation (Greater London Parks and Open Spaces) act 1967, London Borough Councils are allowed to swear in council officers as constables for "securing the observance of the provisions of all enactments relating to open spaces under their control or management and of bylaws and regulations made thereunder". These constables are not legally Police Constables and have no powers to enforce criminal law other than those afforded to every citizen.

History of UK Police

There have always been criminals, but we did not always have police officers. The first steps in policing in the UK, came in 1361 with the Justice of the Peace Act. In each county, three or four men were appointed to, arrest take and chastise offenders.

The industrial revolution caused a huge influx of people from the country to cities. With it came poverty, which caused a law and order crisis. Into this chaos came Henry Fielding, who formed the first paid Police force, known as The Runners.

The Bow Street Runners were a small, plain-clothed force that started in 1750. They sought help from the public by publishing descriptions of criminals. By 1805, The Runners were joined by the Bow Street Horse Patrol, who helped to clear London of highwaymen. Similar to the unofficial 'thief-takers' (men who would solve petty crime for a fee), they represented a formalisation and regularisation of existing policing methods. What made them different from the thief-takers was their formal attachment to the Bow Street magistrates' office, and that they were paid by the magistrate with funds from central government. They worked out of Fielding's office and court at No. 4 Bow Street, and did not patrol, but served writs and arrested offenders on the authority of the magistrates, travelling nationwide to apprehend criminals.

When Henry Fielding retired as 'court' or Chief magistrate in 1754 he was succeeded by his brother John Fielding, who had previously been his assistant for four years. Known as the, "Blind Beak of Bow Street", John Fielding refined the patrol into the first truly effective Police force for the capital, later adding officers mounted on horseback.

Although the force was only funded intermittently in the years that followed, it did serve as the guiding principle for the way policing was to develop over the next 80 years: Bow Street was a manifestation of the move towards increasing professionalization and state control of street life, beginning in London.

Contrary to several popular sources, the Bow Street Runners were not nicknamed, "Robin Redbreasts", this epithet being reserved for the Bow Street Horse Patrol. The Horse Patrol, organised in 1805 by Sir John Fielding's successor at Bow Street, Richard Ford, wore a distinctive scarlet waistcoat under their blue greatcoats.

Peelers and Bobbies In 1822 Sir Robert Peel entered the Cabinet as home secretary in the government of Lord Liverpool. He distinguished himself in this post through a series of penal reforms, including the reform of criminal laws and the reduction of the number of crimes that carried the death penalty. In 1829, convinced of the need for improved methods of crime prevention, Peel reorganized the Bow Street Runners into the London Metropolitan Police force, thereafter called "bobbies", after his first name.

With the Metropolitan Police Bill of 1829. He approved a force of 95 constables, 88 sergeants and 20 inspectors. By 1856, over 200 Police forces were established in England and Wales. These were the true forerunners of modern policing, as we know it.

Uniformed truncheons people hated the new Police so much that uniforms were designed to make them look like civilians. Wearing dark blue coats and a collar with their Constable's number, hence the name caller number still used today. They carried truncheons and a rattle to raise the alarm. By 1864, helmets were introduced and whistles replaced rattles.

History of the Special Constabulary

The history of the Special Constable is a long and honourable one. From time immemorial, ordinary citizens have been called upon to assist the regular forces of law and order.

Traditionally, in the days before Robert Peel introduced professional policing, the Constable of a town or village swore in fellow citizens when a situation arose that he alone could not handle, such as on market days or in times of public unrest.

While the idea of the citizens or populous policing itself dates back to Anglo-Saxon times (with English common law requiring that all citizens have the legal obligation to come to the assistance of a Police officer), it was not until 1673, when Charles II ruled that citizens could be temporarily sworn in as constables during times of public disorder. This ruling was in response to rising public disorder relating to the enforcement of religious conformity, and any citizen refusing to acknowledge the call would have been subject to fines and jail sentences. The 1673 act was enforced for centuries after, but mainly used to call up constables in the north of England.

Public disorder of that nature was renewed during the industrial revolution in the 18th and 19th centuries, which was coupled with falling living standards and starvation. In 1819, mass meetings calling for Parliamentary reform took place across England, including 60,000 demonstrators rioting in Manchester, where a Special Constable was killed. In light of these events, in 1820, an Act was passed allowing magistrates to recruit men as Special Constables.

The earliest legislation relating to Specials was the Special Constables Act of 1831. This officially gave the chief Police officer of a district the power to appoint Special Constables on a temporary basis as a result of specific occurrences. This meant that in the 1840s during the time of the protest marches and demonstrations of the political reformers known as the Chartists, many thousands of specials were enrolled.

During the First World War, the national emergency and the recall of many regular Police officers to their regiments led Chief Constables to enrol many specials. The Special Constables Act 1914 was passed, allowing the Chief Constable to appoint Specials even though "a tumult, riot or felony had not taken place". The outcome of this act was to establish Specials as a permanent feature throughout the war, as opposed to being the temporary force of earlier years. An Inspector of the regular Police was in charge of each district. The superintendent of each of the regular Police Divisions was in overall command of the Specials on the division.

In addition to foot patrols, specials also carried out a number of mounted patrols, with the officers acting as traffic police. Where possible a full uniform with peaked cap was provided and for off duty wear an enamelled lapel badge for civilian clothing was authorised. Many men also wore a badge inscribed "On War Duty". Normally these were issued to persons with reserved occupations. The badge could prevent the presentation of a white feather for cowardice by those misguided members of the public swept away in the patriotic fervour of the early war years.

After the war, decorated truncheons were presented to all Specials, bearing the name of the individual and the coat of arms of the city or borough that he had served. In the 1920s, the Specials were largely disbanded, although the value of their service was not forgotten and the provisions of the 1914 act were reinforced by the 1923 Special Constables Act. This confirmed the permanent nature of the specials and allowed for the employment of them in naval, military and air force yards and stations. It also removed some restrictions on the appointment of Specials in Scotland. Also laid down at this time were regulations regarding the reimbursement of out-of-pocket expenses. However, Specials were enrolled again a few years later during the General Strike of 1926. While civilian volunteers operated buses and the army provided escorts for food lorries and other supplies, many thousands of Specials were required to help maintain vital services. Many volunteers received no uniform, merely an armband, and after the event decorated truncheons were presented by some towns and cities to those who had served. The next great test came during the Second World War when again the call for volunteers was answered, often by men too old for the armed services, but willing to help out on the home front. They topped up police forces depleted by the return of men to the services and stretched by extra duties such as civil defence, air raid precautions and the supervision of foreign nationals - friendly or otherwise.

After the war, the specials remained as a permanent complement to police forces and have remained so until today. At present Special Constables attend a basic recruit training course at a training school. The training includes criminal law, first aid and traffic regulations. Some forces undertake mock court hearings and staged accidents to help to liven up training and boost the Specials' confidence. After training they are posted to Divisions under the guide of a tutor, and are usually required to complete a professional development portfolio. Tours of duty are normally four hours a week as a minimum and, while unpaid, allowances are available and out-of-pocket expenses are reimbursed. Their uniforms and equipment are the same as those used by the regulars. With the decrease in full-time officer numbers Special Constables are in even greater demand with most forces looking to double the number of specials they have.

Police Vehicles

In 1858, the first police vehicle was horse drawn; later secure Police vehicles were introduced. They were called originally Black Marias; a special area in the yard of Bow Street Police court was reserved for the loading and unloading of Marias. From horse drawn the Police moved towards motor vehicles the first was used by the Flying Squad. This was a 1927 Lea Francis with the registration A 209, the registration is still in use today. This car was followed in by 1933 by a Fordson Van. Since then the Police have had a variety of vehicles from Jaguar, Woolsey, Austin, Daimler, Ford, Mini, to name a few including the iconic Ford Zephyr and Rover SD1.

Today's police cars are a mixture of makes and models. With some suppliers being on the, 'Police Preferred' list. These cars range from the Volvo V70 T5/D5, BMW 3 and 5 Series, Vauxhall Astra,Vectra, to the Ford Focus and Mondeo. The Subaru Impreza, Mitsubishi Evo, Range Rover, Land Rover Discovery, Jaguar XF and Skoda Octavia VRS are also used by various police forces as more specialised vehicles.

Along with cars, some Police forces have a variety of motorbikes and vans. In 2010, the government started a list of preferred suppliers Ford being the first on the list followed by Vauxhall, Hyundai, Jaguar, and Peugeot along with some Audi, BMW and Mitsubishi cars.

Many manufacturers create, 'Police demonstrators' one of the more recent ones being the petrol/electric hybrid Vauxhall Ampera as a way of reducing fuel costs. Some forces have trialled various electric vehicles, but other than short trips they do not have the range for a typical shift or patrol. The main aspect of any police car is that it can have the required equipment fitted and be fit for purpose. More forces are going for estates like the Ford Focus, Astra Sports Tourer, Hyundai i30 Estate. With the amount of kit that is required to be carried in the car.

Policewomen

It was not until 1914 that women joined the police ranks when men were away fighting in World War I. In 1915, Edith Smith was sworn in as the first Policewoman with powers of arrest. Initially women were known as WPC (Women Police Constable) and later the W was dropped so that regardless of gender all Police officers are now known as PC (Police Constable).

The modern police service is a varied, multi-layered, responsive institution working to ensure the safety of the public.

The police force is changing. These days it is not just made up of officers and staff, but is augmented by volunteer Special Constables and highly focused Community Support Officers. All three branches walk beats, work closely with the public, and fight crime in their own ways. Forces are working together more closely to share resources and reduce costs. The future may see forces join together to form "Regional" forces or the "Super" force. With the recent 20% cuts, the police service has never had such tight budgets and difficult decisions have had to be made. These have resulted in compulsory redundancies under the "A19" banner. After two years, many forces now need to recruit as the numbers drop below a level that is tenable.

Police Dogs

Dogs and man have co-operated to perform many tasks over the years in war and peace, for hunting, tracking, guarding, hauling and communicating. Dogs have continually shown that they can provide both valuable assistance and warm companionship.

In 19th century Britain, pet dogs often accompanied police on their patrols. The Hyde Park police station in the 1890's had 'Topper a fox terrier who often joined their patrols. Bloodhounds were brought into the 'Jack the Ripper' case in 1888 as public hysteria mounted, but unfortunately, because of confusion in a test session they were not given a proper chance to show their abilities.

The story on the Continent was quite different. The achievements of trained police dogs in Ghent, Belgium spread to several Continental countries, and by World War I, dogs were being scientifically trained to perform specific military duties, as messengers, guards and sentries The German Shepherd, used extensively by the Germans on the Western Front, attracted considerable attention both in England and the United States.

One puppy, abandoned by the retreating Germans in 1918, was taken by an army sergeant to America. There he became world famous as Rin Tin Tin, starring in 122 Hollywood films, showing the popularity of the breed in England and the world.

Continued success with dogs by Continental police forces in the 1920's and 30's, sparked an interest in the Home Office in Britain. An experimental training school was established to examine kinds of training desirable and to show which breeds had greatest aptitude for police work.

Two specially-trained Labradors were officially introduced to the Metropolitan Police Force in 1938 and were based in South London with the idea of accompanying police on beats in the countrified suburbs. Then, the coming of another World War focused police attention on other priorities. After World War II, a small training school was set up at Imber Court in Surrey and more training and experiments were run - including a highly successful test in using dogs to accompany patrols in Hyde Park. On their very first night, one of the dogs foiled a purse snatching attempt, and the crime rate in the park plummeted. At the same time other forces began to trail the use of Police dogs and slowly the usefulness of using dogs for Police work meant that many forces set up their own 'dog sections'. The role of a Dog Unit is to provide police dog and handler teams to support their colleagues across a force area, and to respond to emergency calls where their unique skills can be used or needed.

The dogs and handlers have a variety of skills.

General Purpose Dogs, usually German or Belgian Shepherd Dogs, to patrol with their handlers. They have a range of skills, including:

Searching for suspects and missing people.

Locating objects dropped or concealed during a criminal incident.

Following a track left by a person on the ground.

Chasing and detaining a person who runs away when challenged to stop.

Disarming violent armed suspects and controlling hostile crowds.

Some of the more specialist skills include:

'Line access' work - Some officers and their dogs are 'line access' trained. The officers often have to get themselves and their dogs up and down the outside of buildings or even boats using abseiling skills. The dogs are trained to cope with being tied to their handlers, via a harness, whilst this is done. They are also used to support Armed Response or Public Order Units at a variety of events and incidents

Some dogs, particularly Spaniels and Labradors, are trained to find specific scents such as:

Drugs, both hidden and being carried on a person in public.

Cash, (banknotes).

Explosives, of various types.

Firearms.

Human remains and blood.

Some of the above skills may be combined in one dog team and some dog handlers may handle a German Shepard and a Spaniel for example and the dogs may be trained for more than one scent. In the case of Explosives Search Dogs, the dogs only search for one thing.

Police dogs are trained to be obedient. Which is very important as the dogs must be under control at all times. Commands are given verbally or with a hand signal. Due to the physical demands on police dogs they must be in good physical condition, they are trained to scale a six-foot fence, clear a foot-long jump and complete a hurdle and agility course.

The dogs are trained to bite and will do so under the following conditions; On command, to protect themselves or their handler.

All dogs are tested and must have the correct physical and mental attitude and courage to support their handler in violent situations. The dog will chase and detain criminals who run away, keeping hold of them until told to release by the handler. Police dogs can be used in any violent situation and their presence can be enough to quieten even the most violent of people.

The dogs are used to search for people that are hiding and for property that has been hidden or discarded. The dog uses its strong sense of smell to detect the individual scent of people and property.

Humans are not able to detect these smells, but the dog makes it look easy. The dog will hold the item in its mouth and take it back to the handler. When searching for people the same method is used - the dog will detect a smell, which he is attracted to. On finding the person, the dog will bark to tell the handler where they are located.

Tracking is another common job a police dog will do. This is when the dog is used to track across ground for an offender. Again, the dog uses its sense of smell, sniffing the ground disturbed by the offender. The best ground to do this on is grass. Hard surfaces such as roads and paths are far more difficult.

Weather is another factor. Wind, rain, snow, ice, frost, warm temperatures and time are all factors which will affect tracking.

Becoming a dog handler is a highly sought after position within any police force and competition for the very few posts that come up is very high. If you are lucky enough to be selected as a dog handler, it is most probably a role you will undertake until retirement unless a choice is made to move into management. Most dog handlers enjoy what they do and the dogs they work with so much that they rarely want to leave.

By the time, the dogs are born; bred, reared, and finally operational they represent an investment of almost £6,000 in time and money.

When this dog is on patrol, it is considered one of the Police, most powerful deterrents to crime. Yet these dogs should never be considered vicious. They have been very carefully chosen, evaluated and trained to have an even temperament and exert only the force required by any given police situation -to be only as bold and brave as called for by their handler.

As a team, handler and dog is an extremely sensitive command unit with a level of understanding that often seems to go beyond words. Their temperaments have been matched as carefully as possible, and through living together they can often understand each other in a way that defies description Both dogs and handlers have risked, and sometimes lost their lives to protect each other They are a team, and each part of the team has been carefully selected.

A police officer who volunteers to become a dog handler must have completed two years' service and have passed probation; requirements do vary slightly from force to force. Another requirement due to the handler actually living with their own dog is settled home circumstances. Once approved by a board of senior officers, the prospective handler attends a two-week suitability course to make sure that he has the ability and temperament to work with dogs. If they complete this course successfully, they are allocated a puppy, which is usually 12 weeks old. The puppy then goes to live in the handler's home and becomes part of his family, creating that level of trust that is the essence of a good working relationship.

At the time of allocation, handlers are taught about the care of their puppies and problems that can arise; for example, improper discipline in the home, which can break the dog's spirit. Then there are monthly visits to the training centre until the puppy is ten months old, to check on development. At ten months, dogs go with their handlers on a five-day course to test the dog's ability. Finally, at twelve months they go on a basic training course. If all goes well at the end of that, the dog will be fully schooled as an operational police dog.

Armed Response

A firearms unit is a specialised, armed unit within the police force. Most Police Officers are unarmed however the sad rise in guns and violent crime involving knives, machete's and such like has meant the move from guns just being available at a Police station for the few trained officers to the setting up of dedicated teams who routinely carry weapons. The usual weapons they along with a Taser is the Glock 17 self-loading pistol and the Heckler & Koch MP5SF. Some forces also use the Heckler & Koch G36, a rifle with accurate range of 800 m. A police officer cannot apply to join the firearms unit without first finishing their two-year probationary period, with a further two years in a core-policing role. Firearms unit or Armed Response is the most common name outside of London, while the Metropolitan Police Service call theirs the Specialist Firearms Command, or CO19.

Criminals are less likely to carry firearms due to United Kingdom gun laws, and the presence of an armed officer can often be enough to negotiate their surrender. One particular British police force has only had to use a firearm against a suspect once in its entire history.

Only three forces in the United Kingdom routinely arm officers due to the nature of their work; the Ministry of Defence Police who are responsible law enforcement on MOD property, the Civil Nuclear Constabulary who guard civil nuclear facilities, and the Police Service of Northern Ireland.

Traffic Police

The roads policing unit is not only concerned with catching speeding motorists, but also play an important role in every aspect of road traffic safety. Also in the pursuit and stopping of criminals who operate nationally. Traffic Officers deal with a variety of incidents such as vehicle crashes, pedestrians injured by vehicles, checking the safety standards of cars and Lorries on the road, escorting abnormal loads, pursuing suspect motor vehicles and road safety education.

All road-policing officers are police officers before they become part of the Road Policing Unit. These officers are professionals who work across the force area and are not bound to any geographic areas although each Road Policing crew is based in a territorial Area Command. Some forces have combined their Traffic Police with the Armed Response unit to create a combined unit in which all officers have a dual role.

Sergeants will brief the officers to area issues and problems that they must give attention too. These issues are diverse, possibly needing their expertise as road policing officers with detailed knowledge of traffic law, or their ability as highly trained drivers to ensure the safe stopping of suspected criminals, or to prevent motorists driving under the influence of alcohol or drugs.

Road policing officers will pay particular attention to specific areas at certain time of the year with the aim to reduce casualties. To apply for a post in the Police Traffic Department they must have completed your two-year probationary period and proved to be a competent police officer. They must have also passed their basic police-driving course. They will then need to pass an advanced driver course. So, they can drive the higher-powered vehicles and can pursue and stop vehicles.

British Transport Police (BTP)

British Transport Police is a specialised police service for the railway network across Britain. The goal of the organisation is to provide a policing service that delivers a safe railway environment that is free from disruption and the fear of crime.

BTP currently employs approximately 2,750 Police Officers, supported by 250 Special Constables, 210 PCSOs and 1000 support staff. Together, they are jointly responsible for the whole of the national rail network, the London Underground, Eurostar, the Docklands Light Railway, the Midland Metro Tram System and Croydon Tram link, plus some local light rail and goods services. BTP is a national police service divided into seven geographical areas covering 10,000 miles of track and 3,000 railway stations and depots.

The first railway employees described as "police" can be traced back to 30 June 1826. A regulation of the Stockton and Darlington Railway refers to the police establishment of "One Superintendent, four officers and numerous gate-keepers". This is the first mention of Railway Police anywhere and was three years before the Metropolitan Police Act was passed. They were not, however, described as "constables" and the description may refer to men controlling the trains not enforcing the law.

The modern British Transport Police was formed by the British Transport Commission Act 1949 which combined the already-existing police forces inherited from the pre-nationalisation railways by British Railways, those forces having been previously formed by powers available under common law to parishes, landowners and other bodies to appoint constables to patrol land and/or property under their control. This is distinct from the establishment of a police force by statute, as applicable to the Metropolitan Police in 1829; BTP did not have jurisdiction on a statutory basis until the enactment of the Transport Police (Jurisdiction) Act 1994, which was subsequently amended by the Railways and Transport Safety Act 2003. The jurisdiction now is of any location that either harbours an offender or evidence connected with a crime connected on the railway. The BTP often work with territorial forces especially the Metropolitan Police on joint operations.

BECOMING A POLICE OFFICER

So you want to become a police officer? How do you go about it? What does it mean?

The best place to start is what you will be expected to do and what you might find you will do being as a police officer.

A Police officer is a warranted employee of a police force. Police officers are generally responsible for apprehending criminals, maintaining public order, and preventing and detecting crimes. Police officers are sworn to an oath, and are granted the power to arrest and imprison suspects, along with other practices.

You can either decide to join as a full-time police officer or become a volunteer officer known as a Special Constable.

Short Self-Aptitude Test

Here is a very short test to see if you have the aptitude to be a police officer. Go down the list and choose the course of action you would take.

Question 1

You are on patrol alone at 1.30 am and passing the 'Bright Light' nightclub. You see a group of 10 young men outside the club. Suddenly there is a shout and a man is thrown to the ground. The group of 10 young men start to kick him violently in the head. You can see he is, almost immediately, rendered unconscious and is receiving blows to his head that will cause serious injury, or worse.

A Report what is happening by radio and request back up

B Observe and gather evidence of what happens

C Approach the crowd and shout: 'Police, police – get back!'

D Call for an ambulance because he is likely to be injured

E Draw your baton and body strike the attackers with as much force as is possible

Question 2

You are on patrol alone on a Saturday afternoon at 2 pm and the publican of the Grapes public house flags you down. He tells you there is a fight in his pub. You look through the door and notice there are about 60 people fighting each other. Furniture is being thrown across the bar and substantial damage has been caused.

A Call for back up and observe what is happening
B Go into the pub, shout at them and ask them to stop fighting
C Tell the licensee to close the pub immediately
D Book the licensee for keeping a disorderly house
E Go in and arrest the first person you see fighting

Question 3

You are on patrol with your Sergeant at 8.30 pm. You are passing a young Chinese man walking along the pavement and the sergeant instructs you to stop and search him. You ask the sergeant on what grounds. He replies, "Because he's Chinese"

A Refuse to do it and confront the Sergeant about his racist comments
B Stop and search the man on suspicion of having stolen property
C Refuse to do it because being 'Chinese' is not a ground to justify the stop and search.
D Stop and search the man and later report the Sergeant for being racist
E Tell the Chinese man why the sergeant wanted him stopped and encourage him to make a formal complaint

Question 4

You attend a burglary in a confectionery shop at 3.00 am one morning with another constable. While you await the arrival of the owner your colleague picks up a bag of sweets, opens it and begins to eat them.

A Ask him if he is going to pay for the sweets when the owner arrives
B Ask your colleague for a sweet
C Pretend you didn't see what happened
D Arrest your colleague for stealing the sweets
E Do nothing and report the incident to your sergeant when you get back to the station

Question 5

You attend a domestic dispute at 2.00 am on your own. As you arrive you notice all the lights are on in the house, the front window has been smashed and music is blaring out. You look through the window and see a man. He spots you and immediately grabs a woman by the hair and puts a carving knife to her throat and says, "Get back copper or I'll slice her throat."

A Back off slightly, start talking to him and try to defuse the situation

B Rush into the house and strike the man with your baton to save the woman

C Do what he says and back off from the window so he cannot see you

D Immediately call for back up on your radio

E Call for an ambulance and armed response vehicle

Question 6

You are sitting in the canteen when you overhear two sergeants making sexist and derogatory comments about a woman officer and joking about her being a lesbian.

A Challenge the behaviour and ask them to stop

B Report them to a senior officer

C Ignore the comments

D Smile and laugh at the comments you hear

E Tell someone about it later

Question 7

Whilst on foot patrol at 1.30 pm in the High Street you receive a radio message to indicate that a member of the public has seen a man brandishing a handgun. The description of the man given fits perfectly a man walking about 25 feet in front of you.

A Confirm the description and follow him at a discrete distance

B Approach the man and demand he hands over the gun

C Jump him from behind and disarm him

D Do nothing, it is too risky

E Follow him and observe what he does

Question 8

You are on foot patrol with another colleague who stops to speak to a beggar. Suddenly, the beggar jumps up and punches her in the face. She falls to the ground and the beggar kicks her.

A Restrain and arrest the beggar using reasonable force
B Draw your baton and beat the beggar into submission
C Ask the beggar to stop
D Call for assistance
E Call an ambulance

Question 9

You are off duty and attend a party at a friend's house. There are 15 people at the party who are not police officers. When you get into the house you notice a number of people are smoking cannabis, some are popping ecstasy tabs and a couple are 'chasing the dragon' in the kitchen.

A Telephone the duty sergeant at the local police station, report the situation
B Ignore the drug taking and enjoy yourself
C Confront the people, tell them who you are and ask them to stop
D Try the drugs yourself
E Do nothing and report the incident later

Question 10

You attend a nightclub with a police colleague when you are off duty. As you approach the doorman your colleague takes out his warrant card and flashes it. The doorman turns to the cashier and says' "It's OK they can go in free they are police."

A Challenge your colleague's behaviour and refuse to enter the club
B Enter the night club without paying
C Challenge your colleagues behaviour, then enter the club for free
D Buy the doorman a drink for being so generous
E Insist that you both pay the going rate

If you answered mainly A for all the questions you have strong potential to be a police officer!

Special Constabulary Role

The Special Constabulary forms part of the neighbourhood policing teams, working alongside regular police officers, PCSOs and their partners. The primary role of the Special Constabulary is specifically to provide a high visibility presence (therefore reducing the fear of crime), dealing with anti-social behaviour and gathering and acting upon community intelligence.

A Special Constable is normally part of the neighbourhood team, as part of a larger government initiative. Some Specials do all of their time with these teams whilst some do a proportion of their time with them and the rest being spent with what is known as Response or Reactive. These are the police officers who respond to 999 calls from the public which can be anything from a Road Traffic Collision (RTC) to a fight at a local pub or a theft from a shop. Specials have become more and more integrated into a variety of policing, including roads policing, CID and other specialist teams.

Any constabulary will ensure that you are fully trained to deal with policing problems that are affecting local communities. As a Special Constable you hold the same powers as a full-time officer – powers throughout the whole of England and Wales.

How to Become a Special Constable

To be eligible, you must meet the following basic criteria:

You must be a national of a country within the European Economic Area or, if a national of a country outside the EEA, have the right to reside in this country without restrictions.

You must be 18 years of age or over.

You cannot be working in an occupation that would conflict with your duties as a Special Constable. Some of these occupations include: Traffic Warden, Security, Licencee, private detective, and magistrate. Anything that may bring you into conflict with your role as a Police officer is worth checking. Contact your local force for their list if you feel your current job may be an issue.

If you meet the criteria you can either contact the local force directly, or speak to the Specials recruitment officer. Many constabularies have downloadable application forms and information on their website. You can simply fill out the form, print and post or email it to the recruitment section of the force you are applying to.

As a special, most forces will expect you to be willing to undertake duty time to the equivalent of a minimum of four hours per week, which is the standard minimum. You must be willing to undertake an initial training course and attend regular training at your chosen division or station, in order to maintain your skills.

As a serving Special Constable you will personally benefit from:

New experiences – you can expect to enjoy much of the variety that comes along with police work.

New people – you will be working as one of a team and the experiences you share in working closely together can lead to lasting friendships. You will learn more about life and human nature than most people will ever see.

New skills – you will learn new skills and develop existing ones, such as problem solving, negotiating, decision-making, coping with pressure, communications and interpersonal skills. These skills will help you not only as a Special, but also in your daily life, as well as in your current workplace. This will be supported by the force appraisal system.

Most forces will pay your travelling expenses from home or work to your Police station, and offer a boot allowance of £50-70 or more. Some forces were running bounty schemes for the completion of set hours or objectives. An example is a £500 tax deductible bounty for doing 300 or more duty hours in a year. A few of these schemes have been disbanded as the police cuts have meant money has had to be re-directed into to training and such like.

Being a special can be one of the most exciting ways to volunteer, and find out about the role of a police officer. Being a Special Constable does not guarantee you will get in as a full-time officer, but it will help with scenarios and an awareness of the role of a police officer. You will also find existing officers will be very happy to help you complete your full-time application and give you tips. Some forces run awareness sessions for the application process, to aid your application and give important tips and pitfalls for the application process.

How to Become a Full-time Regular Officer

Full-time officers do pretty much the same roles and duties as Special Constables although being full time they often deal with much more serious crime. They can also undertake training that is not available to special constables. The options open to them during their career are wider and much more varied. All police officers start as police constables regardless of age and experience. Then after their probationary period they can apply to join maybe the Traffic Police, Armed response, Police Dogs Unit, or a Beat Manager for those that want to stay in uniform. You may want to become a detective and move into CID. Other highly sought after roles such as a dog handler, mounted or air support.

Some police officers may be trained in special duties such as; counterterrorism, surveillance, child protection, VIP protection, and investigation techniques into major crime, such as fraud, rape, murder or drug trafficking.

Police Constables Pay as of 1st September 2017

0 - £19,971 (a)
1 - £23,124 (b)
2 - £24,171 (c)
3 - £25,224
4 - £26,277
5 - £28,380
6 - £32,616
7 - £38,382 (a)

(a) Pay point 0 is the entry point for a member appointed to the rank of constable, unless the chief officer of police, after consultation with the local policing body, assigns the member to pay point 1 based on policing qualifications, relevant experience or local recruitment needs. The salary paid to a member at pay point 0 shall be between £19,971 and £23,124 as determined by the chief officer of police, after consultation with the local policing body, on the basis of policing qualifications, relevant experience or local recruitment needs.

(b) On completion of basic training, a member who entered at pay point 0 will move to pay point 1.

(c) All members will move to pay point 2 after one full year at pay point 1, and progression will continue to be at a rate of one pay point per full year of service thereafter.

Alongside the main pay scale under the Windsor review was the addition of an unsocial hour bonus that will be paid pro rata for the hours worked between 8pm and 6am. For a constable, this is up to £1200 for a constable working a standard eight-hour alternating shift pattern.

Shift Pattern

Being a police officer is a 24 hour 7 days a week, 365 days a year job. That is broken down into shift work and an example of a typical set of shifts might be:

2 days 7 till 4pm

2 days 3 till 12am

2 days 10pm till 7am

Followed by 4 days off.

As can be seen, you work at all hours of the day and night at weekends, even Christmas day. The shifts can be difficult to get used to, and your first night shift can feel like the longest night ever. They may even have been an impact on your life in terms of things you use to do regularly might not always fit into your shift pattern. Partners may need to adjust to not seeing you as they may well be at work whilst you are sleeping. You may need to work on Christmas day or New Year's Eve. All this can take its toll on your social and personal life.

As a Special Constable, you will more often than not choose when you want to go on duty, to fit around work commitments or other officers shift patterns. One tip is that if working with full-time officers, always try to work a full shift with them. There may be times when you were due to get off, but end up staying on due to a serious incident or simply needing to complete paperwork. It really is not a job that you can just finish at a set time, and walk away from at a set time on occasions. Imagine being at an RTC controlling the traffic and deciding to just go off duty. What would happen to the traffic? Always worth considering, if maybe you need to be up early for work the next day or have pre-planned event to attend.

Beat Managers or constables working within the NPT teams may work slightly different hours some working till just 12-1am and doing two weekends out of every four.

A local police force will deal with emergencies and non-emergencies within certain agreed times and if you've been a victim of crime, they will agree with you how often and for how long you will be kept informed of progress on your case.

All Police forces across the whole of the England and Wales have signed up to provide the same level of service to their communities. This means that it will be easier for the public to have their say on how they police, the local area, and guarantees that wherever they live, they can expect the same, high level of service.

Wherever anybody lives, they can get the following information by searching for their neighbourhood policing team on their force website:

Contact details of the Neighbourhood Policing Team

Details of the next Neighbourhood Policing meeting

The neighbourhood priorities

Action being taken by the police and follow-up to problems raised by the community

Local crime statistics, information and crime maps

How to get involved and help make your community safer

Neighbourhood Policing

Neighbourhood Policing is a style of policing that provides communities with a visible, familiar, and accessible policing team who work in partnership with other agencies, such as Council Street

Wardens, licensing, local/parish council to reduce crime and anti-social behaviour and address local community safety priorities. All forces are committed to neighbourhood policing within their respective areas.

As such, teams are made up of regular police officers, PCSOs who work on the front-line alongside Special Constables, and Beat Managers. PCSO's provide a visible and reassuring presence on the streets and tackling the menace of anti-social behaviour. PCSOs have different roles in different forces, but they usually patrol a beat and interact with the public, while also offering assistance to police officers at crime scenes and major events.

Depending on where they work, they could: deal with minor offences offer early intervention to deter people from committing offences provide support for front-line policing conduct house-to-house enquiries guard crime scenes provide crime prevention advice.

Although PCSOs do not have the same powers as regular police officers, they still carry a lot of responsibility, and are a crucial part of the police force. Along with Special Constables, they have been established to work with their partners to ensure the right people, the right numbers and with the right skills, are in the right place at the right time. The size of each team depends on the local community needs. Members of the team concentrate on resolving local problems, such as disruptive families, drug misuse and anti-social behaviour.

One of the keys to effective neighbourhood policing is active engagement, consultation and communication with local people to ensure their interests and concerns are reflected in the delivery of policing, community safety and neighbourhood services. Local meetings or "Beat Surgeries" are organised so locals can have a voice.

Due to the unpredictable nature of law enforcement, police officers can encounter many dangerous situations in the course of their career. Officers face an increased risk of infectious diseases, physical injury, or in some cases, death, as well as the potential for emotional disorder due to both the high stress and inherently adversarial nature of police work. These dangers are encountered in many different situations, such as the investigation, pursuit, and apprehension of criminals, motor vehicle stops, crimes, response to terrorism, and intervention in domestic disputes, investigating traffic accidents, and directing traffic. The constant risk, uncertainty and tension inherent in law enforcement and the exposure to vast amounts of human suffering and violence can lead susceptible individuals to anxiety, depression, and alcoholism.

Individuals are drawn to police work for many reasons. Among these often include a desire to protect the public and social order from criminals and danger. A desire to hold a position of respect and authority; a disdain for or antipathy towards criminals and rule breakers; the professional challenges of the work; the employment benefits that are provided with civil service jobs in many countries; the sense of camaraderie that often holds among police; or a family tradition of police work or civil service. An important task of the recruitment activity of police agencies is screening potential candidates to determine the fitness of their character and personality for the work. Often through background investigations and consultation with a psychologist. Even though Police work is very dangerous, police officers are still seen by most people as necessity to maintain order. However, there are also those that dislike the police Force and what it stands for. Becoming a police officer may mean losing friends as well as gaining new ones.

Recruitment Process

The recruitment process can take several months and is very similar for both full-time officers and Special Constables, but can vary from force to force. Specials do not usually have such a rigorous application form and do not attend the assessment day. Their assessment is usually undertaken at a weekend or weekday evening. Specials requirement is not quite as standardised as regular officer recruitment and can vary, although it is becoming more and more standardised between forces. However, the process always includes elements from the regular recruitment assessment day, such as structured interview, IQ test/PIRT and written exercises. Your force will send you a recruitment pack outlining what their recruitment consists of and then you can refer to those specific elements in this chapter.

A typical application process for full-time officers is laid out below. Anything after the application phase can vary between different forces.

Initial Application.
Assessment day.
Security vetting of yourself, your immediate family, and any other adults who may live at your address.
Fitness Test.
An interview.
A full medical.

Of those that apply, only 15% are successful at becoming a Police officer and many have had to apply several times to get in.

The application form is very important, 60% of applicants for the role of police officer and PCSO are rejected at the application form stage. You are marked and graded on your answers to the competency questions and getting these right is a key element of your application form. The questions ask you to give examples that meet with the six core competencies and we will cover these later. In addition, your eligibility requirements will be checked before your application can go to the next stage.

You can even fail on using blue instead of black ink, not following the guidelines properly and even incorrect spelling. As all these things, relate back to the seven core competencies that you will cover later. Expect to spend around twelve hour's completing the application forms, including writing your competency answers. Getting this stage wrong could mean being rejected and having to wait 6 months before you can apply. The time you put in will pay dividends. If unsuccessful, make sure you get feedback so that you know what to improve next time. Don't be disheartened, some of the best police officers I have worked with applied four times before they passed recruitment. Some have failed the paper sift others have had to go through the SEARCH assessment centre two or even three times.

Specials recruitment is not quite as standardised as regular officer recruitment and can vary between forces. With this in mind, the NPIA (National Police Improvement Agency), now College of Policing, has developed a National Recruitment Process and Standards for the Special Constabulary. The new process and standards were formally approved for national roll-out from 1 April 2010 by the Special Constabulary National Consultative Group (SCNCG). With the recruitment of Special Constables has been a local matter, which meant that each of the 43 forces could be running different recruitment processes and using different standards. However, since the launch of the National Strategy for the Special Constabulary in March 2008, the NPIA was working with its partners to produce national standards and an assessment process.

Rollout began on 1st April 2010, and has been extended to March 2012. The NPIA provided each force that adopted the new process with two training courses (assessor training and Quality Assurance training) and other support free of charge during this period.

National Specials Recruit Assessment Process

The National Specials Recruit Assessment Process is a rigorous one involving the observation of candidates' performance across a variety of exercises, assessing their potential to perform the role effectively.

Key features of the assessment process are:

Assessments are made on what candidates do and how they do it.

Trained assessors evaluate each candidate's performance in exercises which relate to identified core competencies

Information from all of the exercises is used to produce the final results.

Assessment exercises include:

A Competency Based Questionnaire (optional) - for forces that wish to sift prior to running further assessments
A written exercise lasting 20 minutes
A situational judgment test lasting 65 minutes
A competency-based structured interview with 4 questions lasting 20 minutes in total.

The assessment exercises are based on the competencies from the Integrated Competency Framework (ICF). The ICF is a series of national standards which sets out, amongst other things, the competencies required for each role within the police force, including that of Special Constable. These competencies are covered later in the chapter.

Forces should also apply the same fitness; medical and eyesight standards as apply to regular officers. Candidates are required to take the following two fitness tests:

Dynamic Strength test (upper-body strength). This requires the candidate to perform seated chest pushes and five seated back pulls on a specially designed device

Endurance fitness. This endurance fitness test involves running to and fro on a 15-metre track in time with a series of bleep

Eligibility Requirements

Eligibility requirements for the police are detailed listed is the main criterion that needs to be met.

Age requirements Applications can be accepted at the age of 18. There's no upper age limit for applying to the Police service, but bear in mind that the normal retirement age is 60 years and that new recruits are required to undertake a two-year probationary period.

Nationality requirements, you must be a British citizen, an EC/EEA national or a Commonwealth citizen or foreign national with no restrictions on your stay in the United Kingdom.

Foreign nationals and UK citizens who have lived abroad may have to wait some time for security and vetting clearance. All applicants must be vetted to the same standard before appointment.

Criminal record - A number of crimes will mean a definite or likely rejection of your application, including anyone who has received a formal caution in the last five years, committed a violent crime or public order offence.

Tattoos, which could cause offence. Tattoos are not acceptable if they are particularly prominent, garish, and offensive or undermine the dignity and authority of your role.

Applicants will have their financial status checked. These checks are carried out because police officers have access to privileged information, which may make them vulnerable to corruption. Applicants with outstanding County court judgments, who have been registered bankrupt with outstanding debts, will be rejected. If you have discharged bankruptcy debts, then you will need to provide a Certificate of Satisfaction with your application.

To ensure you are fit enough for the role, you will undertake a fitness test. There are two elements to the test and you must pass both before you can be appointed. They are looking for no more than the minimum standard needed, to enable you to work effectively as a police officer. You will be given help to improve your fitness and if you prepare yourself properly, there is no reason for you to fail.

There are two elements to the test: dynamic strength and endurance fitness, and health.

Police officers encounter stressful situations, trauma, physical confrontation and work long hours on shifts. They need to be resilient enough to cope with the demands and pressures of Police work. Applicants must therefore be in good health mentally and physically to undertake Police duties.

You will undergo a medical examination to ensure you meet the health standards required.

Applicants will have their eyesight tested at the medical assessment stage. You may be asked to go to an optician to have your eyes tested and the eyesight form filled in. Failure to pass this test will lead to rejection.

You can only apply to one force at any one time. If you have previously applied to join the Police service and been unsuccessful, you must wait six months from your initial rejection before you can apply again.

Applicants from all backgrounds and ethnic groups are encouraged to apply. Applicants are not limited to any particular age group in fact; those who are looking for a career change are encouraged to join with valuable life experience. The minimum age to apply is 18, and there is no upper age limit, though you should bear in mind that the normal retirement age for Police Constables and sergeants is 60 at this present time, but in line with many other sectors will most likely rise. You should also be aware that all new recruits, whatever their age, are required to undertake a two-year probationary period before you can look towards any career advancement.

Get Fit Before You Apply

One of the most rigorous elements of our screening process is the physical fitness training. Police Officers must be able to move quickly while carrying a lot of heavy equipment; they must be in pretty good shape.

If you pass the assessment process, you will then have to take a physical fitness test. To pass, you will need to be reasonably fit, and able to run short distances quickly. The bleep test is the most common test along with a grip test for the fitness element. Later you will also have to pass a medical examination.

Core Competencies/Skills

These are the competencies/skills being looked at within your application, at the assessment centre and are used in the structured interview. They are all based on the Skills For Justice, Policing Professional Framework. You need to try and give examples of when and where you have dealt with each of them. You are graded on your responses. Try to think of good examples that illustrate each competence. Try not to waffle and just show exactly where you have come across each competency in your day to day life. They don't have to be that current either. The aim is to look at your life experience and how you have reacted to each of the competencies. If you have experience of being a Special Constable or a PCSO these will often help you give good examples that you have experienced on duty. Many regular officers will be more than happy to offer advice and guidance by already be part of the police family. Another worthwhile point that is essential to the police force is political correctness and making sure you use the correct terminology and words that are not in any way sexist, racist or homophobic. Diversity is the key here.

Definition of Diversity

The concept of diversity encompasses acceptance and respect. It means understanding that each individual is unique, and recognizing our individual differences. These can be along the dimensions of race, ethnicity, gender, sexual orientation, socio-economic status, age, physical abilities, religious beliefs, political beliefs, or other ideologies. It is the exploration of these differences in a safe, positive, and nurturing environment.

It is about understanding each other and moving beyond simple tolerance to embracing and celebrating the rich dimensions of diversity contained within each individual.

Latest Competencies

Since 1st Nov 2013, the seven competencies were replaced by six skills, from the Policing Professional Framework which are:

Serving the public
Openness to change
Service Delivery
Professionalism
Decision making
Working with others.

Listed below are the latest competencies currently being used at the SEARCH assessment centre and during the force interview. The application form is due to change shortly to reflect the new core competencies.

Serving the public

One of the fundamental roles of the police is to serve the public and respond to their needs. You will be required to build confidence in the public as communities are now far more diverse than ever. You will need to gather intelligence and work with different agencies such as the Local Authority, the Fire Service and other stakeholders to provide a great public service. During the selection process, you must provide a really good service during the role plays and the written report writing. You may also get asked an interview questions that goes along the lines of:

"Can you give an example of when you have delivered excellent customer service to a member of the public?"

Openness to change

The police force has been changing for many years now and they want to recruit new officers who are open to change. You must find better and more cost-effective ways of working in the police force and be open to the changes that are implemented by senior officers. During the selection process, you will have to answer questions based around your understanding of change and how it affects the force. This might be done during a police officer final interview if your chosen force decides to have one as part of the police selection process.

Service delivery

Effective service delivery is crucial to the police force. You must plan and organise your tasks to fit in with the police force's main objectives and goals. During the assessment centre, you will have to organise your actions in the role play and interactive scenarios in order to demonstrate that you have this key quality. An interview question for the assessment centre might be:

"Can you give an example of when you have planned or organised an event to meet someone else's requirements?"

Professionalism

Without doubt, this is one of the most important core competencies. The public expects its police officers to be professional at all times and uphold the principles of great service delivery. You will need to act with integrity and take ownership for resolving problems. During the police assessment centre role play scenarios you will have to act in a resilient manner and take action to solve any problems. You can demonstrate this by saying to the role play actor: "I can assure you that I will take personal responsibility for making things happen and I will act now in order to resolve this issue."

Decision making

As a police officer, you will have to gather information from a range of sources in order to allow you to make effective decisions. Before making a decision, you will need to consider all of the facts of the case. During the report writing stage of the selection process, you must read a summary of events in relation to the Westshire Centre and then come up with a written report solving the problem. Most candidates fail at this stage due to poor spelling and grammar. Make sure you practice these in the build-up to the assessment centre.

Working with others

Finally, as a police officer you must work with others as part of a team in order to solve problems. You will also have to offer support to your work colleagues and be flexible in your approach to tasks. Furthermore, you should be willing to work with anyone regardless of their age, sex, sexual orientation, religious beliefs or otherwise. The police force needs to be diverse in nature, if it is to provide an excellent service to the public.

Regular Application Form

The application form is maybe the first chance a police force will have at seeing what you are all about. It is a very long and detailed application form. Great care needs to be taken when filling it out. Any mistakes or not gaining the required B grade on the competency questions will mean at least a six month wait before you can re-apply. Some may feel using one of the many checking services worthwhile. These will not write your answers, but will check to see if they are good enough to pass and give pointers and corrections so they do pass. The only downside is if you have only a short amount of time to get your application in. It makes for a tight timescale and if looking to apply getting your competency questions correct will help no end.

Hopefully, by having the actual questions listed later on, you can start thinking about and formulating some ideas before you apply or get an application form. I cannot stress enough how important your answers to the competency questions are and they are covered in detail later on in the chapter.

Application Form: Competency Assessment

The Special Constables application form asks for two CBQs (Q1, Q2). The pass mark is lower than the three on the PCSO (Q1, Q2, Q3) and the Regular application forms, although there ay be some local variance. For all filling out and answering the questions, should be the same process. Using the word, "I" not "we" making use of keywords in the core competencies.

The key to success in this part of the form is to understand the purpose of the questions, and to spend some time finding the best example in your life experiences to illustrate the point required. Many applicants simply write down a very brief and superficial experience, with no depth not bringing in key words or phrases. These leads to a low score and the application being rejected. 75% of applicants fail at the application stage due to poor examples and not answering the questions properly. It is essential that the answer is as thorough as possible. As a simple guide, look at each question and consider the following.

Firstly, try to identify what skills areas are being looked for by reading the question thoroughly.

Having done this, outline briefly what the issue or the circumstances of the event were.

State what actions you carried out to address the issue.

Stay what effect this had on the group or others.

Describe the result.

Describe how there was a positive outcome, in that the issue was solved and all parties had a positive learning experience from it.

See where Keywords from the core competencies can be added, this will greatly improve your score.

Do not use an experience from when you were a child, and do not specifically name people.

Your examples must be specific. Don't generalise use a situation that shows a strong response not something minor. At the same time they don't have to be earth shattering examples either.

Add positive phrases like, "I resolved the conflict by staying calm and explaining the situation."

Consider word processing your answers first to check for spelling and grammar before writing your answers on a photocopied page to see if they will fit or can be expanded.

Core words or phrases to include in the answers include the following. "I identified", "I realised" and, "having spoken to him, I discovered that", "having identified the issue, I realised that one of my options was to...", "I decided", and so on. Notice that these are all "I" phrases and all of them demonstrate a sense of purpose and focus. The answer's need to be based around your response and your feelings, which are detailed and cover all the main points. Ensure you points are succinct and to the point. A larger space means a larger and more detailed answer. Try to utilise that space to explain your answer adding in key words/points. Stay gender and diverse neutral if appropriate.

Remember that your answers will be graded, and that some forces may question you on the examples provided later in the recruitment process. In addition, remember whilst everyone exaggerates slightly their involvement in certain incidents. If a force discovers you are blatantly lying, they will have serious doubts about your personal integrity, and any chance of recruitment will be lost.

As well as the four-main competency questions there are another six asking.

Tell us why you want to become a police officer?

Tell us why you have applied to your chosen police force?

Tell us in some detail what tasks you expect to be undertaking as a police officer?

Tell us what effect you expect being a police officer to have on your social and domestic life?

What preparation have you undertaken before making this application to ensure that you know what to expect and that you are prepared for the role of police officer?

If you have previously applied to be a police officer, special constable or police community support officer (PCSO), what have you done since your last application to better prepare yourself for the role of police officer?

These questions are also assessed so need to be well thought out and not just "I want to catch criminals" or "Going around with blue lights flashing". Think about the impact on your local community supporting the public and forging links as some ideas. Have you served as a special constable, PCSO, police cadets or been on a station visit/attended and open day or recruitment event. Remember that spelling, grammar and handwriting is still being assessed as are your responses.

The key to success in this part of the form is to understand the purpose of the questions, and to spend some time finding the best example in your life experiences to illustrate the point required. Try to think of strong examples, as weaker examples tend to score more poorly. Many applicants simply write down a very brief and superficial experience, with no depth not bringing in key words or phrases. This lead to a low score and the application being rejected. 75% of applicants fail at the application stage due to poor examples and not answering the questions properly. It is essential that the answer is as thorough as possible.

Competency Question Results

You will receive the results of the competency assessment with feedback in the post. The come as an overall grade either A, B, C, or D. You need an overall grade B to pass or some forces require each of the four competencies assessed to be a B. You will receive feedback that is relative to the grade and the cohort that you applied with. Here is an example of feedback for a Grade B answer.

The actual score is based on all the candidates that applied for the same application. This means you are competing against the other candidates rather than just a benchmark. It also explains why those that apply against internal applicants find their scores have dropped compared to when they applied with general applicants.

Team Working: How you performed against other candidates:

This performance met the overall standard required. You scored better than 58% of the candidates and only the top 4% candidates scored more highly than you. Candidates who achieved similar scores to you tended to demonstrate that they clearly understood the role they were playing within the team and evidenced clear co-operation between team members. Candidates that scored more highly than you demonstrated that they saw the outcomes as a team effort.

Here is an example of feedback for a Grade C answer that did not make the grade.

Respect for Race and Diversity: How you performed against other candidates:

This performance met some of the requirements, however overall did not meet the standard required. Although you scored more highly than 25% of the candidates, 30% scored better than you. Candidates who achieved similar scores to you tended to use an example where the behaviour challenged was clearly insensitive, bullying or discriminatory. Candidates who scored higher than you evidenced that they directly challenged the behaviour and demonstrated they did so politely. You needed to provide evidence of challenging the behaviour and it was not enough if you dealt with the issue by addressing a group without the individual being clearly told. The evidence of challenging the behaviour had to be clear, and clear to the person who was a bully or discriminatory. If you did not demonstrate clearly telling the person what they had done was wrong, you will have scored less well.

Q1 – Professionalism

Please describe a specific occasion when you have intervened to take control of a situation.

Why was it necessary to intervene in the situation?

What did you do to take control of the situation?

What did you consider when intervening in the situation?

What was particularly good or effective about how you intervened to take control of the situation?

What difficulties did you experience and how did you overcome them?

Q2 - Working with others

Please describe a specific occasion when you have encouraged a person to view an issue more positively.

Why was it necessary to encourage the person to view the issue more positively?

How did you encourage the person to view the issue more positively?

What did you consider when encouraging the person to view the issue more positively?

What was particularly good or effective about how you encouraged the person to view the issue more positively?

What difficulties did you experience and how did you overcome them?

Q3 - Decision Making

Please describe a specific occasion you have considered a number of options before making a decision?

Why was it necessary to consider a number of options before making the decision?

What did you consider when identifying options?

What did you consider when making the decision?

What was particularly good or effective about how you identified the options and made the decision?

What difficulties did you experience and how did you overcome them?

Q4 - Service Delivery

Please describe a specific occasion when you have had to manage your time effectively in order to complete a task.

Why did you have to manage your time effectively in order to complete the task?

How did you manage your time effectively in order to complete the task?

What did you consider to make sure you completed the task?

What was particularly good or effective about how you managed your time?

What difficulties did you experience and how did you overcome them?

Special Constable Application Form

The current application form for the Special Constabulary is now very similar to the full-time police officer application form. You may well find it quite long and arduous to fill out for a volunteer position. However, a Special Constable is now more than ever a professional member of the police family. When out on the streets the public sees a Special Constable the same as any other police officer, and expects the same high level of service and professionalism. Ensuring it is filled out correctly in black ink and readable will aid the recruitment process. The marking and standards of the application form, in terms of the competency assessment part of the application form are not expected to be as high.

The application form has two competency questions compared to the four on the full-time application form (Q1, Q2)

The last six questions are identical to the questions on the full-time application form.

Tell us why you want to become a special constable?

Tell us why you have applied to your chosen police force?

Tell us in some detail what tasks you expect to be undertaken as a special constable?

Tell us what effect you expect being a special constable to have on your social and domestic life?

What preparation have you undertaken before making this application to ensure that you know what to expect and that you are prepared for the role of special constable?

If you have previously applied to be a police officer, special constable or police community support officer (PCSO), what have you done since your last application to better prepare yourself for the role of police officer?

They are looking for answers that show your rationale and commitment to becoming a special constable. Even though you are applying for a volunteer position treat it with just the same care and attention you would if you were applying for a paid position. For those looking to become a full-time officer later it is also good practice!

SEARCH Assessment Centre

Anyone wishing to join the Police Service of England and Wales as a full-time police constable must attend the Police SEARCH® Recruit assessment centre. Once they have been successful on the application form paper sift. The Assessment Centre assessors evaluate candidates' performance in exercises related to core competencies. Information from all of the exercises is used to produce the final results.

Assessment exercises include:

A competency-based interview with 4 questions lasting 20 minutes in total

A numerical reasoning test lasting 12 minutes

A verbal logical reasoning test lasting 25 minutes

Two written exercises lasting 20 minutes each

Four interactive exercises lasting 5 minutes each.

All candidates undertake the same exercises and are assessed on an equal basis. The assessment centre lasts approximately half a day or about five hours.

Assessment Day

One of the most harrowing phase for any prospective applicant is the assessment day. The day will consist of a competency-based structured interview, tests, role plays and written exercises, which is made up of four questions. The assessment day various from around three hours for special constables to five hours for police constable recruits. The special constable assessment centre takes place at the force to which you apply and the police constable at a College of Policing assessment centre. Along with four other exercises all done to see how you compare to the core competencies. The more competencies that can be marked off in theory the higher the score. Although you can also be marked down for showing negative competencies such as not showing understanding, won't work as a team, unable to follow instructions as some examples. It is in some ways a tick box exercise, as the assessors go through a list of competencies or indicators they expect to see in each section. Only the numerical and reasoning multi choice tests, are marked by a computer. At the end of the day all the marks are fed into a computer to generate a score. Usually the results are sent directly to the candidate within two weeks of the assessment along with the police force the applicant has applied to.

Assessment Day Scoring

The assessment centre national pass grade is currently 50% and you must pass Race and Diversity otherwise you will fail the whole assessment. Quite a few forces now require a pass grade of 60%. All elements carry a minimum national standard of 50% less written communication that requires a minimum of 44% to pass. The grading is ABC and D and you are looking to get an overall average grade of a C. However, even if you average a B but get a D in Race and Diversity you will still fail the assessment centre. Overall in an assessment centre there are 123 marks available. If you achieved 50% overall this means you obtained 1/2 of the 123 marks available. If you scored 60% you obtained 73 marks.

For Race and Diversity there are a total of 21 marks available. If you scored 52% this equates to 11 out of the 21 marks. 57% equates to 12 marks. You need to score at least 11 marks to pass Race and Diversity.

In Oral Communications there are a total of 15 marks available. If you obtained 87% this means you scored 13 out of the 15 marks available.

For Written Communications there are just 9 marks available. If you scored 33%, this means you scored just 3 out of the 9 marks.

Even if you obtained 100% in Race and Diversity, Oral and Written Communications, this only accounts for 45 marks out of the 123. So although you may have met the required standard for these 3 competency areas, it is still possible you are rejected because your overall score did not meet the requirement. The remaining 78 marks are accounted for in Team Working, Resilience, Customer Focus, Problem Solving and Effective Communications.

So if you scored:

49% Overall

90% Race and Diversity

100% Oral Communications

100% Written Communications

This means you scored 60 marks out of 123 overall. 19 out of 21 marks for Race and Diversity, 15 marks out of 15 marks for Oral Communications and 9 marks out of 9 for Written Communications. Because you only achieved 60 marks overall (49%), this standard is not sufficient to join any force. As a rule of thumb thinking back to the core competency positive indicators you get a mark for each positive competency you show and loose a mark for each negative competency you show. Having a good working knowledge of the competencies and knowing the keywords will help you to score better.

In order of importance the most marks are awarded to the Role Play (57%) followed by written exercises (26%), structured interview (12%) and finally the IQ tests (5%).

In the interactive and written exercises, you may play the part of a newly appointed customer-services officer at a retail and leisure complex called The Westshire Centre. The Westshire Centre is a made up place created for the assessment centre only. There are other scenarios too. But most are looking at how you deal with various situations in particular diversity issues and effective communication skills. But the scenarios will also bring in resilience, customer service skills, problem solving and maybe team working. Many fall down on diversity or working with others with 30% failing the assessment centre on diversity related issues. It is all too easy to fall into simple traps such as assuming the gender of the complainant or another person.

The four interactive exercises are based around putting you into situations with actors to see how you react. You have five minutes to review the scenario and set out a plan and a further five minutes to deal with the scenario with an actor who is either an ex-police officer or civilian staff but not a professional actor.

Any scenario will have been tried and tested lots of times before you undertake it so you will be able to resolve the issues in the five minutes you have. The scenario may be dealing with an underperforming member of staff. A complaint from the member of the public about the facilities or another member of staff. The key points to being successful I will outline below after I have talked about planning. You will be provided with essential information in the form of memo/email/letter of complaint and they will give you a big hint on what the scenario will be about to aid in the planning.

So many applicants forget or do not plan what they are going to do in the scenario and under the pressure of the moment become flustered and lose valuable marks by missing out key points or elements. Planning is essential and the easiest method I have seen to plan is to use the CAR method.

Circumstances – What important/key details have you been given, look for anything that is diversity and you need to challenge. Any challenges need to be polite and explain why you think what they have said or written is unacceptable.

Action – What are you going to do, maybe list questions you will ask, what you need to say or address.

Results – What are you going to do to resolve the situation, maybe list a few options or action points for each element?

The best way to structure CAR is on the plain sheet of paper you will be provided with, spilt it up into three parts, then put the CAR headings in each section and then work through each section in the five minutes you have.

Some key points for the role playing element

The information you need in the preparation phases of the exercises will be supplied and as part of your assessment day invitation, you will be given a detailed overview of the scenario as part of the information pack. It is important to read and understand all the information fully. The interactive exercises will have you dealing with various situations based on the six core competencies and you are then graded on how you resolve and react to each situation. Actors in the scenario play various customers and leisure centre employees.

Remember, you are a customer service advisor and behave as one, never try to approach the scenarios as a police officer.

Never assume a name you have been given is male or female.

Challenge any diversity issues either said or written in a polite manner explaining why.

Odd scenarios start with an angry customer, stay calm they will have been told to only be angry for a set time. Stay calm, be polite, ask them to sit down and explain the issue in a rational way.

You are watched and observed to see how you behave and interact even with other candidates. Expect the unexpected and be aware at all times during the day.

Remember the assessors are looking for you to solve the problem.

Make sure you question and probe to get all the information. If an employee, maybe look at welfare issues, if a customer find out why that have that particular opinion. You will need to ask questions to get the information needed to give a resolution.

Don't make any assumptions; an underperforming member of staff for example, may have reasons such as problems at home. A customer may have been given the wrong information.

You will need to decide on what to do; the actor will not make the decision for you. The assessors are looking at you to be decisive as part of the core competencies.

Try to keep to a timing schedule of one minute for the initial introduction to the problem, two-three minutes discussing the problem and questioning. Finally, the last minute discussing your solution to the problem.

Each role play will seem to go very quick and will feel quite draining, have a plan, understand the core competencies, ensure no diversity opportunities are missed. Then your chances of getting the marks needed to pass the day will be greatly improved.

Assessment Day Structured Interview

The assessment day interview will last for up to 20 minutes and you will be asked four questions about how you have dealt with specific situations in the past. These questions will be related to the seven key competencies. You will be given up to five minutes to answer each question. The person interviewing you will stop you if you go over the five minutes. As the person interviewing you asks you the question, they will also give you a copy of the question to refer to. They may ask you further questions to help you to give a full response. When you consider your responses to the interview questions, only choose examples that you feel comfortable discussing with the person interviewing you. It is well worth thinking of examples of the seven competencies before you attend your assessment day. You can use the ones you used on your application form if they scored well or think of new ones. Trying to answer these off the cuff will prove to be quite difficult, and reduce your chances of scoring quite so well. It is also all too easy to become flustered or forgetful under pressure.

Written Exercises

The written exercises are very much like the 10-minute role play exercises, in that you must read through information and then deliver a solution. In the case of the written exercises, it is in the form of a letter as opposed to an actor. The written exercises are pass or fail. For the written exercise, you have 20 minutes to plan and then write a response in the form of a letter. Just like the role play exercises use the CAR method and spend only five minutes on the planning, leaving 15 minutes to write a neat and error free letter. You will be graded on punctuation, spelling and grammar. Write neatly and at a pace that enables the least number of mistakes, but still convey all the information you need to get across. If you come across a word you cannot spell, then think of another. Again, make sure any diversity issues are addressed in your response and a solution that is both workable and creative is put in place. Remember these exercises will not be vast and complex as there is simply not the time. They will be quite simple for the average recruit to resolve. You need to look for all the problematic issues and resolve them, and any diversity comment that needs challenging.

As well as the ability to communicate in writing you are being assessed on your ability to understand and summarise information, see both sides of the problem, make a decision, generate creative solutions, evaluate solutions and finally convey that solution with a rationale.

Common scenarios are a parking issue at a school or nursery and a comment is made about silly blonde drivers. Another is a kitchen that has failed a health inspection, complaints about lack of diversity and issues surrounding diversity within a company. All follow the same theme of raising issues that you need to come up with a solution for and more often than not some diversity comment that needs to be challenged in your letter.

For the written exercise, you should really start with a short introduction outlining the issues. Then follow on with how you intend to resolve these issues. Finally, challenge any diversity issues and a short conclusion. It is important to be concise but still write in full sentences. Think about what competencies are being assessed, and tailor your answer towards them. Don't feel you have to remember or throw in key words, just be mindful of what the assessors are looking for. It is undoubtedly going to be Effective Communication and Problem Solving. But may also be Respect for Race and Diversity, Community and Customer. Hence, why having a good working understanding of the core competencies will aid the whole assessment process.

PIRT/IQ Test

The other part is the Police Initial Recruitment test (PIRT) although this has been replaced at assessment centres by two test papers, one is numerical and the other is verbal reasoning. They do follow similar lines and exercises to the (PIRT) and the examples given below will help for both types of testing. There are some examples later to give you an idea of what is expected. One of the best tips is not to try to complete all the answers, but to choose answers that you can give quickly and under pressure. If you find any difficulties, then move onto the next question. Then re-visit any you have failed to complete. The tests are undertaken as part of an assessment day. Some forces still use PIRT for Special Constables entrance tests.

The PIRT test consists of several skills areas.

Verbal Usage Test – the ability to spell words and construct sentences accurately.

Checking Information – the ability to check information quickly and correctly.

Working with Numbers – the ability to solve numerical problems accurately.

Verbal Reasoning – the ability to reason logically when given facts about events.

The new tests being used by some forces consist of a numerical reasoning test, which will ask you to answer multiple-choice questions that will measure your ability to solve number problems accurately. Also a verbal, logical and reasoning test where you will asked to answer multiple-choice questions which will measure your ability to make logical sense of a situation when you are given facts about it.

Example Tests

Verbal Usage Test

1. One hundred officers _____ allocated for _____ control.

A - was / croud
B - was / crowd
C - were / croud
D - were / crowd
E - none of these

2. It is _____ to bring your uniform to the training _____.

A - necesary / centre
B - necessary / centre
C - necessary / center

D - necessery / centre
E - none of these
Answers Verbal Reasoning
1=D
2=B

Checking information test

Look at the two lists below and check to see whether the information in List A has been correctly transferred to List B. If there is a mistake in column A, mark circle A on your answer sheet. If there is a mistake in column B, mark circle B on your answer sheet. If there is a mistake in column C, mark circle C on your answer sheet. If there is a mistake in column D, mark circle D on your answer sheet. If there are no errors in that line, mark circle E on your answer sheet. Note that there may be more than one error in a line.

LIST A

A Date	B Name	C Time	D Ref Num
12.1	Williams	13.30	2613
3.8	Chan	07.29	5971

LIST B

A Date	B Name	C Time	D Ref Num
Jan 12	WILLIAMS	15:30	3612
March 8	CHAN	09:27	579

Answers Checking Information
1=DE
2=CE

Working with numbers/Numerical Reasoning Test

At the assessment centre you will be supplied with a calculator and you need to know how to work out ratios, averages, percentages, area, time, distance and speed. Try he questions below without and then with a calculator.

1. How much will five tins of soup cost at 55p a tin?

A   B   C   D   E
£2.25 £2.55 £2.60 £2.75 £2.95

2. A person saves £35 in four weeks. At this rate how much will have been saved in one year?

A	B	C	D	E
£200	£250	£355	£420	£455

3. What is the total cost of a journey when £1.65 is spent on bus-fares and an Underground ticket costs £2.50?

A	B	C	D	E
£3.15	£3.60	£3.95	£4.05	£4.15

4. What is the average number of people per car, when six cars carry thirty people?

A	B	C	D	E
4.5	5.0	5.5	6.0	6.5

5. If shopping items cost £12.64, how much money remains out of £20?

A	B	C	D	E
£6.36	£6.63	£7.36	£7.46	£7.63

Answers working with numbers

1=D
2=E
3=E
4=B
5=C

Verbal/logical reasoning test

Sometime on the night of 4th November, the Zanzibar Club was burnt to the ground. The Police are treating the fire as suspicious. The only facts known at this stage are:
- The club was insured for more than its real value.
- The club belonged to Jim Tuttle.
- David Braithwaite was known to dislike Jim Tuttle.
- Between 3rd November and 4th November, David Braithwaite was away from home on a business trip.
- There were no fatalities.
- A plan of the club was found in David Braithwaite's flat.

A = TRUE B = FALSE C = IMPOSSIBLE TO SAY

1. A member of Jim Tuttle's family died in the blaze.
A B C
2. If the insurance company pays out in full, Jim Tuttle stands to profit from the fire.
A B C
3. The flat where the plan was found is close to the club.
A B C
4. Jim Tuttle could have been at the club when the fire took place.
A B C
5. There are definite grounds to arrest David Braithwaite for arson.
A B C

Answers Verbal Reasoning
1=B
2=A
3=C
4=A
5=B

What can you do to give your best performance?

Don't be down-hearted if you find the questions difficult or get a lot of them wrong. There are many things you can do to improve your performance. Practice is one answer, another is to simply slow down and take your time. The tests are not designed for you to be able to finish them. It merely assesses that you can undertake tasks efficiently and to a set standard.

Practice doing simple arithmetic without using a calculator. Do number puzzles. Do the scoring when playing games such as darts, card games. Put a ruler or something similar with a straight edge under lists. Take a few deep breaths before you start and don't try to rush.

Make sure that you know what you must do before you start putting pencil to paper – if you do not understand, ask the person who is administering the test.

Read the instructions carefully before each test starts to make sure that you understand. Don't skim through them – you may overlook important details and in consequence make mistakes you could have avoided.

Even if you have taken the test before, don't assume that the instructions (and the worked examples) are the same as the last time – they may have changed.

Once the test begins work as quickly and as accurately as you can. Choose an easy to answer question first to boost confidence.

Avoid spending too much time on questions you find difficult. Find an easier question then go back later if you have time.

If you are uncertain about an answer, enter your best reasoned choice (but avoid simply guessing).

If you have some spare time after you have answered all questions, go back and check through your answers.

Keep working as hard as you can throughout the test – the more correct answers you get the higher your score will be.

Be positive in your attitude. Previous failures in tests or examinations, are in the past and you should not allow that to have a detrimental effect on your performance on this occasion. Focus and believe you can pass the test.

During the whole application process where most candidates fall short is the lack of preparation. You really need to understand the role that you are applying for and then be able to convey your understand of this to the recruitment staff. Understanding what a police officer does along with the core competencies is the first step. For example, during the final interview you are likely to receive a question like the following: "please describe a situation where you have to work as a team, what was the outcome and what role did you play in this.

Now, while this question is obviously referring to the core competency of teamwork, an essential requirement if you want to become a police officer, other questions are not so simple to determine what core competency you are required to demonstrate. However, if you do not these core competencies off by heart you will not be able to work out how you should be answering the question and this will not score you high marks.

Referring to the question above, if you have not thought about a time in your life where you have been able to work as a team it is quite difficult for most people to think about this right there and then. So what starts to happen is panic sets in and you cannot think clearly and so the answer you give is the first example that comes to mind. However, it is only later when you leave the interview do you think "I should have said that" or "why didn't I use that example" and the reason for this is that you are now in a calm and relaxed manner.

On the other hand, a strong candidate will have a couple of examples that that have given considerable thought to before attending the assessment centre so that even if the question doesn't match exactly, they can simply adapt their answer to meet the specific core competency that is being tested. Better still, try to have examples for each of the core competencies. You will have given four on your application form so think of ones for the remaining two.

Some candidates may think that if they give a good example, does it matter if they give the correct core competency? The answer to this question is firstly is shows that you do not understand what is being asked from you and secondly that you have failed to prepare for this role. The recruitment staff are looking for people who have taken their application seriously and given considerable thought to their recruitment. Remember these recruiters have seen many different types of candidates and will have a skill in detecting those that know what they are talking about and have prepared.

As well as preparing a list of examples for particular situations that you can recall and adapt to give specific and related answers the other part of the application process you need to prepare for is the police role play. While many candidates want to be part of the everyday environment that a police officer experiences very few will have experienced this in real life. The role play scenarios will access your abilities to deal with certain situations, your manner and how you apply yourself. In the end, they want to see how many of the core competency indicators you can match. The more positive indicators you match the higher your score and in theory overall grade. The role plays also carry the largest (63%) of the total marks. Therefore, being confident in a role play, being able to ask questions.

Fitness Test

The fitness test will test your dynamic strength, which involves performing five seated chest pushes and five seated back pulls on the dyno machine to measure your strength.

The second part is the endurance part where you will be asked to run to and fro along a 15-metre track in time with a series of bleeps, which become increasingly faster. You can retake your fitness test up to three times.

As said earlier, if you don't consider yourself that fit, then get out and do a little jogging, swimming or cycling. The police fitness test is not that hard as you are not applying to the SAS. However, they do expect a level of fitness to be able to pass at level 13 on the bleep test.

The Final Interview

The final force interview if your chosen force does a final interview. Is where you get a chance to be yourself and also ask questions as well as questions being asked of you. You may well be asked why you want to be a police officer and your career aspirations. Try not to use the usual, "To fight crime" it should be more about supporting your local community and making a difference within the community. Being a police officer is now very much community and customer focused. The panel interviewing you may ask questions to test your knowledge on the local area the force operates in. It is a good idea to revise and understand the area of the force you are applying to join. What is their mission statement and force priorities? Look at a recent HMIC report to find out the challenges the force faces, as well as what they do well and not quite so well.

Try to relax and just be yourself answering questions with some detail, but try not to waffle. There are no questions to try to trip you up, but the questions are to explore your experience, attitudes and the type of person you are. This is why it is so important to, "Just be plain you". You may get asked questions that refer to your original competency questions on your application form or other things that you put down on your application form such as hobbies or interests, military service, current position. Results from various tests may also be looked at in more depth to probe your strengths and weaknesses.

TRAINING

You have passed all the tests and the interview and your final security clearance have been done, you will now receive a date for your training. What will you learn? What will you do? How long will it last?

Training is a vital part of becoming a police officer. It is a very wide ranging job and requires, for example, knowledge of the law, to be able to undertake the job effectively. Don't expect even after training to just walk out onto the beat and have all the knowledge and experience you need. It takes many years to build this up and it is all too easy to get frustrated by your lack of knowledge at times. Experience with dealing with a wide range of offences and incidents will slowly build up your knowledge. A good tutor constable will aid your initial learning period on patrol. Later, you will work with other police officers to give you a good insight into how different officers do their jobs. Once signed off for independent patrol you can attend incidents on your own and be single crewed. That first time out on your own is a little harrowing but at the same time, a sense of achievement that you are thought to be competent enough to work independently. From there on in, the learning never stops. As you attend a plethora of incidents and learn something from each one.

Probation is the first step in your career and this lasts for two years or usually one year for a Special Constable. This is a time where training is intensive and progress is carefully monitored. You will get every assistance to build the skills you will need as an officer - and when you complete the probationary period, you will become a Police Constable or Special Constable. Training is carried out at a force-training centre or maybe an affiliated college depending on the force. Special Constable Training is nearly always carried out at the force's training centre.

Probation's all about continuous professional development - and the first step is induction training. Some forces you'll be issued with your uniform, shown how to maintain it, advised about conditions of service. You will then start an initial phase of training looking at procedures and some aspects of law. Officer Safety Training will also help you deal with confrontational or violent situations and is a mandatory requirement for you to be allowed to go out on patrol with your tutor Constable for both Regular and Special Constables. One important aspect to learn and understand, for all officers is the National Decision Model.

National Decision Model

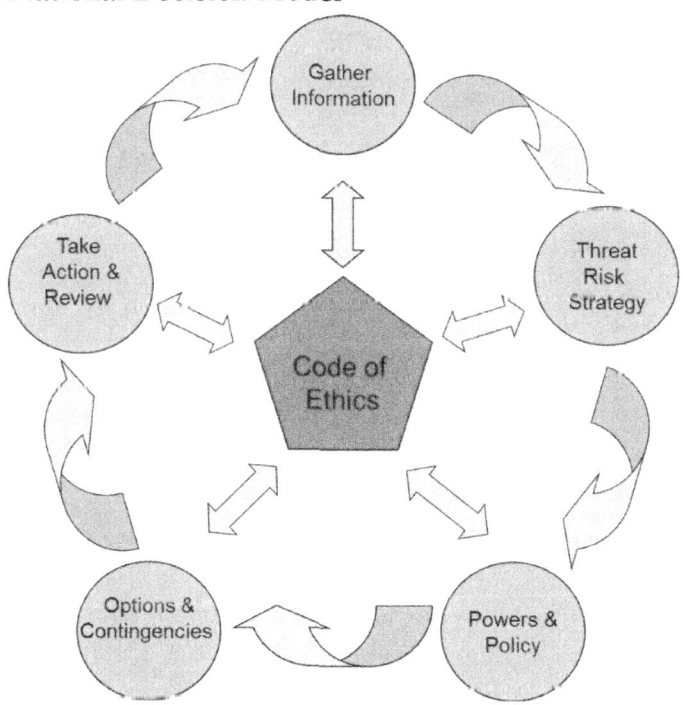

Diagram: A circular flow model with "Code of Ethics" at the centre, surrounded by: Gather Information, Threat Risk Strategy, Powers & Policy, Options & Contingencies, Take Action & Review.

Regular Officer Training

An example of a typical Initial Police Learning and Development Programme (IPLDP) runs over the 18-week course and will consist of:

PHASE 1 – INTRODUCTION

For the first phase of training, you will spend 18 weeks on this section

The modules covered in this phase include:
- health and safety
- first aid

- race and diversity
- ethics and values
- information technology
- problem solving
- team working.
- law
- Equipment usage
- Dealing with different types of crime.

You will also have 3 days of basic personal safety training and start looking at social, community and neighbourhood policing to prepare you for the next phase of your training. At the end of the 18 weeks, there is usually some form of passing out parade, to mark the completion of your initial raining.

PHASE 2 (B) SUPERVISED PATROL

This is for 12 weeks and takes place at a professional development unit or with a tutor from the response shift you will be joining. You will be assigned a tutor on a one to one basis who will support you for the remainder of your probation.

During this phase of the training you will be given time to complete your Student Officer Learning and Development Portfolio (SOLAP) or Professional Development Portfolio (PDP). You will also attend a one week classroom based course where you will be taught the legislation on subjects such as Anti-Social Behaviour Orders (ASBOs) using live local data.

At the end of the 12 weeks, you will be ready to go out on independent patrol.

PHASE 3 - INDEPENDENT PATROL

This is for 4 weeks and is based at your PDU or with your new response shift. If your area has a neighbourhood policing scheme, then you will also spend some time on that.

Either before or during your training you will be attested, which is where you are sworn in as Constable by taking an oath with a magistrate or justice of the peace present.

It takes two years for a regular police officer to be classed as 'substantive' and have completed probation. Probation is a steep learning curve, as the job of a police officer requires a large amount of knowledge, along with the various changes in the law, policies and procedures.

Special Constable Training

Special Constables have a much shorter and more intensive training program. Nearly all use the IL4SC training, which in essence is a cut down version of the regular full-time police officers 18 week IPLDP. With the length of the course they do not cover everything a full-time officer would. Law is one element that is greatly reduced and the training is there to cover the more basic policing role that Special Constable's are normally expected to undertake. Much of what a Special Constable will learn certainly as they progress in service will be learnt on the street from other officers and maybe attending more specialised training.

Below is an outline and content of a typical police force training course. They do vary, but the content for all is very similar and it's mainly the order that changes or local needs in terms of training required in the program.

The first weekend will be designed to introduce you to the force you will be working with and to gain an understanding of policing. This should give you a good grasp of how the force works and what they are trying to achieve. You will learn about the force's aims and policing style and about providing a service that meets the needs of everyone in the community. You may also look at how being a Special Constable affects your life and what being a Special Constable means to you and your family. You will be given the opportunity to discuss with your intake your hopes and fears about becoming a Special. You may well make some lifelong friends along the way. You will also be taken through important issues such as health and safety.

On the second, third and fourth weekends you will receive your Officer Safety Training (OST), which will give you the skills you need to deal with situations on the street. You cover first aid and Unarmed Defence Tactics (UDT) and your Personal Protective Equipment (PPE), like handcuffs, and other force-specific equipment such as the side arm baton, ASP baton and CS or PAVA spray. These weekends will be physically demanding and may be challenging at first.

UDT consists of tactics designed to defend you from attack and techniques to help restrain or move an offender.

Handcuff training will take you through the basic techniques needed to handcuff somebody as well as different types of handcuffing.

CS/PAVA, here you will use an inert CS/PAVA spray filled with water to practice drawing and aiming the spray on an individual and group.

ASP training involves techniques for using the ASP baton both extended and closed, as well as going through the safe areas on the body that that baton can be used on. Training on the side arm baton is also very similar.

You go through the technique and circumstances for using leg restraints, how best to deploy them and the potential risk of leaving them on too long.

The final weekends will provide you with the legal knowledge you require to start your job out on the streets. The legislation you learn will prove invaluable and is just the beginning – from this point you will always be learning and gaining knowledge about criminal legislation and looking at specific offences. Not only will you be revising your law, but you will also be taking part in role-play exercises and learning how to use radios and deal with real-life scenarios. You will also look at diversity, basic use of force, IT systems, filling in crime reports and recording witness statements as well as how to use your pocket notebook.

Officer Safety Training

All police officers must be trained and then re-qualify every year to make use of their personal protective equipment (PPE).

Usually this broken down into a series of Modules that looks at one or maybe several parts of their PPE. This is normally undertaken initially during training before going out on the streets and then every year. The area's covered are:

UDT

Unarmed Defence Tactics is the basic way a police officer and PCSO is taught to defend themselves from attack. It is self-defence training, with home office approved tactics. The idea is to teach a series of strikes and blokes that will enable a police officer to defend themselves. A Palm strike for example is used to push a person away, a Knee strike can be used to cause pain in an assailant's thigh. Another important aspect of UDT is tactical communications. This is used an initial warning to any attacker with the words 'Back off' or similar being used. Using tactical communications is important to alert others and the general public, who more often than not just see a police officer striking someone without realising the reason why. Tactical communications can often work extremely well and resolve a situation before it escalates.

As well as defensive moves and tactical communications, officers are taught pain compliance were pressure points can be used to gain control of a difficult assailant.

Handcuffs

Handcuffs, like UDT is undertaken every year to prevent skill find and update police officers of the changes. The techniques taught are most commonly the different ways to handcuff ie Front, back and stack. Handcuffing a difficult offender and using the handcuffs for pain compliance. Often along with handcuffs limb restraints are also practiced.

The CS spray and Asp again are undertaken once a year. CS spray is practiced with inert canisters filled with water and propelled by compressed air. For the ASP a mixture of 'baton twirling' and hitting real live padded targets is undertaken to practice the various techniques. As part of the Windsor review, usually as part of the

OST training, all frontline officers must undertake an annual fitness test.

First Aid

First aid is very important for every police officer. They may be on the scene of an accident first and must administer first aid before the paramedics arrive. Police first aid is pretty much the same as any other first aid such as 'emergency first aid' or 'full first aid at work'. This section is not intended to be a definitive guide to police first aid but more an aid memoire with the common mnemonics used in police first aid.

On coming across an unconscious casualty y remember the following:

DRSABC

Danger – Check for the safety of yourself and the casualty

Response – See AVPU below

Shout for help either via radio or to someone else

Airways – Check and clear airway of any obstruction

Breathing – Tilt head back, lift chin and listen feel for 10 seconds for any signs of breathing including watching the chest.

Conscious – Place in the recovery position

AVPU

Alert – Are they conscious?

Voice – Do they respond to your voice?

Pain – Does pressing the sides of the neck or squeezing the earlobes induce a response?

Unresponsive – Go through ABC as above.

If unresponsive you should then be doing a top to toe check looking for any signs of injury. For this use the mnemonic:

Respiration – Is their rate between the life sustaining 10 to 30 breaths a minute?

Injury – Check for any visible injury in particular chest/thoracic cavity, especially in a suspected stabbing.

Symmetry – Check for any differences between one side and the other. Check down the sternum to the Zyphoid.

Effort – Check for any difficulty breathing, heaving chest, sucking stomach upwards to indicate phneumothorax

Neck – If there is any effort to breath revisit the neck area and check for:

Any injuries you may have missed

Tracheal Deviation indicating pneumothorax

Subcutaneous or surgical emphesymas that feel like rice crispies under the skin (due to air from the lungs escaping into the chest cavity and into the soft tissue around the neck). If there is internal bleeding this is called a Haema-pnuothorax. If the lung is punctured as well as the chest cavity this is seen by bright red oxygenated blood, coming from the IP's mouth this is known as tension-pnuemothorax.

CPR

CPR is the main way that a person who has no pulse and is not breathing is kept alive with a 30% survival rate. It has been found that just chest compressions will cause enough air to be pulled in to keep a person alive. However, it is still deemed to be best practice to ventilate as well as do compressions.

For CPR on an adult the ratio is 2 breaths to 30 compressions to a depth of 5cm. For a child it is 5 rescue breaths followed by 30 compressions to $1/3^{rd}$ the depth of the chest followed by a continuous cycle of 2 breaths to 30 compressions with either one or two hands depending on size. A baby is the same, as a child, however the compressions are undertaken with one finger and the ventilations will need both the mouth and nose covering.

Bleeding

Severe bleeding can lead to death within minutes therefore severe bleeding must be dealt with as a matter of priority. For bleeding the mnemonic:

PEEPS.

Position – Does the casualty or injury need to be moved

Expose and examine – Check the wound for anything in it

Elevate – Were possible elevate the injury above the heart to slow the flow of blood down

Pressure – Some form of pressure may well need to be applied either direct or indirect, to stem the flow of blood

Shock – Shock is a killer and associated with fluid loss. With blood loss, shock is a real risk and needs to be carefully monitored.

When dealing with any casualty try to get as much information as possible. Such as how did it happen if not obvious? Are they any known medical conditions? When did they last eat or drink? All of this information may help with first aid and aid any further advanced medical care that is needed.

Uniform

Police uniforms and equipment in the United Kingdom have varied considerably from the inception of what was to become the earliest recognisable mainstream police force in the country with the Metropolitan Police Act of 1829. Allowing the formation of the Metropolitan Police Service, and the various County Police Acts, policing became a more standardised practice in the UK throughout the late nineteenth century, the uniforms and equipment became equally standardised. From a variety of home grown uniforms, bicycles, swords and pistols the British police force evolved in look and equipment.

All uniformed officers wear a uniform specified by their individual force. You may have seen when watching TV documentaries or visiting other towns or city's slight variances in what police officers wear. The most common two types of uniform are the new black wicking T-shirts with the words "Police" in white on the sleeves then a stab vest with either a black or high visibility cover. The other style is a white shirt with a black clip on tie and/or a cravat again with a black or high visibility cover on the stab vest. Both styles use similar black trousers and worn normally with boots for extra support and comfort especially when needing to run.

For court attendance, most police officers wear the traditional police tunic with either skirt or trousers for women and the instantly recognisable custodian helmet for men or felt hat for women. You may have noticed that the custodian helmets vary across the forces some have what is called the 'horn' as part of the design or slightly differently designed 'nipple' on the top of the helmet. The modern custodian helmet is actually based on similar construction methods to a cycling helmet to make it lighter and more comfortable to wear. Initially designed for the Special Constabulary who did and still do a large amount of foot patrol it has since been issued to all police officers.

OATH

One of the first things you do after joining as a police officer be it a regular officer or special is to be attested. In simple terms, it is basically saying an oath to be sworn in as a police officer.

English Oath "I, ..(your name) .. of ..(your force) .. do solemnly and sincerely declare and affirm that I will well and truly serve the Queen in the office of Constable, with fairness, integrity, diligence and impartiality, upholding fundamental human rights and according equal respect to all people; and that I will, to the best of my power, cause the peace to be kept and preserved and prevent all offences against people and property; and that while I continue to hold the said office I will to the best of my skill and knowledge discharge all the duties thereof faithfully according to law."

Welsh Oath "Rwyf i...o...yn datgan ac yn cadarnhau yn ddifrifol ac yn ddiffuant y byddaf yn gwasanaethu'r Frenhines yn dda ac yn gywir yn fy swydd o heddwas (heddferch), yn deg, yn onest, yn ddiwyd ac yn ddiduedd, gan gynnal hawliau dynol sylfaenol a chan roddi'r un parch i bob person; ac y byddaf i, hyd eithaf fy ngallu, yn achosi i'r heddwch gael ei gadw a'i ddiogelu ac yn atal pob trosedd yn erbyn pobl ac eiddo; a thra byddaf yn parhau i ddal y swydd ddywededig y byddaf i, hyd eithaf fy sgil a'm gwybodaeth, yn cyflawni'r holl ddyletswyddau sy'n gysylltiedig â hi yn ffyddlon yn unol â'r gyfraith."

Scotland has no specific words that are prescribed within current Scottish Police legislation. Section 16 of the Police (Scotland) act

1967 merely requires that "A person appointed to the office of Constable in a police force shall on appointment make, before a sheriff (or justice of the peace), a declaration in such terms as may be prescribed concerning the proper discharge of the duties of the office." The declaration is typically given in the form:

"I hereby do solemnly and sincerely declare and affirm that I will faithfully discharge the duties of the office of Constable/Special Constable."

Once attested you are entitled to your warrant card, this may be issued any time during your initial training phase, but before you go out on duty and identifies yourself as a Police officer.

Most forces use experiential learning; as the name suggests, you learn from experience. The full cycle is to reflect on your experience and interpret. This is trying to make sense of an event and compiling an action plan for the future. Perhaps it is just like playing a computer game where you have a crash or get killed; you think about it and try it again, maybe changing the way you did it originally.

Training will aim to provide you with the skills and expertise you need to carry out several core tasks that will be built into your probation period.

IT Training, IT is used by all forces for various systems for doing things like recording crime, gathering intelligence, briefing, and showing incidents within the force. Being able to use packages such as Microsoft Word for word processing reports, statements and Microsoft Outlook for Email will be of use.

Probation is about 2 years. It is during this period that you and the force can assess whether the Police Force is right for you and you feel it is the right choice as well.

Most of the ongoing training you need will be delivered in the policing district or area where you work. It will involve a mixture of practical training and further lessons on subjects such as law updates, IT updates, scenes of crime preservation, Victim care and diversity.

All forces have an ongoing training schedule, so that you can learn a new skill or update existing skills. Your force or division will have a training plan in place with dates for training. Some training like UDT, CS, and handcuffs, etc. is mandatory training that you have to take and re-qualify at least once a year.

Regular officers have to complete a PDP or SOLAP while they are on probation. The aim is to collate evidence about your work to show that you have gained experience in all the core tasks. The Portfolio will contain information, such as reports from supervisors, records of attendance on training courses, law notes and other evidence about the work you have carried out. Keeping the profile up to date is the responsibility of individual officers. It does help to see what you have done and what you need to do to complete your probation period.

Key areas you may cover once at your allocated station are:

In the police station, the police station front desk is often where the first point of contact between the police and public takes place. You will learn how to handle enquiries appropriately and effectively, giving advice, taking down information or referring people on to someone who can help.

Dealing with traffic road safety is an important concern for the Police and it is quite likely you will be involved in enforcing traffic law. You will need to know what action you should take and when. You may also be involved in dealing with traffic collisions (RTC) and will need to know how to protect the scene, control traffic and locate and identify witnesses.

Dealing with incidents being a uniformed officer on patrol you may be the first to arrive at the scene of an incident. Whether it is a domestic dispute or a burglary, you will be expected to know what to do. You will be taught how to establish what has happened, who needs to be informed and how to control the scene. It takes time and experience to become proficient, which is why you spend so much time with a tutor Constable and then continue to work with an experienced officer until you are deemed fit to go out on independent patrol.

Making an arrest there will be times when you must arrest a suspect or help other officers make an arrest. Ensuring your safety and that of the people around you will involve knowledge of restraint techniques, how to use equipment such as CS spray and a baton to apply appropriate force. A good legal knowledge of your powers to make an arrest is essential. You will cover some of the basics in the next chapter. You will be taught how to escort detainees to the custody centre and how to search them.

Investigating Another important aspect is the investigation of a crime and obtaining full and accurate statements from victims and witnesses. You will receive instruction on how to take statements and how to write your own if you have been a witness.

Patrolling If patrolling is to be effective, it needs to be well planned and well executed. You will learn about planning a patrol to meet the particular needs of your beat and to tackle the fear of crime. You will need to establish a good network of contacts throughout the community and use the information they give to provide a better policing service on your patch. You will also learn practical skills such as using correct radio procedures by going out on the beat.

Driving As a police officer you will be expected to drive and Police Forces have a wide variety of vehicles from arctic Lorries to a JCB. You start with a standard license to drive marked and unmarked cars up to a set power limit set by the force. You can then undertake further advanced three-week course to be able to use blue lights on lower powered vehicles, then a pursuit course to drive higher power car's and can undertake pursuits. You can also do courses for van driving, motorcycle and various other vehicles the force may have. The Association Chief Police Officers (APCO) has guidelines for the Police Driving competences, which set out the national standards for Police Driving. Very few Forces allow Special

Constables to have anything more than Standard and Van driving on their Police licence.

ON DUTY

It is your first time on duty and in uniform, what can you expect to do? How will you know what to do? The first time you go out in uniform, it is a little nerve-racking but you will soon settle down and your tutor Constable will go through what you need to do. We will start this chapter by looking at what you might do on an average shift. Don't worry if you don't understand all the terminology, you will later on.

02:30pm Arrive at Police station and change into uniform.

02:45pm Go into the parade room and get my radio and CS spray and any other kit I require.

03:00pm Go into a briefing with shift. The Shift sergeant leads the briefing and goes through recent events and priorities for the shift. High visible patrol in burglary hotspots, town centre patrol, checking parks for teenagers who are drinking. At the briefing, everyone is paired up and allocated call sign, i.e. BW66, CB57 or AB24.

03:30pm I have some initial paperwork to complete before going out a couple of tickets need posting and I have a file to complete ready for an interview tomorrow

04:30pm, I get keys to a car and go out on patrol.

05:00pm, I pull a car over and issue a fixed penalty notice for using a mobile phone whilst driving.

6:30pm, now out patrolling the town centre I have been joined by a Special Constable, whom I regularly work with, talking to local pub door staff when the first radio call comes in. A group of teenagers is causing a disturbance outside a fish and chip shop so we go off to investigate.

6:40pm, we arrive at the scene of the disturbance to find a group of 12 teenagers throwing chips and generally being rowdy. We stop and have a chat and use the stop check forms to check details. A couple of them do have previous cases of theft, but nothing current. After giving a verbal warning, we ask them to move on.

7:00pm, back on the patrol, we decide to do a walk through the parks which are just being locked up for the night. A couple of people are making their way to the exit.

7:30pm, we have another call about a group of teenagers drinking and being noisy in the park. The description given fits that of the group we spoke to earlier outside the chip shop. We make our way to the park.

7:40pm, on entering the park some of the group start to run so we pick up the pace a little and manage to catch up with nearly all the group before they have chance to climb over the fence. A few of the group are drunk and two are holding opened bottles of wine and lager. From the previous checks at the chip shop we know they are all under age, so the opened alcohol is seized and poured away. They are warned that they are trespassing, as the park is now closed. One male, who is drunk, becomes abusive and starts to swear and he is given a section 5 warning. One girl is heavily drunk and can barely walk so a decision is made that she needs escorting home. We request another unit to our location to assist. Our male continues to swear and is given a second and final section 5 public order warning.

Another unit arrives and takes the very drunk female home for her personal safety. We then disperse the rest of the group after giving them all a final warning and they are told to go home.

7:55pm, we follow the group out and as we get over the fence the male who swore at us drops his trousers in the distance so we give chase; although he is quick we catch up with him. He is then cautioned and arrested for indecent exposure and being drunk and disorderly. Being on foot patrol, we need to request a van to come and pick him up. We then convey the male to custody where he is booked in and details given. As he is drunk, we cannot interview him about the offence, so we will need to do a handover pack for the morning shift to be able to deal with it.

8:30pm, Back at the Police station we undertake the paperwork for the arrest. This includes an arrest statement as to why and under what circumstances the arrest was made. The crime reporting paperwork and handover pack needs compiling and that includes all the paperwork that the morning shift will need to continue the investigation and see if he can be charged.

09:30pm, a call comes in with reports of a fight outside a pub. As it is an immediate we are authorised to use the blue lights and quickly get to the fight. On arrival, there is nothing to be seen; a few people walking to taxis and to the various takeaways but nobody matching the description. We talk to the door staff and they have not seen anything either. We then get back into the car and do an area search to see if we can find any of the offenders, but there is no trace. With that call-out checked we resume patrol work.

09:45pm, the next call reports domestic violence at a house. We put on the blue lights. On arrival, there is still some shouting going on and the door is slightly open. We enter the property to find the couple still arguing, so we part them and take one into the kitchen and one in the living room to try and ascertain what has happened. Both have been drinking and the fight is down to the mother-in-law coming to stay the next day. Both parties are still quite emotional and as soon as they catch sight of each other start to argue. As we feel there could be further breaches of the peace we ask if the male can go and stay somewhere else for the night. He replies he can go to a mate's house so we offer to take him there to make sure he does not go back to his home address.

10:30pm, back on patrol. We will have some paperwork to do for the domestic fight we have just been too, but for the moment, on a busy Friday night, the greater need is to be on patrol and available for jobs as they come in.

10:45pm, the third call comes in asking us to go to a driver, possibly drunk and seen wandering across the road. We head off and follow the car, checking its details and pull the car over using the blue lights. I go around and ask the driver to step out of the car whilst my colleague gets the breathalyser out. I can smell alcohol on the man's breath and on breathalysing him, he is over the legal limit. He is duly cautioned and arrested for drink driving and then conveyed to custody. Once booked into custody we take him to the intoxylyser for further samples of breath and on both readings, he is twice the legal limit of 35mg at 70mg. He is then taken back to the cells to be charged in the morning.

00:30amm, finally all paperwork is complete and time to book off duty and go home should have finished at 12 but we cannot go off duty until all the paperwork needed by the morning shift is completed for our arrests.

As can be seen, whilst on duty you can come across a whole variety of incidents and crimes and no two shifts are ever the same. Another shift may be spent doing nothing but paperwork. Taking a statement from a victim of crime then putting all the required paperwork together to interview the suspect. You never stop coming across new incidents and never stop learning.

Equipment

Going out on the beat does require you to have various bits of equipment for protection known as PPE and equipment to gather and record information. Equipment does vary from force to force.

Pocket Note Book - this low-tech piece of equipment is one of the most important. Some forces make greater use of it than others do. It is a legal document that can be used in court and outlines what you have done each time you are on duty: it can be used to record details of incidents and take brief statements.

Blackberry – More and more frontline officers are equipped with smartphones the most common one being issued is the blackberry. These can be used as normal mobile phones/smart phones. They also have the capability for officers to do PNC checks, do crime reports, add intelligence, and other information onto the various police systems. Being a mobile phone they do suffer the same issues as any other mobile phone in turns of reception and data speeds.

Torch - this is essential for helping to search at night or even during the day in unlit buildings or a dark area within a car like under the seats.

Stab Vest - the Police Patrol body armour style has been designed to provide you with a light and easy to wear a stab proof vest. The item is made in hard-wearing poly cotton fabric and supplied with epaulettes, radio loops and two large utility pockets. The inserts are made of Kevlar and consist of one at the front, one at the back and two in each of the shoulders. It's imperative that it is fitted correctly and zipped up fully to give maximum protection. These normally have a life of around five years, after which they need replacing to guarantee their effectiveness. The stab vest will deflect all knives and does have minor ballistic stopping power as well as from small calibre weapons. However, extra steel plates are inserted as worn by UK military forces and armed response officers to fully stop bullets

Utility Belt - if issued holds all your personal equipment outlined below. It can also hold a first aid kit and have pockets to hold paperwork such as stop search forms or fixed penalty notices. There are many quick release type belts that some officers find easier to use than the more conventional leather hook and eye belts.

CS Spray - CS spray is classed as a firearm and can only be stored securely at the Police station and used by a trained officer whilst on duty.

The CS is in the form of a hand-held aerosol canister, with the solution being 5% CS, with Methyl isobutyl ketone, which is propelled by Nitrogen. The liquid stream is directed where the user points the canister, and is accurate up to 4 meters. It has been noted that the solvent MiBK that the CS is suspended in, is itself harmful, and can cause inflammation, dermatitis, burns to the skin and liver damage in isolated cases.

The biggest issue with CS spray is what is called 'splash back' in that wind or other environmental factors can cause some of the spray to end up on officers, especially in close confines and officers using it need to be tactically aware of the impact of using it in a situation. Another issue is that dogs and some people are immune to CS crystals which look like a snowflake and it is the sharp spines on the crystal that cause the irritation.

PAVA spray - this is used by some forces, and others have been trialing its use. It is dispensed from a handheld canister similar to CS spray, in a liquid stream that contains a 0.3% solution of PAVA (Pelargonic Acid Vanillylamide) in a solvent of aqueous ethanol. The propellant is nitrogen the same as CS spray.

This solution has been selected because this is the minimum concentration which will fulfil the purpose of the equipment; namely to minimise a person's capacity for resistance without unnecessarily prolonging their discomfort. It should be noted that PAVA is significantly more potent than CS.

The liquid stream is a spray pattern and has a maximum effective range of up to 4 meters. Maximum accuracy, however, will be achieved over a distance of 1.25 - 2 meters. The operating distance is the distance between the canister and the subject's eyes, not the distance between the officer and the subject.

Limb Restraint – this is used by many forces now to restrain offenders. The straps come as a pair and are wound round the ankle and just below the knee and held together with strong Velcro. They reduce the risk of the offender being able to kick at officers as they are placed into a prison van or Police car. They can only be left on for around 30 minutes otherwise they could cause deep vein thrombosis that causes a clot to form that potentially when it becomes loose could clog and stop the heart.

ASP - a tactical baton that works by using a friction lock system of telescopic tubes, which can be deployed almost instantly. This allows the ASP to quickly extend at the flick of the wrist. It can be used either extended or retracted and works as a visual deterrent. It should only be used where appropriate force is required or as a defence when searching a property or area where offenders could be present. The ASP can also be used to break windows to gain access to properties or vehicles.

Radio - all Police forces use the Airwave system, which is a secure digital communication system that offers many benefits, such as the ability to talk directly with other officers (point to point), text and use GPS and have an emergency button that will give you air priority if you need it. They are very similar in operation to, and look like, mobile phones. Sepura are one major supplier and Motorolla another. Police officers can contact another officer directly using what is called point to point. The control room can also contact officers directly to relay or gather further information. The GPS function is very useful in knowing where an officer is both for safety reasons and operational reasons, so that the nearest resource can be sent to an incident.

Handcuffs - restraint devices designed to secure an individual's wrist closer together. Speed cuffs are used by most forces and are handcuffs made by Hiatt & Company. They are characterised by their rigid design, the two cuffs being joined by a rigid metal bar and a black plastic grip, replacing the chain of earlier types of cuff. Their rigidity and the design of the grip makes them effective for gaining control over a struggling prisoner even if only one cuff has been applied.

Taser – Whilst not standard issue the Taser is becoming used by more and more officers as opposed to just armed response officers when it initially came into service. Now many traffic police and public order units also carry the Taser. Tasers were introduced as non-lethal weapons to be used by police to subdue fleeing, belligerent, or potentially dangerous people, who would have otherwise been subjected to what they consider more lethal weapons (such as a firearm). Since teaming up with police forces in 1999, Taser has had widespread success, with a 2009 Police Executive Research Forum study stating that officer injuries drop by 76% when a Taser is used. Although non-lethal there has been some controversy over several incidents where Taser use resulted in serious injury or death. However, the side effects are much less than those of CS or PAVA spray. Often it is enough to 'red dot' an offender with the built-in laser to gain compliance. Tasers are "prohibited weapons" under the Firearms Act 1968 and possession is an offence. The maximum sentence for possession is ten years in prison and an unlimited fine

The Taser works by initially placing a red laser dot on the target, usually the chest or back area and firing. The Taser fires two metal barbs that will penetrate medium clothing, but not really padded jackets so a different area of the body would need to be targeted. Although newer Taser versions like the X26 and C2 give an extra pulse to enable better penetration of thicker clothing. The air cartridge contains a pair of electrodes and propellant for a single shot and is replaced after each use. There are a number of cartridges, designated by range, with the maximum at 35 feet (10.6 m). The two barb electrodes look like fish hooks and when they penetrate the skin become lodged in and allow a 50,000 volt charge to penetrate. Once contact is made, the voltage drops to about 1,200 volts at about 19 pulses per second to cause neuromuscular incapacitation to the offender. They work by interrupting the ability of the brain to control the muscles in the body, so are not pain based and as such cannot be overcome. Further short bursts of electricity can be given to regain compliance as and when needed. Much debate is going on as to if and when these will be rolled out to all front-line officers.

Paperwork - part of Police work is doing various form filling or paperwork. Some of this paperwork you may carry with you, such as stop search forms or Fixed Penalty Notices - all forces have a wide variety of paperwork for associated crimes and incidents. The exact layout and procedure does vary from force to force. It is worth getting to know the more commonly used ones.

Radio Usage

Using the radio can seem a little scary at first. What do I say? How do I say it? Again, radio protocol does vary from force to force. All Police Forces use the Airwave system, which is essentially technology based on mobile phone technology that offers secure communication. It was originally set up by O2 and is due for renewal from 2015. Police Forces use either a Sepura or a Motorolla handset, the Sepura handset being the most widely used. The radios allow as well as normal radio usage, the ability to call an individual officer, sent text messages and status updates, along with normal telephone calls. They have an orange 'emergency' button to enable an officer to get hands free air priority should the need arise.

A - Alpha (or "Alfa")
B - Bravo
C - Charlie
D - Delta
E - Echo
F - Foxtrot
G - Golf
H - Hotel
I - India
J - Juliet (or "Juliett")
K - Kilo
L - Lima
M - Mike
N - November
O - Oscar
P - Papa
Q - Quebec
R - Romeo
S - Sierra
T - Tango
U - Uniform
V - Victor
W - Whisky
X - X-Ray
Y - Yankee
Z - Zulu

A large proportion of radio usage on a system called Airwave ad is basically an encrypted digital radio system similar in operation to a mobile phone network. This training is restricted and operationally varies slightly from force to force, although many elements are standard such as Airwave speak. However, it cannot really put into this book for security reasons. But the best way to learn how to use the radio is listen to how existing regular Police officers use theirs and you will be amazed at how quickly you pick it up. The radio is the main device used to deploy officers.

A central control room will direct officers to the various jobs. Often these are graded due to their nature and importance. A red job or immediate for instance is an emergency, usually given when there is a risk to life or property and allows immediate response with the use of blue lights. Other jobs may not pose an immediate threat, but still require a response within an hour, those are then graded as even lower may require a police presence within 24 hours. Lower grade jobs may include some anti-social behaviour, a theft where nothing was seen or heard and no description of an offender, an assault that happened on a previous day or much earlier time than reported. The grading is often based around either a crime being in progress or an offender on the scene. All forces have their own requirements for grading of jobs.

To the customer or victim when they ring the police to report something it will always be of high importance to them. As a police officer, you often have to manage their expectations and explain the course of action and why you will carry out that action.

When a member of the public phones the police, their call is taken by a customer service advisor, who will take the basic details and create an incident, usually on a system called Vison. They may also carry out some basic PNC (Police National Computer) checks as required. The incident is then passed onto a dispatcher, who has the job of managing resources, in other words the police out on the streets and sending the most appropriate resource to an incident.

PNC

The Police National Computer is used to check individuals (Nominals) and Vehicles. All UK vehicles are on PNC via the DVLA and any foreign vehicle that have been stolen or involved in some form of a crime and been reported or recorded. Also within vehicles is insurance details. Nominals are a little more complex with various elements, which are:

DD – Disqualified Driver
WM – Wanted Missing
FC – Firearms Certificate
DD – Disqualified Driver
DE – Description
MS – Marks and Scares
DS – Disposal Summary (Conviction history)
IX – Internal cross reference
LX – Local cross reference
BC – Bail and Care (Bail Conditions)
WS – Warning signals (Things to be wary of about the nominal)

To be able to carry out PNC checks a four-day user course and a refresher every three years is required. PNC is an invaluable tool to the police.

MoPI

MoPI (Management of Police Information) work stream represents a huge programme of policy, process and cultural change across the whole of the police organisation. Any police force works on intelligence and ensuring it collects and disseminated data to the relevant and authorised people. Any force has various systems for collecting data, be it Memex for intelligence, CRMS for the recording and reporting of crimes or newer more integrated systems such as Niche. It is essential that all this data can be linked and shared with other forces or agencies. The data also needs to be relevant and fit for purpose and data no longer needed or relevant is disposed of.

MoPI has been implemented by all police forces in England and Wales. Most forces have achieved the targets they set for themselves through their local MoPI action plans to ensure they manage information effectively and efficiently. MoPI is now business as usual to ensure continuity in the management of information. MoPI supports national standards across the police service. MoPI is about making information relevant and accessible; ensuring that all police operational information is managed effectively. MoPI covers the whole of the information life cycle, through collection & recording, evaluation, sharing and review, retention & disposal.

MoPI Code of Practice

The murder of Holly Wells and Jessica Chapman in August 2002 by Ian Huntley and the subsequent inquiry by Sir Michael Bichard had a profound and far reaching effect on how the police service now gathers, manages, use and share information. As a result of the inquiry, in 2005 the home secretary issued a statuary code of practice on the management of police information this then became referred to as MoPI.

The code ensures that:

Should only be retained if required for a 'Policing Purpose'

Should be grouped according to the nature of the information

Must undergo a Review/Retention and deletion process after a period of time commensurate with the nature of the information.

This code is intended to:

Ensure that information is managed consistently, throughout its entire lifecycle.

Allow information known about individuals to be readily identified and shared between police agencies across the UK.

Create a consistent national standard.

Help develop national information with the PND (Police National Database).

PACE

The Police and Criminal Evidence Act (PACE) and the PACE Codes of Practice provide the core framework of Police powers and safeguards around stop and search, arrest, detention, investigation, identification and interviewing detainees.

Code A Deals with the exercise by police officers of statutory powers to search a person or a vehicle without first making an arrest. It also deals with the need for a police officer to make a record of a stop or encounter.

Code B Deals with police powers to search premises and to seize and retain property found on premises and persons.

Code C Code C sets out the requirements for the detention, treatment and questioning of suspects not related to terrorism in police custody by police officers.

Code D Concerns the main methods used by the police to identify people in connection with the investigation of offences and the keeping of accurate and reliable criminal records.

Code E Deals with the audio recording of interviews with suspects in the police station

Code F Deals with the visual recording with sound of interviews with suspects. There is no statutory requirement on police officers to visually record interviews. However, the contents of this code should be considered if an interviewing officer decides to make a visual recording with sound of an interview with a suspect.

Code G deals with powers of arrest under section 24 the Police and Criminal Evidence Act 1984 as amended by section 110 of the Serious Organised Crime and Police Act 2005.

Code H sets out the requirements for the detention, treatment and questioning of suspects related to terrorism in police custody by police officers.

Revised PACE codes

Following consultation in November 2011, revised versions of PACE codes C and H are now in operation. The revised code G came into effect from November 2012. The codes above are the revised versions. The changes to the codes are highlighted below.

Codes C and H

Many of the changes to code C are mirrored (with modifications as necessary) in code H and vice versa to ensure consistency. Particular changes include:

Allowing the custody officer to direct custody staff to carry out certain actions in relation to a detainee's rights and entitlements, need for medical treatment and the risk assessment process

Supporting code G (Arrest) concerning 'voluntary' interviews by police and explaining the arrangements for obtaining free legal advice if a police interview takes place allowing those in whose welfare the detainee has an interest to visit. Updating the arrangements for access to legal advice and safeguards for detainees who change their mind about wanting advice.

Simplifying arrangements for mandatory notification of the arrest of foreign nationals and asylum claims. Updated provisions on the self-administration of controlled drugs and the application of safeguards for detainees suspected of being under the influence of drink or drugs or both. Detention without charge in terrorism cases

Post-charge questioning and detention in terrorism cases, for the purposes of which a new code of practice for video recording of interviews also comes into operation

Code G (Arrest)

The revisions to code G are updated provisions and guidance for police about their statutory power under section 24 of PACE to arrest any person without warrant for any offence

Clarify and emphasise the application of the necessity criteria in section 24(5) of the Act and reflect a number of court judgments about the need to arrest to interview ('voluntary interviews') where the only investigative action required is to interview the suspect and victim

Make it clear that arrests may not be made solely to obtain fingerprints and DNA

Additional notes for guidance, refer to the law on self-defence, which may be particularly relevant to officers dealing with allegations of assault; this includes provisions specific to teachers, which allow the use of reasonable force to prevent their pupils from committing any offence, injuring persons, damaging property or prejudicing the maintenance of good order and discipline

Identification of Suspects

There are a number of methods of identifying suspects. They may be conveniently grouped as identification by:

1. Witnesses

By video

Identification parades

Group identification

Confrontation

Photographs

2. Fingerprints

3. Examination e.g. to find marks such as tattoos or scars

4. Body samples and impressions e.g. blood or hair to generate DNA profile.

Normally the arrangements for, and the conduct of, identification procedures and the circumstances in which they are held, are the responsibility of an officer not below the rank of inspector. However, arranging and conduct of such procedures may, under supervision, be delegated to other officers of civilian staff. No person involved in the investigation of the case against the suspect may take any part in these procedures.

Prior to any formal identification procedure taking place, where a witness has been identified, is purported to have been identified, expresses an ability to identify, or there is a reasonable chance of him being able to identify, a suspect, and the suspect disputes being the person the witness claims to have seen, an identification procedure shall be held (unless it is not practicable to do so or it would serve no purpose).

If a procedure is held, the suspect should initially be offered video identification unless:

It is not practicable

An identification parade is both practicable and more suitable than a video identification.

The officer in charge of the investigation considers that a group identification is more suitable than a video identification parade and the identification is more suitable than video identification or an identification parade and the identification officer considers it practicable to arrange.

Identification by Witnesses

A record must be made of the suspect's description as first given by a witness, before the witness takes part in any of the procedures applicable to cases were the suspect is known.

When the suspect identity is not known

A witness may be taken to a neighbourhood or place to see whether they can identify the person. The principles applicable to identification by video, identification parades, or group identification must be followed as far as practicable, e.g. a record to be kept of the witness's description of the suspect. The witness attention is not to be directed to any individual, but this does not prevent them being asked to look towards a group or a particular direction to ensure that a possible suspect is not overlooked. Where there is more than one witness, they should be kept separate and taken to an area independently. Once there is sufficient information to justify an arrest, the provision applicable to 'where a suspect is known and available' should be followed for any subsequent witness. A record of action taken is to be recorded in the officer's pocket note book as soon as possible.

A witness must not be shown photographs, composite likeness or pictures. If the identity of the suspect is known to the police and the suspect is available to take part in video, parade or group identification. If the suspect's identity is not known, the showing of such images must be done in accordance with the showing of photographs procedure.

When the suspect is known and available

If a suspect is known, then the following procedures can be used:

1. Video where a witness is shown moving images of a suspect together with similar images of others who resemble the suspect

2. Identification parade where the witness sees the suspect in a line of others who resemble the suspect.

3. Group identification were the witness sees the suspect in an informal group of people.

Arranging Identification procedures

Normally the arrangements for and the conduct of identification procedures along with the circumstances in which they are held as said before are the responsibility of an Inspector or higher. However, arranging and conduct of such procedures may under supervision, be delegated to other officers of civilian staff. No person involved in the investigation of the case against the suspect may take any part in these procedures.

Notice to suspect

Before any identification procedure is arranged it needs to be explained to the suspect and a written copy given to them to sign. They need to be informed of the following:

Purpose of identification.

Entitlement to free legal advice.

Procedures including right to have a solicitor of friend present

They do not have to consent or co-operate.

If they do not give consent or co-operate, their refusal may be given in evidence, and the police may proceed covertly without their consent or make other arrangements.

For video identification, whether images have previously been obtained and that they may provide further images instead.

Any special arrangements for juveniles, mentally disordered or otherwise mentally vulnerable people.

That if they significantly alter their appearance between being offered a procedure and any attempt to hold it will be given in evidence and other forms of identification considered.

A moving image or photograph may be taken when they attend for any identification.

They or their solicitor will be provided with the description first given by the witness.

Power of Arrest

As a police officer in England or Wales you have the power to arrest a person within England and Wales. If you are a police officer in Scotland, then your arrest power only extends to Scotland. This power of arrest is:

"Arrest is the apprehending or restraining of a person in order to detain him at the police station while the alleged or suspected crime is investigated and in order that he be forthcoming to answer an alleged or suspected crime."

The most important reason, but not the only reason, for the suspect being arrested is to allow him to be questioned about the offence of which he is suspected. Other reasons for arresting a person include the prevention of a breach of the peace or the protection of that person from harm while they are drunk or mentally ill.

A Police officer has wide powers of arrest under s24 Police and Criminal Evidence Act 1984. A lawful arrest requires two distinct elements :(a) Suspected or has attempted involvement in the commission of a criminal offence; and

(b) Compliance with the necessity test.

A Miranda warning, known as the "Caution", is a warning given by police to criminal suspects in police custody, or in a custodial situation, before they are questioned. A custodial situation is one in which the suspect's freedom of movement is restrained although they are not under arrest.

An arrest begins with what the person is being arrested for e.g. I am arresting you for section 5 public order, theft of a bottle of wine or ABH (actual bodily harm), this is followed by the caution.

"You do not have to say anything. But it may harm your defence if you do not mention when questioned something which you later rely on in court. Anything you do say may be given in evidence."

The caution above is worth learning and should roll off your tongue as and when it is required. Although minor deviations from the words of any caution do not constitute a breach provide the sense of the caution was preserved.

At this point it is important to mention human rights, which apply during arrest, detention and in the interview process. Human rights apply as they do in our day to day lives. The Human Rights Act 1998 sets out the rights in the UK which are protected by the European Convention on Human Rights (ECHR).

The act did not invent human rights for British people; instead, it introduced into our domestic law some of the rights set out in the Universal Declaration of Human Rights and other international documents.

More specifically, it gave greater effect within the UK to the rights and freedoms protected by the ECHR, a treaty that British lawyers helped to draft. The main part of human rights is the belief that everybody should be treated equally and with dignity, no matter what their circumstances.

This means that nobody should be tortured or treated in an inhuman or degrading way. It also means that everybody should have access to public services and the right to be treated fairly by those services. This applies to all public services, including the criminal justice system. If you arrest someone and they are charged, they should not be treated with prejudice and their trial should be fair. Another example is if you arrest someone for shop theft you should not parade them through the store unless you have no alternative.

UK law includes a range of human rights which protect us from poor treatment and prejudice, and which require everyone to have equal and fair treatment from public authorities.

When must a caution be given?

A caution must be given when there are grounds to suspect a person of an offence, they must be cautioned before any questions are asked about an offence, or further questions if the answers provided the grounds for suspicion are put to them. This applies if the person's answers or silence may be given in evidence. But no caution is necessary if questions are for other purposes, e.g. to establish identity or ownership of a vehicle. At the same time as the caution a person must be told that they are not under arrest and free to leave.

If a person is arrested, or further arrested they must be informed at the time or as soon as practicable thereafter, that they are under arrest and the grounds for their arrest. They must also be cautioned unless:

1 It is impracticable to do so by reason of their condition or behaviour at the time.

2 They have already been cautioned immediately prior to arrest when being questioned.

Reasonable Force

Police officers are empowered by common law and statute to use force to protect life, preserve order, prevent the commission of crime or arrest or detain offenders. Common law powers are also afforded to all members of the general public.

Use of reasonable force by a police officer must be, proportionate, reasonable in the circumstances and the minimum amount necessary to accomplish the lawful objective concerned. Persons being taken into police custody should not have greater force used towards them than is required to achieve restraint. Force should not be used in a manner that is arbitrary, unreasonable or based on irrational considerations. This is why all Police officers are provided with appropriate training in self-defence and the controlled use of force and are equipped accordingly, so as to protect their safety and that of others.

Opinions can differ on what is a reasonable amount of force, but one thing is certain the person who is applying the force does not have the right to decide how much force it is reasonable to use. If it ends up in court, the person who applied the force would always believe he or she was acting reasonably and would never be guilty of any offence. It is for the jury, as ordinary members of the community, to decide the amount of force which it would be reasonable to use in the circumstances of each case. It is relevant that the person was under pressure from an imminent attack and might not have had time to make entirely rational decisions, so the test must balance the objective standard of a reasonable person by attributing some of the subjective knowledge of the defendant, including his or her beliefs as to the surrounding circumstances, even if mistaken. However, even allowing for any mistakes made in a crisis, the amount of force must be proportionate and reasonable given the value of the interests being protected and the harm likely to be caused by use of force. The classic test comes from the Jamaican case of Palmer v The Queen, on appeal to the Privy Council in 1971:

"The defence of self-defence is one which can be and will be readily understood by any jury. It is a straightforward conception. It involves no abstruse legal thought. Only common sense is needed for its understanding. It is both good law and good sense that a man who is attacked may defend himself. It is both good law and good sense that he may do, but may only do, what is reasonably necessary. But everything will depend upon the facts and circumstances. It may in some cases be only sensible and clearly as possible to take some simple avoiding action.

Some attacks may be serious and dangerous. Others may not be. If there is some relatively minor attack it would not be common sense to permit some action of retaliation which was wholly out of proportion to the necessities of the situation.

If an attack is so serious that it puts someone in immediate peril, then immediate defensive action may be necessary. If the moment is one of crisis for someone in imminent danger, he may have (to) avert the danger by some instant reaction. If the attack is all over and no sort of peril remains, then the employment of force may be by way of revenge or punishment or by way of paying off an old score or may be pure aggression.

There may no longer be any link with a necessity of defence... If a jury thought that in a moment of unexpected anguish a person attacked had only done what he honestly and instinctively thought was necessary, that would be most potent evidence that only reasonable defensive action had been taken."

In R v Lindsay (2005) AER (D) 349 the defendant who picked up a sword in self-defence, when attacked in his home by three masked intruders armed with loaded handguns, killed one of them by slashing him repeatedly with that sword. The prosecution case was that, although he had initially acted in self-defence, he had then lost his self-control and demonstrated a clear intent to kill the armed intruder. In fact, the defendant was himself a low-level cannabis dealer who kept the sword available to defend himself against other drug dealers. The Court of Appeal confirmed an eight year term of imprisonment. In a non-criminal context, it would not be expected that ordinary householders who "go too far" when defending themselves against armed intruders would receive such a long sentence.

Self-defence in English law is a complete defence to all levels of assault, and can't be used to mitigate liability, say, from murder to manslaughter where a Police officer acting in the course of their duty uses a greater degree of force than necessary for self-defence. Hence, self-defence is distinguishable from provocation, which only applies to mitigate what would otherwise have been murder to manslaughter (i.e. provocation is not a complete defence).

Due to the completeness of the defence, self-defence is interpreted in a relatively conservative way to avoid creating too generous a standard of justification. The more forgiving a defence, the greater the incentive for a cynical defendant to exploit it when planning the use of violence or in explaining matters after the event. Thus, although the juries in self-defence cases are entitled to consider the physical characteristics of the defendant, that evidence has little probative value in deciding whether excessive force was actually used. The general common law principle is stated in Beckford v R (1988) 1 AC 130:

"A defendant is entitled to use reasonable force to protect himself, others for whom he is responsible and his property. It must be reasonable."

Conveying a Prisoner

Once an arrest has been made you have a duty of care for the prisoner and as such should endeavour to convey them in a safe manner. The use of handcuffs to the rear is always a recommendation, as you never know how a person may react later on to being arrested, especially if the person being arrested is being placed in the back of a car. A violent offender is best conveyed in a prison van, where possible, to reduce risks further. You should check that the cuffs are on correctly and not too tight. Once arrested, a prisoner should not smoke or use a mobile phone.

Once in custody the detainee is taken in front of the custody sergeant who can authorise detention based on the account you have given and what they have been arrested for. The detainee will need to empty all their pockets and remove any belts, chains, shoelaces, or anything that it is deemed they could harm themselves with this property needs to be recorded and booked into custody. Pay particular attention to money and record individual amounts of coins and notes. Get the detainee, where possible, to agree with the amount of money and the property booked in. All property will be given back on the detainee's release. Once all details have been taken you will either take the detainee to a cell or a custody officer will take them down for you. At this point, you are free to leave custody.

Suspect Interviews

Suspect interviews can seem quite complicated at first, but with practice, you will become proficient although many officers still have a script as an aide memoir. Often the PEACE model is followed as a structure.

Plan – Plan the interview/questions

Explain – Explain to the suspect what is going to happen

Account – Suspect gives their account

Conclusion – Conclude interview, recap, probe, summarise

Evaluate – Evaluate the interview

Your first interview will only be conducted after you have sat in on quite a few interviews and understand the procedure and how it is carried out. The actual interview is the suspect's chance to give their account of what has happened and to either agree or deny an allegation.

The interview has set guidelines which have to be followed; this includes the actual questions that are asked.

Interviews must be carried out under caution. The person being interview must be informed of the nature of the offence.

If arrested, the interview must take place at the police station or other authorised place of detention, unless the consequent delay would be likely to:

Lead to interference or harm to evidence or people, or serious loss of, or damage to property.

Lead in alerting other people suspected of committing an offence, but not yet arrested for it.

Hinder the recovery of property obtained by the commission of an offence.

Interviewing hinder these circumstances must cease once the risk has been averted, or the necessary questions have been put in an attempt to avert it.

Before any interview at a police station or other authorised place of detention, the suspect should be reminded of their entitlement to free legal advice, and that the interview can be delayed to obtain it.

At the beginning of the interview, the suspect shall be asked whether they confirm or deny any significant statement or silence which occurred before the start of the interview.

Answers and statements may not be obtained by oppression. Such an approach is likely to mean that any evidence obtained is inadmissible. The interviewer may not volunteer information on what action will be taken as a result of the suspect answering questions, making a statement or refusing to do so.

Where a person has not been charged, or has been told they may be prosecuted, the interview must cease when all relevant questions have been put, account has been taken of any evidence, and there is sufficient evidence for conviction.

The interview should be conducted sitting down and as far as possible in comfort, with proper breaks for refreshment (normal meal breaks and at least 15 minutes every two hours). The interview should take place in an adequately heated, lit and ventilated room. Before the start of the interview, it is advisable to ensure that all persons' present have switched off mobile telephones, pagers, etc to avoid interruptions. The suspect should be given the option to have legal representation and, if a minor, an appropriate adult present - a parent, guardian or an impartial Police designated appropriate adult (volunteer).

When there are grounds to suspect that a person has committed an offence, you must caution them before any questions about it are put to them, to ensure that the answers (or any failure to answer) are capable of being admissible in evidence in a prosecution. You should then put to them any significant statement(s) or silence(s) which occurred in your presence, or of any other interviewing officer, before the interview, and which have not been put before the suspect in a previous interview. You should ask the suspect whether they confirm or deny that earlier statement or silence and if they wish to add anything.

You should also give the suspect the opportunity, where practicable, to read the record and sign it as correct, or to indicate the respects in which they consider it inaccurate. If the suspect agrees the record is correct, they should be asked to endorse the record with, for example, 'I agree this is a correct record of what was said' and add their signature. Where the suspect disagrees with the record, you should record the details of any disagreement and ask the suspect to read these details and sign them to the effect that they accurately reflect their disagreement. Any refusal to sign should also be recorded.

Tape Recorded Interview Guide

Persons Present

I am…. (State name rank and number). The date is…… The time is…….

This interview is being recorded at….(Police Station) and may be given in evidence if the case comes to trial.

I am interviewing……(suspect). Please state your full name, date of birth and address…..

Also present is my colleague……..(state name, Rank, and number if present).

If Solicitor is present - state your name and the firm you represent.

If an appropriate adult, interpreter, etc is present - Please state your name and relationship to the suspect.

There are no other persons present in this interview.

If a solicitor is not present - I must remind you that you are entitled to free and independent legal advice. You are entitled to this at any time during this interview. You may contact a solicitor by telephone and the interview can be delayed for you to obtain that advice. Do you understand?

Do you want a solicitor at this time?

Legal Advice

If the right to legal advice is waived - Ask why

If previously asked for legal advice and has now changed their mind - you previously said you wanted legal advice, I understand you have now changed your mind. Is this correct?

Caution

You do not have to say anything. But it may harm your defence if you do not mention when questioned something you later rely on in court. Anything you do say may be given in evidence.

Do you understand?

The reason for this interview is because you have been arrested on suspicion of (include "What. Where and When" for the offence).

Significant Statement/Silences

I wish to speak to you about the comments/silences made at the time of your arrest, prior to your arrival at the Police station, in addition to any other comments made prior to interview.

You said…….Do you agree this was said?

This is my opportunity to question you with regards to this matter. It is also your opportunity to give an explanation if you wish.

The wording of the Special Warning

I am investigating an offence of…….(state offence).

I want your account for…..(state fact/item).

I believe that……(state fact/item) may be due to you taking part in the commission of the offence…..(state offence).

I must inform you that a court may draw a proper inference if you fail or refuse to answer satisfactorily questions about (state fact/item).

That a record is being made of the interview and it may be given in evidence if you are brought to trial.

If previously stated 1) and 5) do not need to be repeated.

I have explained to you what may occur. Do you understand what I have said?

Explanation – It means that if you are reported/charged for the offence and you have failed to answer these questions, the magistrate or jury can ask themselves the question "Why didn't they explain when given the chance?" Whatever they consider the answer to be it can be taken into account when deciding guilt or innocence.

Closure

Do you wish to clarify anything?

Have you said all you wish to say about this matter?

The time is now……The date is……..

Do you agree I am handing you a form explaining access to the tapes?

I am now stopping the recording.

Everything is done to set guidelines so that the crown prosecution service (CPS) can put a case before the court. That is unless a Police caution has been given by the custody sergeant, or a decision that there are no charges to answer has been made by the CPS.

Interview Records

Interview records must be kept for every interview stating the place, time it began and ended, breaks, and the names of persons present. It must be made and completed during the interview unless not practicable or would interfere with the conduct of the interview, in which case it must be made as soon as practicable afterwards and the reason recorded. It must be a verbatim record of what has been said or an account which adequately and accurately summarises it. The record must be timed and signed by the maker. Unless impracticable, the suspect (and appropriate adult and or solicitor) should be allowed to read it and sign it as correct. If a person cannot read or refuses to read it the interviewer should read it to the suspect and record what has occurred. Any refusal to sign must be recorded.

Interpreters

Arrangements must be in place for the provision of suitably qualified interpreters for people who are deaf, or do not understand English. There is also something called Language Line to aid with talking to suspects. An interpreter can then speak to a suspect via a telephone and interpret for you. Wherever possible, interpreters should be drawn from the National Register of Public Service Interpreters.

A person must not be interviewed in the absence of a person capable of interpreting if:
They have a difficulty understanding English
The interviewer cannot speak the person's own language and the person being interviews wants and interpreter present
The interpreter must make a note of the questions and answers in the interview at the time, in the person's own language, and certify its accuracy. The person

should be allowed to read the record or have it read to him and sign it as a contract.

Where the person makes a written statement other than English, the interpreter records the statement in the language it is made, the person is invited to sign it, and an official English translation is made.

If a person appears to be deaf or there is doubt about their hearing or speaking ability, they must not be interviewed without a suitable interpreter unless they agree in writing to be interview without one. The same applies if the parent or appropriate person has such a disability and a juvenile is to be interviewed.

Stop and Search

Stop and search is another common aspect of police work. You may be doing a stop check on a group of teenagers or a stop search on a person suspected to be carrying drugs. Stop and Search is so that Police officers are allowed to combat street crime and anti-social behaviour and to prevent more serious crimes.

You have to have grounds to stop somebody, even more so to actually search a person, and that is what we will go through in this section. Although you can still talk to anybody you meet and public interaction is a key part of good policing. You no longer have to record a stop only a search.

What is a stop? There are three different types of stops that you may utilise:

Stop - when a police officer or PCSO stops a person or persons in a public place and asks them to account for themselves. They may ask the following questions:

What are you doing?
Where have you been?
Where are you going?
What are you carrying?

Stop and Search - when a police officer stops and searches a person.

Vehicle - a police officer can stop any vehicle and ask the driver for driving documents. This is not the purpose of stop and search, but you can give documentation relevant to road traffic matters. It becomes a stop if:

The driver or any passengers are asked to account for themselves.

A search is carried out on the vehicle, driver or any passengers present.

The police officer or PCSO must explain why they are doing a stop and held to account for the stopped person's presence in an area.

There are plenty of occasions when you might talk to the public, and most of these do not qualify as either a 'stop' or 'stop and search'.

You have not officially 'stopped' someone if, for example:

You are asked for directions or information.

A person has witnessed a crime and is questioned about it to establish the background to the incident.

The person has been in an area where a crime recently occurred and is questioned about what they might have seen.

In March 2011, the government introduced changes to the Police and Criminal Evidence Act (PACE) Code of Practice A which you will cover later, which governs the use and recording of stop and search. These changes are to the monitoring structures that were in place. Police forces have been given the discretion to choose whether or not to record stop and account and to reduce the recording of stop and search.

So you may still need to fill out a form outlining the reason for stopping the person, the outcome of the stop and search and your collar number and name, and give them a copy. This information will not be held on file unless the person stopped is charged with an offence. However forms are still required to be filled out whenever a search has taken place although, the name and if any items were found during the search don't actually need to be recorded.

Searching

A police officer has various powers to undertake searches. There has been a recent crackdown on the use of searching and ensuring it does not target certain minorities and is used proportionately. The pneumonic GOWISELY is often used to aid in the correct procedure.

Grounds for search
Object of search
Warrant card-collar number
Identity of officer-name
Station to which officer is attached
Entitlement to a copy of the search record
Legal power used
You are detained for the purpose of a search

The main search power comes under Section 1 of PACE, then you have Section 23, misuse of drugs act and also Section 43 terrorism act. Finally, once a person is arrested and not in the police station, they can be searched under Section 32 of PACE.

The most important element is undertaking the search correctly. Ensure you have the grounds to search them in the first place. Ideally, any search should where possible be undertaken by the same sex. Transgender can elect to be searched by the gender they identify with. The first element of a search is to tell them who you are and what police station you are based at. Tell them the grounds and reason for the search, even if they have just been arrested. For most searches, they are entitled to a copy of the search and ensure you offer it to them. Remain professional, polite and courteous, even if dealing with difficult people. It sounds obvious, but can change not only public perception, but lead to a more positive outcome with the individual. If they are shouting at you and you are being polite back, how does that make them look?

If in a public place, then you can search using the mnemonic JOG (Jacket, Outer Clothing, Gloves). In simple terms ask them to hand you their jacket and search thoroughly, linings, pockets, hood storage area. Searching is a skill that needs to be practised to become proficient. Use your hands to feel along arms, shoulders, back and front. Check the belt line carefully and ask the person being searched to empty their pockets. Maybe place the contents in a clear plastic bag if they are going to be arrested. Ask them if they have anything on them that may cause harm or they should not have on them. Check legs, and finally feel around the ankle area.

In custody, they can remove footwear and you can check their feet, feeling around the toe and sole of their foot. A metal detector is used in custody as a final check once you are happy all areas and pockets have been searched. Another tip is to always check your vehicle before and after a detained person has been placed in it. To see if they have tried to hide anything. A search in custody is not just about finding prohibited or stolen items. It is about the safety of the detained person and ensuring they cannot harm themselves. Being in custody can be very stressful for some people, who may try to harm themselves if various procedures were not put in place. Anyone in custody is risk assessed and anything that they could use to harm themselves with removed, including shoelaces, cords in trousers and tops, chains and earrings.

Warrants

In England & Wales, arrest warrants can be issued for both suspects and witnesses. Arrest warrants for suspects can be issued by a justice of the peace under section 1 of the Magistrates' Courts act 1980 if information (in writing) is laid before them that a person has committed or is suspected of having committed an offence. Such arrest warrants can only be issued for someone over 18 if:

The offence to which the warrant relates is an indictable offence or is punishable with imprisonment, or

the person's address is not sufficiently established for a summons to be served on him.

Arrest warrants for witnesses can be issued if:

a justice of the peace is satisfied on oath that:

any person in England or Wales is likely to be able to give material evidence, or produce any document or thing likely to be material evidence, at the summary trial of an information by a magistrates' court,

It is in the interests of justice to issue a summons under this subsection to secure the attendance of that person to give evidence or produce the document or thing, and

It is probable that a summons would not procure the attendance of the person in question.

or, if:

A person has failed to attend court in response to a summons, the court is satisfied by evidence on oath that he is likely to be able to give material evidence or produce any document or thing likely to be material evidence in the proceedings

it is proved on oath, or in such other manner as may be prescribed, that he has been duly served with the summons, and that a reasonable sum has been paid or tendered to him for costs and expenses, and

It appears to the court that there is no just excuse for the failure.

Search Warrant

Search warrants are issued by a local magistrate and require a Constable to provide evidence to support the warrant application. In the vast majority of cases where the Police already hold someone in custody, searches of premises can be made without a search warrant under Section 18 of the Police and Criminal Evidence Act (PACE), which requires only the authority of a Police Inspector.

Searches under section 18 Police and Criminal Evidence Act can be conducted immediately by a Constable without the requirement for an Inspector's authorisation under section 18(5)a of PACE. This subsection allows a Constable to search the address of a suspect(s) under arrest in their presence before being presented to a Police station (or other custody suite).

If a person is arrested on their own property or just after leaving their premises, a Constable may immediately search both them and the immediate area where the person was under Section 32 of PACE.

Evidence Seizure and Crime Scene Preservation

The crime scene is a highly important source of physical evidence and is where forensic science investigations begin. From the point of collection to the time of archiving, evidence must be kept within a strict chain of custody to ensure no possible cross-contamination with any other objects. The methods employed to collect and preserve evidence are crucial and it is important that fundamental practices are adhered to.

Arrival at the crime scene

Upon arrival at the scene of the crime, the first officer must record the time, date and weather conditions and take action to preserve and secure the area to the maximum extent possible.

This may involve putting a cordon in place to prevent any further contamination of the crime scene.

The administering of medical assistance to victims at the crime scene takes priority, although any unauthorised access most minimal and where possible disallowed as any individual present poses the risk of contaminating or destroying physical evidence.

Once the scene has been secured, the investigating officer must evaluate the scene and decide on the system for examination to be employed by the crime-scene investigators. Immediate action must be taken to protect items of evidence, which may be destroyed by weather conditions or fire etc. Any persons present at the scene of the crime who may be witnesses should be removed and their details taken. It is also necessary to record all movements at the scene and any items moved or touched by individuals.

Recording at the crime scene

Recording the scene in its original state is highly important both as an aid for the subsequent investigation and also as evidence in court when the details of the crime scene and location of physical evidence must be provided. Various methods of recording the crime scene can include photography, sketches and written notes. Thorough in most instances recording usually require that all three methods be employed.

The crime scene will firstly be photographed as thoroughly as possible and from various angles; suspected entrances and exits, any surrounding areas or areas where events in relation to the crime occurred should be included. Items of physical evidence should be photographed to show their position and location relative to the scene. Close-up photographs should then be taken to show the evidence in as greater detail as possible and alongside a measuring scale to ascertain size. If a body is present at the crime scene, this also should be photographed from various angles to show all injuries and weapons; the surface beneath the body is then be photographed upon its removal.

Rough sketches are made at the crime scene to give an accurate portrayal of the scene, including dimensions and the location of items of physical evidence in relation to each other. The locations of approaches such as roadways, paths, entrances, exits and windows should be depicted. The size and dimensions of the area or building should be measured, with all measurements being made with a tape measure and the compass direction of north should be indicated. The exact locations of objects are determined by distance measurements from two fixed points, for example the walls of a room. Generally, objects are indicated by the assignment of letters, which are then referred to below the sketch with a description of the item. The initial sketch is usually a rough one, used to give maximum information, but without care and attention to appearance. This sketch is then used to prepare a finished sketch, usually carried out by a skilled worker, which is drawn to scale and includes details of the articles of evidence.

Alongside both the sketches and photographs, note taking will play an important role throughout the processing of the crime scene. A detailed written description of the scene and physical evidence should be included, along with the times of discovery and the individuals coming in contact with the evidence. Tape-recording notes can often be more beneficial as it is a much quicker method of note taking, but this must later be transcribed into a written document for use as evidence.

Searching the crime scene for evidence

A systematic search of the crime scene is highly important so that no evidence is left unrecorded and for maximum information to be obtained; the more evidence gathered, the stronger the case. The investigator in charge of the crime-scene generally co-ordinates the search for evidence to ensure that all necessary areas are covered but also to ensure there is no duplication of effort. A forensic scientist is not usually present at the scene of a crime, unless the evidence is very involved. Trained field evidence technicians who are skilled in photography and examination, are sometimes employed to locate and collect physical evidence. The choice of search method is that of the evidence collectors and usually depends on the size and type of the crime scene and on the number of individuals participating. Search methods include the spiral search method, in which the collection of evidence is carried out in a circular pattern working towards a fixed point at the centre; the grid method in which the area is searched along horizontal and vertical lines of a grid; a strip or line search; and the quadrant method where the area is divided into segments for individual searching. Experiences of the investigating officer and the type of crime committed will generally determine the search method employed.

While searching the crime scene, any doubted item should be treated as evidence until it can be proven otherwise. Gloves and protective clothing should be worn to prevent contamination of the scene. Along with collecting evidence, it is also important to collect known standards, for example, fibre samples from carpets and furnishings. For any material stained with biological fluids collected for analysis, a clean piece of the same material should be collected separately as a control.

Maintaining the chain of custody

The chain of custody of an evidential item begins at the initial collection of the evidence at the scene of crime. It must be presented if the evidence is used in court. The authenticity and integrity of the evidence relies upon the detailed recorded history of the item, including the persons who came into possession of the item and the examination tests performed upon it. Establishing set guidelines on recording and labelling of the history of the evidence during its time retained by the police is the most effective way to ensure this of custody is maintained.

You may find yourself being asked to take part in a search of a house using a warrant or to search an area following a crime. You may even find an item whilst out on patrol.

In all cases, you need to make a record of what you have found and the location it was found. An item found on the street on patrol will often just be recorded in a lost property book or something similar, but it must be recorded.

If the item found is linked to a crime, then it needs to be recorded as a seized exhibit, with a seizure statement being.

Always consider carefully the evidence that may need to be collected.

When taking items into possession, seek, whenever possible, to obtain the best evidence available.

Consider proportionality, and issues of evidential significance.

Record in your notebook all objects (including evidential documents) taken.

Consideration needs to be given to the type of bag or container the exhibit needs to be placed in.

Packaging

Physical evidence must then be properly packaged and labelled, with different samples requiring different methods of packaging. For example, while hairs and fibres can be contained within plastic containers, any items containing biological evidence such as blood or semen must be air-dried before packaging and placed in paper bags to remove the problem of moisture build-up and contamination from bacterial growth.

Packages should be labelled with the time and date of packaging, the name of the packager and any history of any known contact with the evidence. Where possible, the actual item of evidence should be labelled for identification, in addition to labelling the packaging in which it is placed.

Any items apart from clothes - place each item into a separate plastic police evidence bag. Package firearms and ammunition separately; seek individual force advice. Knives can be placed into a special knife container.

Clothing - empty pockets. Place each item of clothing into a separate paper police evidence bag (but put any wet/blood soaked item inside an open plastic police evidence bag first).

Hold seal away from your face and expel air from bag; close bag by folding top twice.

Sign two signature seals and place over fold.

Wrap 2-inch sticky tape around the fold to form an airtight seal. Any potential for leakage must be eliminated - especially at the corners; go right to the edge of the bag.

Fold bottom of bag once (or twice if your model has blue tabs).

Complete and affix a label.

Finally, (in case the label might come off) write exhibit number, date, taken by, description of the exhibit and exhibit name directly onto the bag.

Dealing with Exhibits Tips

All items seized under PACE which we will cover next and are being retained must be recorded in some kind of property book or booking in system and then placed in an approved temporary or holding store immediately. Exhibits may need to be retained whilst further enquires and interviews are carried out. Ensure that there is always an audit trail and any movements are fully recorded. Keep a copy of any exhibit number or exhibit reference even if it is just in your pocket notebook. If any exhibits are needed for court as soon as you are warned which is usually 2/3 weeks in advance, make sure you request any exhibits to ensure they are ready in time if they are being stored at a different location.

Once any exhibits are no longer required ensure they are released to their legal owner if they are the type of exhibit such as a bike, mobile phone or even a car that the legal owner may well want returning. Seized items are often what get police officers into the most strife, especially when amounts of money are seized. Correct recording as well as keeping the required audit trail also mean that any issues or claims made later are easily refuted.

Computer Forensics and Cyber Crime

The plethora of digital devices has surged in the last ten years. People have homes full of them like tablets, PC, Macbook, routers, PS4, Xbox One, Smartphones, Set top boxes, TVs to name the obvious ones. All of these devices can access the internet giving a further source of data. 10 years ago, mobile phones stored around 15 pages of A4 paper in data terms, today it is more than 67 million pages of A4 on high end Smartphone.

Computer forensics of Forensic IT is a branch of digital forensic science pertaining to legal evidence found in computers and digital storage media. The goal of computer forensics is to examine digital media in a forensically sound manner with the aim of identifying, preserving, recovering, analysing and presenting facts and opinions about the information.

Although it is most often associated with the investigation of a wide variety of computer crime, computer forensics may also be used in civil proceedings. The discipline involves similar techniques and principles to data recovery, but with additional guidelines and practices designed to create a legal audit trail.

Evidence from computer forensics investigations is usually subjected to the same guidelines and practices of other digital evidence. It has been used in several high-profile cases such as Harold Shipman.

With the onset of mobile phones in particular Smartphones that store useful data they are also becoming more sought after exhibits.

Records of texts, phone calls, email and data stored on a phone can all be useful evidence.

When seizing evidence, if the machine is still active, any information stored solely in RAM that is not recovered before powering down may be lost. One application of "live analysis" is to recover RAM data (for example, using Microsoft's COFEE tool, windd, WindowsSCOPE) prior to removing an exhibit. CaptureGUARD Gateway bypasses Windows login for locked computers, allowing for the analysis and acquisition of physical memory on a locked computer.

RAM can be analysed for prior content after power loss, because the electrical charge stored in the memory cells takes time to dissipate, an effect exploited by the cold boot attack. The length of time that data is recoverable is increased by low temperatures and higher cell voltages. Holding unpowered RAM below −60 °C helps preserve residual data by an order of magnitude, improving the chances of successful recovery. However, it can be impractical to do this during a field examination.

Some of the tools needed to extract volatile data, however, require that a computer be in a forensic lab, both to maintain a legitimate chain of evidence, and to facilitate work on the machine. If necessary, law enforcement applies techniques to move a live, running desktop computer. These include a mouse jiggler, which moves the mouse rapidly in small movements and prevents the computer from going to sleep accidentally. Usually, an uninterruptible power supply (UPS) provides power during transit.

Hard drives or solid memory are very easy to work with, the most important factor is ensuring that some form of write blocker is in place. To ensure data is only downloaded off the drive and not written too to maintain data integrity and ensure the drive can be returned in the same condition it was found.

Hard drive acquisitioning is the technique of imaging, or copying, the entire contents of a hard drive to another hard drive. This could arguably be the most critical part of the forensic process. The imaging allows complete data transfer without modifying the original drive and forensically preserves all content, as well as date and time stamps. At this point, an exact duplicate has been created, thereby allowing a full recovery and forensic analysis without altering the original drive. The most crucial element of Digital Forensics in terms of police is ensuring that the four ACPO principles are adhered to. The four principles are

Conflict Resolution

Conflict resolution is a range of processes aimed at alleviating or eliminating sources of conflict. As a police officer, many of the incidents you may attend will require conflict resolution, so what is it? The term "conflict resolution" is sometimes used interchangeably with the terms "dispute resolution" or "alternative dispute resolution". Processes of conflict resolution generally include negotiation, mediation and diplomacy.

Talking at the right level without aggression can often calm people down. Once you have stepped up a level of aggression, it is nearly impossible to step down. People will often respond well to being spoken to in a quiet and polite manner even if they have a very aggressive demeanour themselves. Stay calm, listen and reply in a positive manner

There are many tools available to, persons in conflict. One option would be not to fight over it, no violence, only talking out the problem. How and when they are used depends on several factors (such as the specific issues at stake in the conflict). Sometimes taking away a person or persons, either through arrest or simply a distance apart could help. That could be down the street, or into another room to talk through what has happened and help calm the situation down. The tools you can use to aid conflict resolution include negotiation, advocacy, diplomacy, activism, nonviolence and critical pedagogy: you can also utilise outside agencies who can arrange or use a community building, mediation and counselling for a longer-term resolution. For those wanting to learn more about this exciting subject matter are recommend to look at CompTIA material, A+ and Security+ are two that are now being delivered to police officers to upskill them in the digital age.

Open Source Investigation

Open-Source Intelligence or OSI refers to a broad array of information and sources that are generally available, including information obtained from the media (newspapers, radio, television, etc.), professional and academic records (papers, conferences, professional associations, etc.), and public data (government reports, demographics, hearings, speeches, etc.). It has been estimated that roughly 90% of valuable intelligence comes from open sources compared to traditional covert intelligence. According to the CIA open sources often equal or surpass classified information in monitoring and analysing issues including terrorism, proliferation and counterintelligence. To an online investigator OSI provides access to a plethora of intelligence which if knowing where to look and how to look can be the life blood of a modern day investigation.

To most searching the Internet is simply about using a search engine such as Google or its close rival Bing to run a key word search. This type of search and sites such as Google are typically referred to as the surface or visible web. In simple terms the surface web is a portion or segment of the World Wide Web that is indexable by a search engine such as Google for example. Search engines typically construct a database of the Web by using programs called spiders or robots (web crawlers). The spider gets a copy of each page and indexes it, storing useful information that will let the page be quickly retrieved again later. Google uses a slightly more refined approach using what is commonly termed the 'page rank algorithm'.

When it comes to searching online there are many tools available with some being more popular than others so which are the most effective for the online investigator? This is a difficult question as it depends on many circumstances based on the type of search being carried out. However the following section explores some of the options available to the online investigator when exploring the world of social media.

The main search tools include Google and Bing with both having the ability to filter text, images, video and offer the investigator the ability to filter by time, location, site or related pages. Both have good advanced features and offer the ability to translate (although this is very basic). Whilst both these search engines are good they do not cover every possible angle of searching which some investigators have come to expect. Meta search engines, search or the search engines and two examples are Duck & Go and Dogpile. One weakness is that by default they do not automatically search the vast wilderness of social media including everything from blogs, photos, videos, geo-location data to name but a few.

Social Media

Social Media has become both a useful tool and one of frustration by the sometimes way it is used to post material that can cause offence or be deemed as harassment. However, it is a key component to profiling a subject as part of an investigation. The pool of information about each individual can form a distinctive social signature.

Twitter, Facebook, LinkedIn to name but a few have embedded themselves in people's lives. Posting to walls, tweets, video and image updates are emerging as a new trove of intelligence.

Social media evidence can be a valuable addition to an investigation, revealing the kind of information that, years ago, would have been difficult, if not impossible, to find. But it has to be gathered in a way that will hold up in court. Because it's such a new source of evidence in investigations, case law is

developing rapidly. A forward-thinking investigator would be well-advised to stay on top of the latest legislation both locally and internationally.

Once the access to social media information has been secured, either through court order or simply due to public accessibility, evidence must be gathered in a way that is legal and useful. Collecting evidence from social media sites can be challenging for several reasons.

The world of social media is constantly changing, and users can easily update and delete material that could be evidence in a case, although once a user is aware of an ongoing investigation, he or she is under an obligation to preserve social media evidence just as if it were any other type of evidence. Deleting photos, posts and other information is akin to shredding documents and the courts have been clear about the consequences, handing out hefty fines and sanctions for spoliation.

There are a series of specialist search tools available which offer options to the online investigator especially as these tend to excel in searching social media. The following selection of sites each has their own unique strengths whether it is looking at photos, finding user profiles or even establishing geo-social footprints – collectively they provide a powerful toolkit to the online investigator.

The dark or deep web, is an area of the web which sits below the 'Google' level and specialist software such as TOR is required to be able to search. Here you can find sites that sell, drugs, guns and stolen credit cards. Silk Road and Silk Road II were almost eBay for drugs. It is an area that can be fraught with danger and even though TOR adds in anonymity, there is really no such thing, just the ability to be anonymous to varying levels. However, if someone wants to find out who you are especially law enforcement such as the FBI, then they can.

Victim Care

Victim care may seem like something simple but it is all too easy to overlook. A victim of a crime is looking to you to investigate and, if possible, solve the crime. It may be the first time that person has spoken to, or needed, the Police. Try to treat a victim the same way you would treat a member of your family. Spend time reassuring and explaining what you can do. If further investigation is needed, then keep them updated with what is happening. All victims, or indeed anyone who comes into contact with the Police, deserve a positive experience and should be treated fairly and with empathy and understanding. Never give false hopes or promises and never feel embarrassed to say "I will find out and get back to you", but make sure you do get back to them. In the end the public are our customers and more and more the word customer care is banded about in police force training.

As mentioned in the radio section, "managing expectation's" is another key term. Everyone has expectations of what they expect to happen or to be done. Sometimes the expectations are not part of the police remit. For example, civil matters or when you have not turned up as quickly as the victim would have expected. It is important to remain polite and fully explain what you are able to do as well as what you are unable to do.

This all sounds basic but it is all too easy to forget when you want to make an arrest or resolve an incident quickly if there are several other jobs coming in.

Human Rights

The Human Rights Act 1998 gives further legal effect in the UK to the fundamental rights and freedoms contained in the ECHR. These rights not only impact matters of life and death, they also affect the rights you have in your everyday life: what you can say and do, your beliefs, your right to a fair trial and other similar basic entitlements.

Most rights have limits to ensure that they do not unfairly damage other people's rights. However, certain rights – such as the right not to be tortured – can never be limited by a court or anybody else.

If any of these rights and freedoms are breached, you have a right to an effective solution in law, even if the breach was by someone in authority, such as a Police officer. This means that as a Police officer it is important to be aware of the Human Rights Act and know how a detainee for example should be treated.

Article 2: Right to Life

(1) Everyone's right to life shall be protected by law. No one shall be deprived of his life intentionally save in the execution of a

sentence of a court following his conviction of a crime for which the penalty is provided by law.

(2) Deprivation of life shall not be regarded as inflicted in contravention of this article when it results from the use of force which is no more than absolutely necessary- (a) in defence of any person from unlawful violence;

(b) in order to effect a lawful arrest or to prevent the escape of a person lawfully detained;

(c) in action lawfully taken for the purpose of quelling a riot or insurrection

Article 3: Inhuman treatment

No one shall be subjected to torture or to inhuman or degrading treatment or punishment.

Article 4: Slavery

(1) No one shall be held in slavery or servitude.

(2) No one shall be required to perform forced or compulsory labour.

(3) For the purpose of this article the term "forced or compulsory labour" shall not include:

(a) any work required to be done in the ordinary course of detention imposed in accordance to the provisions of article 5 of this convention or during conditional release from such detention;

(b) any service of a military character or, in the case of conscientious objectors in countries where they are recognised, service exacted instead of compulsory military service;

(c) any service exacted in case of an emergency or calamity threatening the life or well-being of the community;

(d) any work or service which forms part of normal civic obligations.

Article 5: Right to Liberty

(1) Everyone has the right to liberty and security of person. No one shall be deprived of his liberty save in the following cases and in accordance with a procedure prescribed by law:

(a) the lawful detention of a person after conviction by a competent court;

(b) the lawful arrest or detention of a person for non-compliance with the lawful order of a court or in order to secure the fulfilment of any obligation prescribed by law;

(c) the lawful arrest or detention of a person effected for the purpose of bringing him before the competent legal authority on reasonable suspicion of having committed an offence or when it is reasonably considered necessary to prevent his committing an offence or fleeing after having done so;

(d) the detention of a minor by lawful order for the purpose of educational supervision or his lawful detention for the purpose of bringing him before the competent legal authority;

(e) the lawful detention of persons for the prevention of the spreading of infectious diseases, of persons of unsound mind, alcoholics and drug addicts or vagrants;

(f) the lawful arrest or detention of a person to prevent his effecting an unauthorised entry into the country or of a person against whom action is being taken with a view to deportation or extradition.

(2) Everyone who is arrested shall be informed promptly, in a language which he understands, of the reason for his arrest and of any charge against him.

(3) Everyone arrested or detained in accordance with the provisions of paragraph 1(c) of this article shall be brought promptly before a judge or other officer authorised by law to exercise judicial power and shall be entitled to trial within a reasonable time or to release pending trial. Release may be conditioned by guarantees to appear for trial.

(4) Everyone who is deprived of his liberty by arrest or detention shall be entitled to take proceedings by which the lawfulness of his detention shall be decided speedily by a court and his release ordered if the detention is not lawful.

(5) Everyone who has been the victim of arrest or detention in contravention of the provisions of this article shall have an enforceable right to compensation.

Article 6: Right to a fair trial

(1) In the determination of his civil rights and obligations or of any criminal charge against him, everyone is entitled to a fair and public hearing within a reasonable time by an independent and impartial tribunal established by law. Judgment shall be pronounced publicly, but the press and public may be excluded from all or part of the trial in the interests of morals, public order or national security in a democratic society, where the interests of juveniles or the protection of the private life of the parties so require, or to the extent strictly necessary in the opinion of the court in special circumstances where publicity would prejudice the interests of justice.

(2) Everyone charged with a criminal offence shall be presumed innocent until proved guilty according to law.

(3) Everyone charged with a criminal offence has the following minimum rights –

(a) to be informed promptly, in a language which he understands and in detail, of the nature and cause of the accusation against him;

(b) to have adequate time and facilities for the preparation of his defence;

(c) to defend himself in person or through legal assistance of his own choosing or, if he has not sufficient means to pay for legal assistance, to be given it free when the interests of justice so require;

(d) to examine or have examined witnesses against him and to obtain the attendance and examination of witnesses on his behalf under the same conditions as witnesses against him;

(e) to have the free assistance of an interpreter if he cannot understand or speak the language used in court.

Article 7: Retrospective crimes

(1) No one shall be held guilty of any criminal offence on account of any Act or omission which did not constitute a criminal offence, under national or international law at the time when it was

committed. Nor shall a heavier penalty be imposed than the one that was applicable at the time the criminal offence was committed.

(2) This article shall not prejudice the trial and punishment of any person for any Act or omission which, at the time it was committed, was criminal according to the general law recognised by civilised nations.

Article 8: Right to privacy

(1) Everyone has the right for his private and family life, his home and his correspondence.

(2) There shall be no interference by a public authority with the exercise of this right except such as is in accordance with the law and is necessary in a democratic society in the interests of national security, public safety or the economic well-being of the country, for the prevention of disorder or crime, for the protection of health or morals, or for the protection of the rights and freedoms of others.

Article 9: Freedom of conscience

(1) Everyone has the right to freedom of thought, conscience and religion; this right includes freedom to change his religion or belief and freedom, either alone or in community with others and in public or private, to manifest his religion or belief, in worship, teaching, practice and observance.

(2) Freedom to manifest one's religion or beliefs shall be subject only to such limitations as are prescribed by law and are necessary in a democratic society in the interests of public safety, for the protection of public order, health or morals, or for the protection of the rights and freedoms of others.

Article 10: Freedom of Expression

(1) Everyone has the right of freedom of expression. This right shall include freedom to hold opinions and to receive and impart information and ideas without inference by public authority and regardless of frontiers. This article shall not prevent states from requiring the licensing of broadcasting, television or cinema enterprises.

(2) The exercise of these freedoms, since it carries with it duties and responsibilities, may be subject to such formalities, conditions, restrictions or penalties as are prescribed by law and are necessary in a democratic society, in the interests of national security, territorial integrity or public safety, for the prevention of disorder or crime, for the protection of health or morals, for the protection of the reputation or rights of others, for preventing the disclosure of information received in confidence, or for maintaining the authority and impartiality of the judiciary.

Article 11: Freedom of Assembly

(1) Everyone has the right to freedom of peaceful assembly and to freedom of association with others, including the right to form and to join trade unions for the protection of his interests.

(2) No restrictions shall be placed on the exercise of these rights other than such as are prescribed by law and are necessary in a democratic society in the interests of national security or public safety, for the prevention of disorder or crime, for the protection of health or morals or for the protection of the rights and freedoms of others.

This article shall not prevent the imposition of lawful restrictions on the exercise of these rights by members of the armed forces, of the Police or of the administration of the state.

Article 12: Marriage and the family

Men and women of marriageable age shall have the right to marry and to found a family, according to national laws governing the exercise of this right.

Article 14: Discrimination

The enjoyment of the rights and freedoms set forth in this convention shall be secured without discrimination on any ground such as sex, race, colour, language, religion, political or other opinion, national or social origin, association with a national minority, property, birth or other status.

Protocol No 1

Article 1

Every natural or legal person is entitled to the peaceful enjoyment of his possessions. No one shall be deprived of his possessions except in the public interest and subject to the conditions provided for by law and by the general principles of international law.

The preceding provisions shall not, however, in any way impair the right of the state to enforce such laws as it deems necessary to control the use of property in accordance with the general interest or to secure payment of taxes or other contributions or penalties.

Article 2

No person shall be denied a right to an education. In the exercise of any functions which it assumes in relation to education and to teaching, the state shall respect the right of parents to ensure such education and teaching in conformity with their own religious and philosophical convictions.

Article 3

The High Contracting Parties undertake to hold free elections at reasonable intervals by secret ballot, under conditions which will ensure the free expression of the opinion of the people in the choice of the legislature.

LAW AND OFFENCES

What is the law and what laws do I need to know? What is crime and what do I do if I see a crime and what crime can I arrest for?

The law in itself is a wide subject so we will look at the law and crimes that you would typically come across on the beat as a police officer.

We will start by asking what is the law?

The easiest way is to give the definition of law from the English dictionary

"– Binding or enforceable rule: a rule of conduct or procedure recognised by a community as binding or enforceable by authority piece of legislation: an Act passed by a Parliament or similar body - legal system: the body or system of rules recognised by a community that are enforceable by established process."

As a Police officer, it is your duty to uphold the law and gather evidence. You do not make the direct decision to prosecute or bring the case to court; that is the job of the CPS.

From this we can see that a law is something we all abide by and should not break in our day to day lives. Law itself is broken down into different types of law; ones you will come across are common law, criminal law, and civil law.

Common Law

The definition - this is evolved law - the body of law developed because of custom and judicial decisions, as distinct from the law laid down by legislative assemblies - and forms the basis of all law that is applied.

Criminal Law

Criminal Law has three main objectives: to protect people, to maintain order in society, and to punish criminals. Some believe that Criminal Law should also enforce moral values, but this is controversial, and there basically two schools of thought as represented by the Wolfenden Committee and Lord Devlin:

The Wolfenden Committee in 1957 determined that law should only interfere with private lives in order to preserve public order and protect citizens

Lord Devlin's, 'Enforcement of Morals' in 1965 stated that, 'there are acts so gross and outrageous that they must be prevented at any cost.'

This basic difference in views is unresolved, and this is illustrated by the inconsistent sentencing of those brought to trials for engaging in mutually agreed sado-masochistic activities – there are examples of convictions for assault causing actual bodily harm, and others where S&M defendants have been found not guilty.

What is Strict Liability?

Strict liability is an interesting concept in criminal law. In some crimes, there is a guilty act (actus reus) which, has an identified consequence, but the defendant did not know about, or intend for that.

Elements of a Criminal Offense

Usually a person can't be found guilty of a criminal offense unless both actus reus (guilty act) and mens rea (guilty mind) are present. We covered actus reus in a previous article, and now we will go on to.

What is considered a crime?

A crime is anything that the State has determined as being criminal and punishable. Thus there is a big variation in the definition of crimes between countries, as the governments' different values are reflected within their laws. Furthermore, within a country the definitions of crimes change as their values change over time.

If you take a look at the age of consent in various countries, you will see a significant difference as to below what age it is considered criminal to engage in sex. For differences in what is considered criminal changing within a country just take a look at booming pornography industry under the Clinton administration, and the legal problems it faced under the Bush administration. Another example is the evolving acceptance of homosexuality in Western countries as it is shifted from criminal, to lower and lower ages of consent, through to gay marriage.

However, not all criminal law is passed by the state: sometimes the rulings of judges create new criminal definitions by creating a consistent case history that creates a new criminal classification, as it did in the case of marital rape.

For almost all crimes both actus reus and mens rea must be present.

Actus Reus

The terms actus reus and mens rea developed in English Law are derived from the principle stated by Edward Coke, namely, actus non facit reum nisi mens sit rea which means: "an act does not make a person guilty unless (their) mind is also guilty"; hence, the general test of guilt is one that requires proof of fault, culpability or blameworthiness both in behaviour and mind.

Mens Rea

Mens rea is Latin for "guilty mind". In criminal law, it is viewed as one of the necessary elements of a crime. The standard common law test of criminal liability is usually expressed in the Latin phrase, actus non facit reum nisi mens sit rea, which means "the act does not make a person guilty unless the mind is also guilty". Thus, in jurisdictions with due process, there must be an actus reus accompanied by some level of mens rea to constitute the crime with which the defendant is charged (see the technical requirement of concurrence). As a general rule, criminal liability does not attach to a person who acted with the absence of mental fault. The exception is strict liability crimes. The key thing an officer uses with a criminal offence is 'points to prove' the actions an individual must have undertaken to be guilty of the criminal offence. An example is theft – Dishonestly appropriate with the intention to permanently deprive.

Here you have two points to prove. Did they:

Dishonestly appropriate – stole the item

Permanently deprive – had no intention to return to the owner

How are crimes classified?

There are many different types of crimes, and many ways to classify them.

Classifying Crimes: The Method Used by Criminals, Attorneys and Prosecutors

Crimes are tried in different ways, and can be classified as such:

"Indictable Offences" – these are tried on indictment at the Crown Court, and include serious crimes like murder and rape

"Triable Either Way" – these are tried on indictment at the Crown Court or at the Magistrates Court, and include crimes such as burglary, theft and some forms of assault

"Summary Offences" – these are tried only at the Magistrates Court, and cover crimes that have less than £5,000 of damage in terms of cost, and offences such as common assault.

The magistrate's court has the powers to fine or send to prison. 90% of offences are heard in a magistrate's court.

Classifying Crimes: The Method Used by Academics

Another way to classify crimes is by their source, but such a classification is more the concern of law professors, than a practical one. The sources of crimes are:

"Common Law" - these are made by judges

"Statutory" - these are defined in an Act of Parliament

Regulatory – these are defined in delegated legislation

Classifying Crimes: The Method Used by Policemen

Whilst academics have their classification, the police tend to look at crimes in terms of what their powers are in relation to the treatment of suspects:

"Serious Arrestable Offences" – Police can detain the suspect for 36 hours, extended up to 96 with the permission of magistrates. Crimes such as rape, murder and manslaughter fall under this category

"Arrestable Offences" – these are defined in the Criminal Justice Act of 1967 and cover any offence with a sentence fixed by law, any offence where the maximum sentence is in excess of five years, and any crime which Parliament makes arrestable

Non-arrestable offences

Classifying Crimes: The Victim's Perspective

There are three main categories when one considers the harm done by the crime:

A crime against a person

A crime against property

A crime against public order

How do you prove a crime?

It is down to the prosecution to prove that a crime has been committed, and the defendant is presumed innocent until proven guilty. The prosecution must demonstrate both actus reus and mens rea, and the proof must be 'beyond reasonable doubt.'

Whist the defendant is not obliged to raise a defence, it is typical for them to do so. The prosecutor must then set out to negate this defence. For example, if a defendant states that a vehicle ran over the victim accidentally, a prosecutor seeking a conviction for murder may set out to prove it was intentional. There are, however, some defences that the defendant must make, for example, if he is pleading insanity.

Importantly, you can still be liable for helping another person's criminal Act - aiding and abetting an offender or conspiring to do something prohibited, or merely attempting to commit an offence, like attempted criminal damage. Defences exist to some crimes, so that in some jurisdictions a person who is accused can plead they are insane and did not understand what they were doing, that they were not in control of their bodies, they were intoxicated, mistaken about what they were doing, acted in self-defence, acted under duress or out of necessity, or were provoked. These are issues to be raised at trial and form part of the defence for the accused, for which there are detailed rules of evidence and procedure to be followed. As a Police officer, it is your role to gather all the facts and evidence, investigate the crime and prove the intent so that the CPS can see if there is a case to be proven at court. We shall look at evidence and its importance later on in the chapter.

Civil Law

The definition - law of citizens' rights: the law of a state dealing with the rights of private citizens.

English law is the legal system of England and Wales. It was exported to Commonwealth countries, while the British Empire was established and maintained, and it forms the basis of the jurisprudence of most of those countries. English law prior to the American Revolution is still part of the law of the United States through reception statutes, except in Louisiana, and provides the basis for many American legal traditions and policies, though it has no superseding jurisdiction.

English law in its strictest sense applies within the jurisdiction of England and Wales. Any legislation which the Welsh Assembly enacts is enacted in particular circumscribed policy areas defined by the Government of Wales Act 2006, other legislation of the UK Parliament, or by orders in council given under the authority of the 2006 act. Furthermore, that legislation is, as with any by law made by any other body within England and Wales, interpreted by the undivided judiciary of England and Wales.

Scottish law is a unique legal system with an ancient basis in Roman law. Grounded in uncodified civil law dating back to the Corpus Juris Civilis (Roman Body of Civil Law), it also features elements of common law with medieval sources. This means Scotland has a pluralistic, or mixed legal system. South Africa has a similar system to Scotland.

Since the Acts of Union, in 1707, it has shared a legislature with the rest of the United Kingdom. Before 1707 Scotland retained a fundamentally different legal system from that of England and Wales, but the Union brought English influence on Scots law. In recent years, Scots law has also been affected by European law under the Treaty of Rome, the requirements of the ECHR (entered into by members of the Council of Europe) and the establishment of the Scottish Parliament, which may pass legislation within its areas of legislative competence as detailed by the Scotland act 1998.

There are substantial differences between Scottish and English law. Some of the more important practical differences between the jurisdictions include; the age of legal capacity (16 years old in Scotland, 18 years old in England); the use of a 15 member jury in Scotland rather than the usual 12 members; the fact that the accused in a criminal trial does not have the right to elect a judge or jury trial; judges and juries of criminal trials have the "third verdict" of "not proven" available to them, and the fact that Equity does not exist in Scots law. Some of the more important practical similarities between the jurisdictions include the similar protections for consumers under the Sale of Goods Act 1979, very similar treatment under various taxation legislation and similar protections for employees and agents.

Common Law - the essence of English common law is that it is made by judges sitting in courts, applying their common sense and knowledge of legal precedent (stare decisis) to the facts before them. A decision of the highest appeal court in England and Wales, the House of Lords, is binding on every other court in the hierarchy, and they will follow its directions. England and Wales are constituent countries of the United Kingdom, which is a member of the European Union. Hence, EU law is a part of English law. The European Union consists mainly of countries that use civil law and so the civil law system is also in England in this form. The European Court of Justice can direct English and Welsh courts on the meaning of areas of law in which the EU has passed legislation.

The oldest law currently in force is the Distress act 1267, part of the Statute of Marlborough, (52 Hen. 3). Three sections of the Magna Carta, originally signed in 1215 and a landmark in the development of English law, are extant, but they date to the reissuing of the law in 1297.

Apart from a very few examples of local custom and tradition that survive in England's legal system, law that is not contained within a specific act is known as common law. It is built up by the courts and their judgments. This means that, in deciding a particular case, the court must have regard to the principles of law laid down in earlier reported cases on the same or similar points, although the law may be extended or varied if the facts of the particular case are sufficiently different.

In fact, many aspects of the law shown here are also controlled by statute law (which is the law made by Parliament) but as a general heading, these matters can be grouped together as based on, or originating in, common law.

There are several examples relevant to the countryside and used by rangers and others who are required to enforce laws and bye-laws.

Scottish common law is often different from English, and sometimes significantly so. The following examples apply to English law.

Trespass - as applied to a piece of land open to the public which is not common land, open access land, or a public right of way. This is one of the areas where the laws of England and Scotland are significantly different. It is against the law to trespass on any land (and inland that includes land covered by water, such as rivers or lakes) or in any building. Ignorance of that fact is no defence under this law. The word trespass covers much more than people usually realise. All land in this country belongs to someone. If you go on to land without the owner's permission, you are trespassing unless there is some right of access for the public, or for you specifically (for example, if you have acquired a right to pass over the land to reach some land of your own).

Any person can enter a place if the landowner permits it. However, this does not necessarily make a permanent right of access, and unless they have dedicated a bit of land to be permanently open it is within the power of the landowner to ask any person to leave, assuming that person does not have some other lawful reason to be there. The landowner does not have to give a reason. If the person does not go immediately, by the shortest practical route, then they are trespassing. Despite the well-known sign 'trespassers will be prosecuted', trespass is not a criminal offence and trespassers cannot usually be prosecuted. They can, however, be sued. There is little chance of such a matter ever being so serious as to be worth suing over, and so this rarely happens.

People in a park will often protest (if asked to leave) that it is public land. However, the ownership of the land is not relevant. Even if the land is owned by a public body, such as the local council, this does not mean necessarily that they have a right to be on it at all times - they do not. If the place closes at a certain time and a visitor remains after that time, they can then be considered to be trespassing. If a visitor misbehaves at any time and refuses to leave when asked to do so by someone with a right to do so (usually the landowner or a representative), then the visitor could become a trespasser because they no longer have the landowner's permission to be there, even if they entered legally. Note: this also gives landowners the absolute right to close off paths (other than rights of way) and areas without notice or explanation. You may well come across a lot of trespassing by young people using parks after closing time. This is often just for a social meeting, but it can also be to consume alcohol or to take drugs.

This law is of little practical use, but might be employed when arguing with more reasonable people. It does not apply to people on a public footpath or other right of way, or on open access land. The problem is that if someone is trespassing, they are unlikely to comply with a polite request to leave, and if they do not, the landowner has little, if any, further recourse. Section 61 of the Criminal Justice and Public Order Act 1994 allows the senior Police officer attending the scene of an incident involving a trespass or nuisance on land to order trespassers to leave the land and to remove their vehicles as soon as reasonably practicable. The power can only be used when there are two or more people there and they "are present there with the common purpose of residing there for any period, (and) that reasonable steps have been taken by or on behalf of the occupier to ask them to leave" and either the trespassers have six or more vehicles between them, or they have caused damage to the land or to property on the land or used threatening, abusive or insulting words or behaviour - or both. So really, it's not likely to cover anything other than a major invasion. This power is not often used, but for practical purposes, this is the only instance where you might get the Police to come and remove trespassers.

Sometimes, people go onto private property, which is not apparently fenced off and where the owners do not seem to mind. The fact that there is no fence or any sign saying that the land is private does not mean that people can go there. Wandering on to farmers' fields or other places which are obviously private is clearly trespassing. So is wandering over land which may not be so clearly private, if the public has no right of access.

It is not normally possible to be a trespasser whilst legitimately on a right of way. However, if the user is not using the right of way as a route to get from one place to another, but using it for some other reason, such as to interfere with the landowner, they can be considered to be a trespasser. A real example of this (before open access land was in existence) concerned a hunt saboteur who was deemed by a court to be a trespasser for shouting and waving flags, whilst on a footpath, on a grouse moor. This important distinction was the purpose for which the person was there. This does not mean that it is always wrong to shout and wave flags on a footpath.

Murder comes under common law as there is no statute making murder illegal. It is a common-law crime - so although there is no written Act of Parliament making murder illegal, it is illegal by virtue of the constitutional authority of the courts and their previous decisions Common law can be amended or repealed by Parliament; murder, by way of example, carries a mandatory life sentence today, but had previously allowed the death penalty.

Crime and Offences

Crime - for the final part of this chapter we shall look at what a crime is and go through some examples of crime that you may come across. Society defines crime as the breach of one or more rules or laws for which some governing authority or force may ultimately prescribe a punishment.

Authorities employ various mechanisms to regulate behaviour, including rules codified into laws, policing people to ensure they comply with those laws and other policies and practices designed by the Police, government or local authorities to prevent crime. In addition, authorities try to provide remedies and sanctions, and collectively these constitute a criminal justice system. Not all breaches of the law, however, are considered crimes, for example, breaches of contract and other civil law offences.

Offence definition - legal or moral crime: an official crime or a crime against moral, social, or other accepted standards; anger or resentment: anger, resentment, hurt, or displeasure, cause of displeasure or anger. Something that causes displeasure, humiliation, anger, resentment, or hurt.

Below is a list of some of the more common crimes and offences you may come across whilst on duty.

Mainstream Cyber Crime

The Internet is a global system of interconnected computer networks that use the standard Internet protocol suite (TCP/IP) to serve several billion users worldwide. It is a network of networks that consists of millions of private, public, academic, business, and government networks, of local to global scope, that are linked by a broad array of electronic, wireless and optical networking technologies.

The Internet carries an extensive range of information resources and services, such as the inter-linked hypertext documents on the World Wide Web (WWW), the infrastructure to support email, and peer to peer networks. The internet is unregulated and any form, of information can be freely distributed, although the information that is of a really offensive nature or breaks copyright/legal can be removed or blocked depending on a countries legal and internet regulations.

Examples of this are peer to peer material such as the Pirate Bay, where illegal copies of movies, music and games can be downloaded. Paedophiles use the internet to distribute their images and although blocked or tracked in many circumstances, now hide their pornographic images within innocent pictures requiring encryption to view and are much harder to track.

Organised crime groups have used the internet to set up sites to conduct fraud, money laundering or even phishing sites to collect personal information. These sites are located around the world the main ones currently coming from Africa and Russia. The current main use of the internet after email is social networking and the growth of social networks such as Facebook, Twitter and LinkedIn has been rapid over the last few years. The three most popular current websites are Google, Facebook and YouTube. Chrome is the most popular current web browser followed by Firefox and Internet Explorer.

Cyber Crime is not something new, but is something that is becoming more and more widespread. It includes a variety of terms linked with various types of cyber crime.

Identity theft - (assuming someone's identity having acquired their personal details or payment details) can be done online or offline (therefore it isn't a 'pure' offence)

Flaming – hostile interaction between internet users, usually involving profanity (also known as bashing). Whilst some arises out of normal discussion some individuals (flamers) set out to deliberately provoke a reaction

Hacking – generic term for accessing someone else's computer without their permission

DoS Attack – Denial of Service attack is an attempt to make a machine or network resource unavailable to its intended users.

Social Engineering – seeking personal information about someone in order to use their identity to commit fraud or other activities (ID theft). This can be done online or offline. Such as ringing someone and purporting to be from a financial institution or law enforcement body, and getting them to disclose bank card details and other security information.

Phishing – (Offender driven) Use fraudulent e-mails to obtain personal financial data. Large volumes of e-mails are sent out often with branding that appears credible. The e-mails may link to fraudulent websites

Farming – (Victim has driven) slightly different from phishing in that victims' access a fraudulent website or malware/virus whilst seeking a genuine site

Stalking – can be done online or offline (and sometime using both)

At present, many of these crimes go unreported or undetected, as people feel it is not a police matter. However, they are all crimes and fall under various acts - Computer Misuse Act 1990, Malicious Communications Act 1988, RIPA (The Regulation of Investigatory Powers Act) 2000. Cyber Crime is treated like any other crime and the collection of evidence is just the same. However, instead of having tangible evidence, such as a jacket or a letter, we have filed or screenshots that can be taken.

Open Source

The collection, evaluation and analysis of materials from sources available to the public, whether on payment or otherwise to use as intelligence or evidence within investigations'.

Open Source Information

'Open Source is defined as publicly available information (i.e. any member of the public could lawfully obtain the information by request or observation). It includes books, newspapers, journals, TV and radio broadcasts, newswires, Internet WWW and newsgroups, mapping, imagery, photographs, commercial subscription databases and grey literature (conference proceedings and institute reports)

The information must be available in the public domain although it is recognised that commercial subscription databases may contain some data not available to the public but are still considered open source due to their nature.

It is worth noting that any activity carried out over the Internet leaves a trace or digital footprint, which can identify the device used and, in some instances, the individual carrying out that activity. Staff engaged in investigation/research over the Internet must take precautions to protect the security of themselves and of police computer systems. Internet Service Providers (ISP) maintain a record of Internet Protocol (IP) addresses and the sites visited. An IP is a numerical number assigned to any device that uses the Internet Protocol. As well as being tracked IPs can be used to block or deny access to sites if unauthorised or fraudulent activity has taken place. A media access control address (MAC) can also be traced back to the actual device along with the IP address. A MAC address is usually assigned during manufacture and embedded in the hardware of the device.

Websites may record IP addresses as well as other details about the computer used, including the Browser, Operating System, computer name etc. Records are often kept of the time and date of each visit in addition to the sites the visitor came from and went to. Websites can install cookies on to a computer to identify the user, should they return to that site. Therefore, when undertaking any Level 2 or 3 surveillance, it is imperative that the computer and IP cannot be traced back to the police and must be stand alone with its own separate internet access. On the completion of any surveillance it is imperative that a computer has all traces of cookies, passwords, browsing history removed to ensure any compromise of the computer or investigation is minimised.

All computers have an IP (Internet protocol) address, and the devices themselves a MAC address (Machine Access Code) these can be used to help trace the offending computer and then user.

Long headers in emails can also be sued to trace the origin of the email, through the IP was sent through.

Malicious Communication

A person is guilty of malicious communications if they send to another person any form of communication of any description which conveys a message of indecent or grossly offensive, threatening, information which is false or unknown or believed to be false by the sender. For the purpose to cause distress or anxiety to the intended person of the communication.

The defence is that the threat was used to reinforce a demand on reasonable grounds and that it was believed on reasonable grounds that the use of the threat was a proper means of reinforcing the demand.

Hate Crime

Hate crime is any criminal offence committed against a person or property that is motivated by hostility towards someone based on their disability, race, religion, gender identity or sexual orientation.

The Association of Chief Police Officers (ACPO) and the Crown Prosecution Service have a nationally agreed definition of Hate Crime. Hate crimes are taken to mean any crime where the perpetrator's hostility or prejudice against an identifiable group of people is a factor in determining who is victimised. This is a broad and inclusive definition. A victim does not have to be a member of the group. In fact, anyone could be a victim of a hate crime.

The CPS and ACPO have agreed five monitored strands of hate crime. A hate crime is any criminal offence that is motivated by hostility or prejudice based upon the victims:

disability
race
religion or belief
sexual orientation
transgender identity

Hate crime can take many forms, including:

Physical attacks such as physical assault, damage to property, offensive graffiti and arson threats of attack, including offensive letters, abusive or obscene telephone calls, groups hanging around to intimidate, and unfounded, malicious complaints

verbal abuse, insults or harassment - taunting, offensive leaflets and posters, abusive gestures, dumping of rubbish outside homes or through letterboxes, and bullying at school or in the workplace

Racist or Racially Aggravated

A racist or racially motivated offence that has been based on a victim having received verbal or physical hostility based upon race or religion.

Generally, a racist or racially aggravated offence is when:

At the time of committing the offence or immediately before or after the offence, the person demonstrates towards the victim hostility based on a victim's membership of a racial or religious group, sexual orientation or gender,

The offence is motivated by hostility towards members of a racial or religious group based on their membership of that group.

Public Order

Public Order comes in different sections outlined below, but as an overview it is to deal with public disorder or violence. It is dealt with under the 1986 Public Order Act, which replaced the common law and Public Order act of 1936.

Section 1 – Riot

(1) Where 12 or more persons who are present together use or threaten unlawful violence for a common purpose and the conduct of them (taken together) is such as would cause a person of reasonable firmness present at the scene to fear for his personal safety, each of the persons using unlawful violence for the common purpose is guilty of riot.

(2) It is immaterial whether or not the 12 or more use or threaten unlawful violence simultaneously.

(3) The common purpose may be inferred from conduct.

(4) No person of reasonable firmness need actually be, or be likely to be, present at the scene.

(5) Riot may be committed in private as well as in public places.

(6) A person guilty of riot is liable on conviction on indictment to imprisonment for a term not exceeding 10 years or a fine, or both.

Section 2 - Violent Disorder

(1) Where three or more persons who are present together use or threaten unlawful violence and the conduct of them (taken together) is such as would cause a person of reasonable firmness present at the scene to fear for his personal safety, each of the persons using or threatening unlawful violence is guilty of violent disorder.

(2) It is immaterial whether or not the three or more use or threaten unlawful violence simultaneously.

(3) Same as section 1.

(4) Same as section 1.

(5) A person guilty of violent disorder is liable on conviction on indictment to imprisonment for a term not exceeding five years or a fine, or both, or on summary conviction to imprisonment for a term not exceeding six months or a fine not exceeding the statutory maximum or both.

Section 3 - Affray

(1) A person is guilty of affray if he uses or threatens unlawful violence towards another and his conduct is such as would cause a person of reasonable firmness present at the scene to fear for his personal safety.

(2) Where two or more persons use or threaten unlawful violence, it is the conduct of them taken together that must be considered for the purposes of subsection (1).

(3) For the purposes of this section words cannot be made by the use of words alone.

(4) Same as section 1.

(5) Same as section 1.

(6) A Constable may arrest without warrant anyone he reasonably suspects is committing affray.

(7) A person guilty of affray is liable on conviction on indictment to imprisonment for a term not exceeding three years or a fine or both, or on summary conviction to imprisonment for a term not exceeding six months or a fine not exceeding the statutory maximum or both.

Section 4 - Fear or provocation of violence

(1) A person is guilty of an offence if he - a) uses towards another person threatening, abusive or insulting words or behaviour, or b) distributes or displays to another person any writing, sign or other visible representation which is threatening, abusive or insulting, with intent to cause that person to believe that immediate unlawful violence will be used against him or another by any person, or to provoke the immediate use of unlawful violence by that person or another, or whereby that person is likely to believe that such violence will be provoked.

(2) An offence under this section may be committed in a public or a private place, except that no offence is committed where the words or behaviour are used, or the writing, sign or other visible representation is distributed or displayed, by a person inside a dwelling and the other person is also inside that or another dwelling.

(3) A Constable may arrest without warrant anyone he reasonably suspects is committing an offence under this subsection.

(4) A person guilty of an offence under this section is liable on summary conviction to imprisonment for a term not exceeding six months or a fine not exceeding level 5 (currently £5,000) on the standard scale or both.

Section 5 - Harassment, alarm or distress

(1) A person is guilty of an offence if he - a) uses threatening, abusive or insulting words or behaviour, or disorderly behaviour, or b) displays any writing, sign or other visible representation which is threatening, abusive or insulting, within the hearing or sight of a person likely to be causing harassment, alarm or distress thereby.

(2) An offence under this section may be committed in a public or a private place, except that no offence is committed where the

words or behaviour are used, or the writing, sign or other visible representation is displayed, by a person inside a dwelling and the other person is also inside that or another dwelling.

(3) It is a defence for the accused to prove - a) that he had no reason to believe that there was any person within hearing or sight who was likely to be caused harassment, alarm or distress, or b) that he was inside a dwelling and had no reason to believe that the words or behaviour used, or the writing, sign or other visible representation displayed, would be heard or seen by a person outside that or any other dwelling, or c) that his conduct was reasonable.

(4) A Constable may arrest without warrant if - a) he engages in offensive conduct which the Constable warns him to stop, and b) he engages in further offensive conduct immediately or shortly after the warning.

(5) In subsection (4) above 'offensive conduct' means conduct the Constable reasonably suspects to constitute an offence under this section, and the conduct mentioned in paragraph (a) and the further conduct need not be of the same nature.

(6) A person guilty of an offence under this section is liable on summary conviction to a fine not exceeding level 3 (currently £1,000) on the standard scale.

Breach of the Peace

Constables are permitted to arrest a person to "prevent a further breach of the peace" which allows Police Constables to arrest a person before a breach of the peace has occurred. This is permitted when a Constable holds a reasonable belief that should the person remain, that they would continue with their course of conduct and that a breach of the peace would occur. Arrest for breach of the peace is usually used to remove violent or potentially violent offenders from a scene rapidly. The only punishment that can be inflicted by a court for this offence is for the offender to be bound over to keep the peace.

Drink related Offences

Drunk in a public place If the police think a person is drunk in a public place they can arrest and place in custody. They may do this if they think it is necessary for the person's safety.

Drunk and disorderly in a public place Disorderly' behaviour is acting in a way that disturbs the peace or interferes with the comfort of people who may be nearby. The police can arrest and charge for this if they think the person's behaviour is intended to disturb, even if no one is actually disturbed by it.

Drunk and behaving in a riotous or disorderly manner. Riotous behaviour is behaviour that frightens a member of the public and makes them fear that some breach of the peace is likely to occur. Disorderly has the same meaning as above, but the police may charge with this more serious offence if they think your disorderly behaviour is severe.

Drunk and Incapable

Drunk and incapable means that an individual has consumed alcohol to the point of being unable to either walk unaided or stand unaided or is unaware of their own actions, or unable to fully understand what is said to them."

As a guide, it is suggested that, if someone appears to be drunk and showing any 'aspect' of incapability which is perceived to result from that drunkenness, then that person should be treated as being drunk and incapable.

A person found to be drunk and incapable should be treated as being in need of medical assistance and hospital and an ambulance should be called.

If a drunk and incapable person who is under arrest declines or is refused medical treatment, they should, only as a last resort, be taken into custody at a police station.

The fact that a person has declined or has been refused treatment does not absolve the police or medical services of their responsibility.

Offensive Weapon

"Any person who without lawful authority or reasonable excuse, the proof whereof shall lie on him, has with him in any public place any offensive weapon shall be guilty of an offence."

Punishable on summary conviction by three months' imprisonment or level 5 fine; on indictment by two years' imprisonment and/or maximum fine.

Although there is no express power of arrest for this offence, an arrest can be carried out if the general arrest conditions under PACE are satisfied. In any event the Constable may seize the weapon in question.

Section 1(4) provides a definition of an offensive weapon.

'Offensive weapon' means any article made or adapted for use for causing injury to the person, or intended by the person having it for such use by him (or some other person).

Hence, weapons become offensive in two ways:

(a) Some weapons are offensive because they have been made for the purpose of causing injury or have been so adapted.

(b) Any article which has the potential of causing injury is offensive if the possessor has it with the intention of causing injury.

The question of whether the article is offensive or not has an important bearing on the burden of proof: if the weapon is offensive and it can be proved that they had it with them in a public place, the burden shifts to the offender to prove that they had lawful authority or reasonable excuse.

Hence, for example, in the case of spray cans or improvised whips - unless it can be shown that they are offensive, by showing that they had the item with them with the intention of causing injury, they will not be classed as offensive weapons.

If a prosecution proves that the article is offensive, then they would have to prove, on the balance of possibilities, that they had a "reasonable excuse" for the possession, and this question of reasonableness is one for a jury.

Possession of a Controlled Drug

It is unlawful to have a controlled drug in your possession unless you have authorisation in the form of a licence, or if you did not know the substance was a controlled drug.

Three elements constitute the offence of possession:

The substance is in the possession or under the control of the individual. The substance must be in an individual's physical custody or under their control. This can include the substance being at the property of someone who is not present but has control over that property.

The individual knows the 'thing exists'. The individual must know of the existence of the substance and they must know that the substance is a controlled drug.

The substance is a controlled drug. The substance must in fact be a controlled drug. Therefore, if the individual thought they were in possession of cannabis but they were in fact in possession of tea leaves, no offence has been committed. Although there could be still a conviction for attempted possession.

It is a defence against a possession charge if the defendant can prove that, as soon as was practicable, they intended to destroy the substance or give it to someone who had legal authority to possess it.

The severity of the penalty applied in relation to drugs offences will depend on the individual circumstances of the case and the class of the drug. Below is a list of the more common drugs and their classification, Class A being the most severe.

Class A – heroin, methadone, crack, cocaine, ecstasy, magic mushrooms and 'crystal meth'

Class B – amphetamines, barbiturates and dihydrocodeine, Cannabis. Certain class B drugs are reclassified to Class A if they have been prepared for injection. These include amphetamines, dihydrocodeine and codeine.

Class C - benzodiazepines, steroids and subutex (buprenorphine).

Possession with intent to supply

It is an offence for a person to have a controlled drug in their possession, whether lawfully or not, with the intent to supply it to another. This offence is known as possession with intent to supply.

A person charged with possession with intent to supply can enter a plea of guilty to the charge of possession and not guilty to supply, on the grounds that the drugs seized were for personal use. At this point the prosecution may adduce evidence to attempt to prove guilt. Prosecutions for this offence may be based on circumstantial evidence, statements made by the defendant at the time of arrest and expert evidence.

Examples of relevant circumstantial evidence would include the possession of drug supply paraphernalia such as scales, bags, Clingfilm and large sums of unexplained cash. The manner in which the drugs were wrapped could also be used as evidence of intent to supply or to support the defendant's case (if the offence is denied) that the drugs were for personal use.

Statements at the time of arrest can be important. For example, a young person who is caught in possession of two ecstasy tablets and tells the Police, 'I was holding them for a friend,' could face a charge of possession with intent to supply.

In many cases the prosecution case will be built largely on the quantity of drugs seized, on the basis that the quantity was so large that it could not have been for personal use. Expert evidence can be crucial in such cases, to help the court to determine whether this is the case.

Criminal damage

Criminal damage is where somebody damages an item or property. "A person who without lawful excuse destroys or damages any property belonging to another intending to destroy or damage any such property or being reckless as to whether any such property would be destroyed or damaged shall be guilty of an offence."

An example would be to break the windows on a bus shelter or to run a key down the side of a car, scratching the paintwork.

False accounting

CPS Fraud, False Accounting, Fraudulent evasion of VAT, False statement for VAT purposes, Conduct amounting to an offence.

False accounting is an indictable offence contrary to section 17 of the Theft Act 1968; and where a person destroys, conceals, or falsifies an account; or dishonestly provides information which is false, misleading or deceptive with a view to gain for himself or another or with intent to cause loss to another, they commit the offence.

Section 17 Theft Act 1968 provides:

(1) Where a person dishonestly, with a view to gain for himself or another or with intent to cause loss to another, —

(a) destroys, defaces, conceals or falsifies any account or any record or document made or required for any accounting purpose; or

(b) in furnishing information for any purpose produces or makes use of any account, or any such record or document as aforesaid, which to his knowledge is or may be misleading, false or deceptive in a material particular; he shall, on conviction on indictment, be liable to imprisonment for a term not exceeding seven years.

(2) For purposes of this section a person who makes or concurs in making in an account or other document an entry which is or may be misleading, false or deceptive in a material particular, or who omits or concurs in omitting a material particular from an account or other document, is to be treated as falsifying the account or document.

Theft

Section 1(1) of the Theft Act 1968 (TA 1968) creates the offence of theft. It states:

"A person is guilty of theft if he dishonestly appropriates property belonging to another with the intention of permanently depriving the other of it."

Theft is triable either way. The maximum punishment that can be imposed where a defendant has been convicted of theft following trial on indictment, was reduced from ten years to seven years by s26 of the Criminal Justice Act 1991.

Whilst s1(1) creates the offence, ss 2-6 provide complete or partial definitions of the elements of theft. As s1(3) provides:

"The five following sections of this Act shall have effect as regards the interpretation and operation of this section (and, except as otherwise provided by this Act, shall apply only for the purposes of this section)."

The Actus Reus of Theft

1. Appropriation

The definition of "appropriation" is provided by s3(1) which states:

"Any assumption by a person of the rights of an owner amounts to an appropriation, and this includes where he has come by the property (innocently or not) without stealing it, any later assumption of a right to it by keeping or dealing with it as an owner."

Thus, although theft usually occurs when a person takes property belonging to somebody else, there are many other situations where it can arise. For example:

A lends a book to D. If D sells or gives the book to X, or destroys the book, D will have appropriated it, and may therefore be guilty of theft. Only A, the owner of the property, has the right to do those things and D would therefore be treating the book as if he owned it.

D who finds a book in the street, and later discovers that it belongs to his neighbour, A, decides to keep it, would also be within s3(1). D came by the property innocently and later assumes the rights of an owner.

Innocent appropriation

Some protection is offered to the bona fide (in good faith) purchaser by s3(2) which provides:

"Where property or a right or interest in property is or purports to be transferred for value to a person acting in good faith, no later assumption by him of rights which he believed himself to be acquiring shall, by reason of any defect in the transferor's title, amount to theft of the property."

Where therefore, A buys stolen property from D, unaware that it is stolen, and he gives value for it, he will not be guilty of theft if he later discovers the truth and decides to keep the property; neither will he incur any liability for handling stolen goods.

Appropriation by consent or authorised acts

The House of Lords has held that a person can appropriate property, even where the owner consents to the taking of property.

The House of Lords has also made it plain that an assumption of any right of an owner will be an appropriation.

2. Property

Section 4(1) provides a general definition of property for the purposes of theft, where it states:

"Property" includes money and all other property, real or personal, including things in action and other intangible property.

General

Things in action are rights which can only be enforced by taking legal action, as they have no physical existence. For example, a man owes £500 to a company. This debt is a chose in action. It exists in the sense that the company could sell it to somebody else, who would then have the right to collect the money from the man.

Other examples of intangible property are copyrights, trademarks and patents. However, confidential information has been held to fall outside the definition of property:

Land

Section 4(2) provides that land cannot be stolen except in three particular circumstances:

(a) Where a person is dealing with land in a special capacity, for example as a trustee (and makes a dishonest appropriation). (b) Where a person not in possession of the land severs something from it, for example crops or turf.

(c) Where a person in possession of the land as tenant appropriates a fixture or structure let with the land, for example by selling an outbuilding. (Note that in this situation, it does not matter whether the object is actually removed from the land or not.)

Plants and flowers

The question of the extent to which plants constitute property for the purposes of theft is provided for by s4(3) which states:

'A person who picks mushrooms growing wild on any land, or who picks flowers, fruit or foliage from a plant growing wild on any land, does not (although not in possession of the land) steal what he picks, unless he does it for reward or for sale or other commercial purpose. For purposes of this subsection "mushroom" includes any fungus, and "plant" includes any shrub or tree.'

Simply stated, it is not theft to take mushrooms or flowers, fruit or foliage from a wild plant. It would, however, be theft to take the whole plant, or to take anything for a commercial purpose. Thus, it would be theft if mushrooms were picked in order to sell them later.

Wild animals

About animals in the wild, they are referred to in s4(4) which provides:

"Wild creatures, tamed or untamed, shall be regarded as property, but a person cannot steal a wild creature not tamed nor ordinarily kept in captivity, or the carcass of any such creature unless either it has been reduced into possession by or on behalf of another person and possession of it has not since been lost or abandoned, or another person is in the course of reducing it into possession."

Thus, animals in zoos, safari parks and domestic pets can all be stolen, even if they are appropriated having escaped from captivity. A wild animal, whether live or dead, cannot be stolen unless it has already been taken into possession by somebody else. Note, however, that there are other statutes which create specific criminal offences for poachers.

3. Belonging to another

The general rule

Section 5(1) provides an extended meaning for the phrase "belonging to another" where it states:

"property shall be regarded as belonging to any person having possession or control of it, or having in it any proprietary right or interest ... "

Clearly this section does not require that property should be owned by the person from whom it is appropriated; mere possession or control is enough. For example, suppose that A lends a book to B and B is showing it to C when D snatches the book from C's hands and makes off with it. Here D has stolen the book from C (who has control of it), and B (who has possession of it), and A (who also has a proprietary interest, ie ownership, in it).

Provided he has the necessary mens rea, a person can steal his own property from someone with a lesser interest:

Ownerless property

A person cannot steal property that is not owned by another at the time of the appropriation. Property which has at one time been owned may become ownerless by abandonment. But abandonment is not something to be lightly inferred - property is abandoned only when the owner is indifferent to any future appropriation of the property by others; property is not abandoned because the owner has lost it and has given up the search. Consider the following situations:

(a) A man deliberately leaves his newspaper on a train and it is picked up by D who occupies the seat after him. The newspaper would not be regarded as property belonging to another as against D.

(b) A wife loses her wedding ring and long since given up the search but she will not have abandoned it.

The vital distinction between the two situations is that in example (a), the owner intends to relinquish his rights of ownership, and if property is ownerless it cannot be stolen. One should be cautious, however, before concluding that a person has relinquished his rights of ownership:

Property subject to a trust

Property subject to a trust is regarded under s5(1) as belonging to the beneficiaries as well as to the trustees. Special provision for charitable trusts where there are no beneficiaries (in the legal sense of persons owning a beneficial interest in the trust property) is made under s5(2), the consequence of which is that if trustees hold property on trust for charitable purposes, the Attorney-General, as a person who, though not a beneficiary, has the right to enforce such a trust, is someone to whom the property belongs, and the trustees may be convicted of theft if they dishonestly appropriate it.

Property received for a particular purpose

Sometimes the recipient of property is obliged to deal with property in a particular way. Section 5(3) provides that it is theft if a person receives property under an obligation to deal with it in a certain way but instead uses it for his own purposes:

"Where a person receives property from or on account of another, and is under an obligation to the other to retain and deal with that property or its proceeds in a particular way, the property or proceeds shall be regarded (as against him) as belonging to the other."

The defendant must be under a legal obligation to retain property or its proceeds in a separate fund. Further, the defendant must be aware that such an obligation exists. Whether an obligation exists or not, and if it does, the nature of the obligation, is to be determined by construing the express and implied terms of any contract between the parties:

Where a person receives money or other property for onward transmission to another there is clearly an obligation, to the person entrusted it for transmission, to retain and deal with it on its process in a particular way (to keep it or its equivalent separate and to hand it over):

Property Received by Another's Mistake

If a person is given property by mistake it will still be treated as belonging to the person who gave it (subject to some complex civil law rules as to whether there is a civil obligation to return the property or not). Section 5(4) states:

"Where a person gets property by another's mistake, and is under an obligation to make restoration (in whole or in part) of the property or its proceeds or the value thereof, then to the extent of that obligation the property or proceeds shall be regarded (as against him) as belonging to the person entitled to restoration, and an intention not to make restoration shall be regarded as an intention to deprive that person of the property or proceeds."

The Mens Rea of Theft

An appropriation of property belonging to another amount to theft if it is done (1) dishonestly, and (2) with the intention of permanently depriving the other of it.

1. Dishonesty

Dishonesty is dealt with in s2 but it only provides a partial definition.

Defences

Section 2(1) sets out the situations where as a matter of law a person is not dishonest:

"A person's appropriation of property belonging to another is not to be regarded as dishonest- (a) if he appropriates the property in the belief that he has in law the right to deprive the other of it, on behalf of himself or of a third person; or (b) if he appropriates the property in the belief that he would have the other's consent if the other knew of the appropriation and the circumstances of it; or (c) … if he appropriates the property in the belief that the person to whom the property belongs cannot be discovered by taking reasonable steps."

If there is evidence of a belief which is covered by s2(1), the judge must tell the jury that as a matter of law they must acquit the accused unless the prosecution disproves his alleged belief beyond reasonable doubt.

Other Cases

Two further subsections touch on the question of dishonesty:

A defendant can be dishonest where he does not act with a view to making a gain for himself or another. It is sufficient that he acts with a view to causing loss to the owner, this being the effect of s1(2):

"It is immaterial whether the appropriation is made with a view to gain or is made for the thief's own benefit."

The other provision is s2(2) which states:

"A person's appropriation of property belonging to another may be dishonest notwithstanding that he is willing to pay for the property."

This subsection meets a possible argument that an appropriation cannot amount to theft by virtue only of the fact that the defendant is willing to pay for the property.

Dishonesty not Covered by S2

In cases where the defendant cannot avail himself of s2(1), and where there is nevertheless some debate as to whether or not his actions were dishonest, the matter should be left to the jury (or magistrates) who should apply the standard of ordinary decent people. In determining whether the prosecution has proved that the defendant was acting dishonestly, the Court of Appeal in R v Ghosh [1982] QB 1053 (a case involving s15 TA 1968) held that:

(1) A jury (or magistrates) must decide whether according to the ordinary standards of reasonable and honest people what was done was dishonest. If it was not dishonest by those standards, that is the end of the matter.

(2) If it was dishonest by those standards, then the jury (or magistrates) must consider whether the defendant himself must have realised that what he was doing was by those standards dishonest. It is dishonest for the defendant to act in a way which he knows ordinary people would consider to be dishonest.

Here, the Court of Appeal added a second, subjective test to that laid down in R v Feely [1973] QB 530. In R v Roberts (1987) 84 Cr App R 117, the Court of Appeal ruled that this second point need only be put to the jury in those cases where the defendant raised the special plea that he did not think he was being dishonest by his own standards.

2. Intention to permanently deprive

The defendant must have taken the property "with the intention of permanently depriving the other of it", although the owner does not have to be permanently deprived of his property. In the vast majority of situations the presence or absence of such a state of mind should be evident. The facts (the history of what the defendant did with the goods) will often have an important bearing on the proof of the defendant's intent. For example:

If D was found respraying the car which he took from V without his permission, the jury is likely to favour the inference that D's intent was to deprive V permanently of it. If on the other hand, D had taken V's lawnmower without permission, and left it in full view of V's house after he had used it to mow his lawn, the jury is likely to favour the inference that it was not D's intention to deprive V permanently of it.

In every case it is for the jury to determine, on the evidence, whether the defendant did so intend, so that where the evidence as to the defendant's intent is circumstantial the judge will instruct the jury that they may infer the intent from evidence pointing to that conclusion. Note two particular circumstances:

Even long-term or indefinite borrowing will not amount to theft:

It is not a defence to claim that money that has been taken would have been repaid:

3. Special forms of borrowing

Section 6 provides that in certain circumstances, where a person disposes of or borrows property, that person is to be regarded as having had the intention of permanently depriving the other of it. Section 6 states:

"(1) A person appropriating property belonging to another without meaning the other permanently to lose the thing itself is nevertheless to be regarded as having the intention of permanently depriving the other of it if his intention is to treat the thing as his own to dispose of regardless of the other's rights, and a borrowing or lending of it may amount to so treating it if, but only if, the borrowing or lending is for a period and in circumstances making it equivalent to an outright taking or disposal.

(2) Without prejudice to the generality of subsection (1) above, where a person, having possession or control (lawfully or not) of property belonging to another, parts with the property under a condition as to its return which he may not be able to perform, this (if done for the purposes of his own and without the other's authority) amounts to treating the property as his own to dispose of regardless of the other's rights."

In R v Lloyd [1985] QB 829, (a case concerning a charge of conspiracy to steal) it was made clear that s6 should only be referred to in exceptional cases; for most purposes it would be unnecessary to go beyond s1(1). Reference should only be made to s6 where the defendant does not mean the other person permanently to lose the thing, but has acted in a way which may fall within s6.

Section 6(1) deals with two separate situations where a defendant is deemed to intend to deprive the other permanently of the property:

(i) If his intention is to treat the thing as his own to dispose of regardless of the other's rights.

(ii) Borrowing or lending for a period and in circumstances making it equivalent to an outright taking or disposal. For example, the use of a season ticket followed by its return to the owner.

Under s6(2) a person is to be treated as having an intention to permanently deprive the owner of his property if he parts with the property under a condition which he may not be able to perform. This is meant to provide for the case where a person takes another's property and pledges it with a pawnbroker without the owner's permission. Such a defendant will be deemed to have an intention to permanently deprive as it may be uncertain whether the defendant will be able to redeem the goods - the very fact that he has pawned them tends to show that he is lacking in funds.

Robbery

A person is guilty of robbery if he steals, and immediately before or at the time of doing so, and in order to do so, he uses force on any person or puts or seeks to put any person in fear of being then and there subjected to force.

An example would be a teenager walking home is stopped by a group of teenagers. They are then threatened with violence to hand over his mobile phone and mp3 player.

Common Assault

It is committed by a person who causes another person to apprehend the immediate use of unlawful violence by the defendant. This is any act by which a person intentionally or recklessly causes another to apprehend immediate unlawful violence. Such an act must be with the intent being calculated in that person's mind to cause apprehension or fear in the mind of the victim. Therefore, where there is no intent, there will be not be an assault, UNLESS, that the person who assaulted another, (and it was conclusive by way of evidence), that the person was indeed reckless as to the other person would in all probability have indeed apprehended that immediate unlawful violence would be used.

An assault is used to describe both an assault and battery, and indeed, there is often confusion between both the two offences.

Battery – contrary to section 39 of the Criminal Justice Act 1988

Common Assault – contrary to section 39 of the Criminal Justice Act 1988

Common assault and battery are summary offences, which means that the matter may only be tried in a Magistrates Court, and if found guilty have a maximum penalty not exceeding six months' imprisonment or a fine not exceeding £5,000.00

However, an offence of common assault (to include battery) may be tried on indictment that is the Crown Court.

An example, may be:

A person throwing a wine bottle at another, and misses, will be an assault.

A person kicks another person causing no injury.

A person who uses a dog as a threat only, being an intention that the dog bite, but does not do so, will be an assault.

When assault is included to the term battery, this is defined as an act whereby a person intentionally or recklessly causes the other person to apprehend immediate unlawful personal violence or to sustain unlawful personal violence.

Battery is the act of intentionally or recklessly asserting unlawful force to another person.

Recklessness is common assault, which involves the foresight of the possibility that a person would fear immediate and unlawful violence, and that person takes the risk of doing the act. It is basically taking the risk, which is being reckless.

Arson

At Common Law, the malicious burning or exploding of the dwelling house of another or the burning of a building within the curtilage, the immediate surrounding space, of the dwelling of another.

The main elements necessary to prove arson are evidence of a burning and evidence that a criminal act caused the fire. The accused must intend to burn a building or other structure. Absent a statutory description of the conduct required for arson, the conduct must be malicious, and not accidental. Malice, however, does not mean ill will. Intentional or outrageously reckless conduct is sufficient to constitute malice. Motive, on the other hand, is not an essential element of arson.

At common law an offence and is defined by Lord Coke to be the malicious and voluntary burning of the house of another, by night or day. 3 Inst. 66. To make this crime complete, there must be, 1st, a burning of the house, or some part of it; it is sufficient if any part be consumed, however small it may be. The burning must have been both malicious and wilful. The offence of arson at common law does not extend further than the burning of the house of another.

ABH

ABH is an assault that has caused a non-serious injury that has not broken the skin. In England and Wales, and in Northern Ireland, the offence is created by section 47 of the Offences against the Person Act 1861. "Whosoever shall be convicted upon an indictment of any assault occasioning ABH shall be liable to be kept in penal servitude".

An example would be somebody who has been punched in the face and has a black eye.

GBH

Grievous Bodily Harm is a more serious assault where a wound has been caused that breaks the skin. It comes under Section 18 and Section 20 of the Offences against the Person Act 1861.

Section 18 - "Whosoever shall unlawfully and maliciously by any means whatsoever wound or cause any grievous bodily harm to any person, with intent to do some grievous bodily harm to any person, or with intent to resist or prevent the lawful apprehension or detainee of any person, shall be guilty of an offence and, being convicted thereof, shall be liable to imprisonment for life."

Section 20 - "Whosoever shall unlawfully and maliciously wound or inflict any grievous bodily harm upon any other person, either with or without any weapon or instrument, shall be guilty of an offence and, being convicted therefore, shall be liable to a term of imprisonment not exceeding five years."

The two parts are for specific intent: Section 18 is wounding with intent and carries a harsher sentence.

An example would be where a knife has been used to stab somebody and caused a non-life-threatening injury and would be section 18. A section 20 could be causing a nosebleed to the injured party (IP) during a fight.

Burglary

Burglary is defined by section 9 of the Theft act 1968 which created two variants:

"A person is guilty of burglary if he enters any building or part of a building as a trespasser with intent to steal, inflict grievous bodily harm (or raping any person therein), or do unlawful damage to the building or anything in it. (section 9(1)(a))"

"A person is guilty of burglary if, having entered a building or part of a building as a trespasser, he steals or attempts to steal anything in the building, or inflicts or attempts to inflict grievous bodily harm on any person in the building (section 9(1)(b))"

For the crime to be complete certain elements outlined below need to be met.

Enters - although physical evidence of entry is not normally difficult to obtain, it can be difficult on occasions to decide whether an entry has occurred in law.

Building or part of a building - the Theft act 1968 does not define a building, so this must be a matter of fact for the jury, however, section 9(3) specifically states that the term includes an "inhabited vehicle or vessel"; hence motor homes, caravans and houseboats are protected by the section even when temporarily unoccupied. Burglary can also be committed in "part of a building" and in R v Walkington 1979 the defendant had entered a large shop during trading hours but went behind a counter and stole money from the till. The court held that he had entered that part of the building normally reserved for staff as a trespasser and was therefore guilty of burglary.

As a trespasser - the essence of trespass is entering or remaining on another's property without authority; a person having permission to enter property for one purpose who in fact enters for another purpose may become a trespasser: an example being, a friend invited you into their property and you then stole some jewellery. In recent years, the terms "distraction burglary", "artifice burglary" and "burglary by trick" have been used in crime prevention circles when access to premises is granted as a result of some deception on the occupier, usually by pretence that the burglar represents somebody who might reasonably request access such as a water, gas or electricity supplier. There is no separate legal definition of this variant.

With intent - the intention to commit an offence, being an essential element of burglary, requires proof beyond reasonable doubt. For example, if entry is made to regain property which the defendant honestly believes he has a right to take, there is no intention to steal and the defendant is entitled to be acquitted. However, it has been held that a conditional intent to steal anything found to be of value is enough to satisfy this requirement.

Sexual Offences

The Sexual Offences Act 2003 (the Act) came into force on the 1st May 2004. The purpose of the Act was to strengthen and modernise the law on sexual offences, whilst improving preventative measures and the protection of individuals from sexual offenders. The Act extends the definition of rape to include the penetration by a penis of the vagina, anus or mouth of another person. The 2003 Act also changes the law about consent and belief in consent.

The first part of the Act covers sexual offences. The second part covers offenders with an emphasis on the protection of vulnerable individuals.

It gives a comprehensive list of sex offences to protect individuals from abuse and exploitation, and is designed to be fair and non-discriminatory.

Rape

Rape is a type of sexual assault usually involving sexual intercourse, which is initiated by one or more persons against another person without that person's consent. A person who commits an act of rape is known as a rapist. The act may be carried out by physical force, coercion, abuse of authority or with a person who is incapable of valid consent

Rape is a crime that can have deep and profound effects on the victim and care needs to be taken both gaining witnesses details and taking sensitive samples.

The word "consent" in the context of the offence of rape is now defined in the Sexual Offences Act 2003. A person consents if he or she agrees by choice, and has the freedom and capacity to make that choice. The essence of this definition is the agreement by choice. The law does not require the victim to have resisted physically in order to prove a lack of consent. The question of whether the victim consented is a matter for the jury to decide, although the Crown Prosecution Service (CPS) considers this issue very carefully throughout the life of the case.

The new measures of consent are designed to redress the balance in favour of victims without prejudicing the defendant's right to a fair trial, to help juries reach just and fair decisions on this difficult area of criminal law:

Consent is defined by law as: a person consents if he or she agrees by choice to the sexual activity and has the freedom and capacity to make that choice.

All the circumstances at the time of the offence will be looked at in deciding whether the defendant is reasonable in believing the complainant consented.

People will be considered most unlikely to have agreed to sexual activity if they were subject to threats or fear of serious harm, unconscious, drugged, abducted, or were unable to communicate because of a physical disability.

Child Sex Abuse

Those accused of child rape can no longer argue that the child consented. Any sexual intercourse with a child under 13 will be treated as rape. Other non-consensual offences against children under 13 are sexual assault by penetration, sexual assault, and causing or inciting a child to engage in sexual activity.

There are new offences of sexual activity with a child under 16. These cover a range of behaviour, involving both physical and non-physical contact. As children and young person's commit sexual crimes on other children, these offences apply also to persons under 18.

Prosecutions of persons under the age of 18

The age of consent is 16. Because children can and do abuse and exploit other children, the Act makes it an offence for children under 16 to engage in sexual activity, to protect children who are victims.

However, children of the same or similar age are highly unlikely to be prosecuted for engaging in sexual activity, where the activity is mutually agreed and there is no abuse or exploitation.

The Crown Prosecution Service has issued guidance to prosecutors, which sets out the criteria they should consider when deciding whether or not it is in the public interest to bring a prosecution.

How does the law affects those who advise children?

A person does not commit an offence of aiding or abetting a child sex offence if they give advice to children in order to:

protect them from sexually transmitted infection,

protect their physical safety,

prevent them from becoming pregnant, or

promote their emotional well-being.

This means that parents, doctors, other health professionals, in fact anyone can provide sexual health advice to children as long as their only motivation in doing so is the protection of the child.

However, people who cause or encourage the child to engage in the activity, or 'advise' children for their own sexual gratification, will be liable to prosecution.

Child sex offences cover not only assaults by blood relatives but also foster and adoptive parents and live-in partners.

To protect vulnerable 16 and 17 year olds, the offences of 'abuse of a position of trust' prohibits sexual contact between adults and children under 18 in schools, colleges and residential care.

Sexual Offences involving the Internet, and 'grooming'

To combat increasing sexual approaches to children on-line, there is a new offence of meeting a child following sexual grooming. This makes it a crime to befriend a child on the Internet or by other means and meet or intend to meet the child with the intention of abusing them. The maximum sentence is 10 years' imprisonment.

A new civil preventative order, the Risk of Sexual Harm Order, may be imposed which will prohibit adults from engaging in inappropriate behaviour such as sexual conversations with children on-line.

Convicted sex offenders must:

report each year to their local police regardless of whether their circumstances have changed

inform the police if they change their name or address within three days (previously fourteen days)

disclose if they spend seven days or more away from home

supply their national insurance number

Failure to report is a criminal offence that carries a prison term of up to five years.

Other preventative measures include:

Sex Offender Preventative Orders can be imposed on anyone convicted of a serious violent offence if there is evidence that they pose a risk of causing serious sexual harm.

"Sex tourists" convicted of sex crimes abroad may have to comply with the notification requirements.

Courts in certain circumstances, can prohibit those convicted of a sexual offence against a child under 16 from travelling abroad.

Police can apply for a Risk of Sexual Harm Order against any person thought to pose a risk to children under 16.

Other Offences in the 2003 Sexual Offences Act

There are offences against:

trafficking persons for the purposes of sexual exploitation;

child abuse through prostitution and pornography. These include:

buying sexual services of a child,

causing, encouraging, arranging or facilitating child prostitution or pornography, and

controlling any of the activities of a child involved in prostitution or pornography;

sexual abuse of vulnerable persons with a mental disorder. These include situations where:

they are unable to refuse because of a lack of understanding,

they are offered inducements, threatened or deceived, and

there is a breach of a relationship of care, by a care worker;

voyeurism, that criminalises those who watch for sexual gratification people engaged in a private act without their consent;

exposure, where a man or woman exposes their genitalia with intent to cause alarm or distress;

preparatory offences, such as:

drugging a person with intent to engage in sexual activity with that person;

committing any offence with intent to commit a sexual offence; and

trespassing on any premises with intent to commit a sexual offence;

engaging in sexual activity in a public lavatory.

Sexual Assault

Sexual assault is an act of physical, psychological and emotional violation, in the form of a sexual act, which is inflicted on someone without consent. It can involve forcing or manipulating someone to witness or participate in any sexual acts, apart from penetration of the mouth with the penis, the penetration of anus or vagina (however slight) with any object or the penis, which is rape.

Manslaughter

Manslaughter is the unlawful killing of another person without the intention to kill or cause grievous bodily harm. Manslaughter is sally called either voluntary or involuntary. It is a common-law crime under the offences against the person act 1861.

Voluntary where death follows an intended injury (but if the injury is serious, then this may be murder). It normally occurs as a result of sudden 'frying of temper' or following some degree of provocation.

Involuntary where injury is not intended, but nevertheless caused through gross negligence or a lawful act.

Murder

Murder is the unlawful killing, with malice aforethought, of another human, and generally, this state of mind distinguishes murder from other forms of killing such as manslaughter when there was no intent to kill. It is up to the CPS and jury to decide if there was the intent to kill.

Murder is an offence under the common law of England and Wales. It is considered the most serious form of homicide, in which one person kills another with the intention to unlawfully cause either death or serious injury. The element of intentionality was originally termed malice aforethought although it required neither malice nor premeditation. In certain circumstances intent, can be 'transferred' when harm was intended to one person but a different person was killed, or acquired due to a common intent to commit serious harm with other people who go further and commit murder.

Firearms offences

A firearm is "a lethal barrelled weapon of any description from which any shot, bullet or other missile can be discharged" (section 57 (1) Firearms Act 1968), it includes:

any prohibited weapon whether it is such a lethal weapon as aforesaid or not; and

any component part of such a lethal or prohibited weapon; and

any accessory to any such weapon designed or adapted to diminish the noise or flash caused by firing the weapon.

Lethality is a complex issue and although case law exists (Moore v Gooderham [1960] 3 All E.R. 575), only a court can decide whether any particular weapon is capable of causing "more than trifling and trivial" injury and is therefore is a "firearm" for the purposes of the Acts. The Forensic Science Provider (FSP) will be able to advise in any case where "lethality" is likely to be an issue. See also: R v Thorpe 85 Cr. App. R 107 CA.

"barrelled" is a question of mixed law and fact

"from which any shot, bullet or other missile can be discharged" has to be capable of discharging a missile either in its present state or with adaptation. To prove that a weapon is a firearm, it is essential to call evidence as to whether a bullet or missile can be discharged from the weapon or which can be adapted to discharge any missile: Grace v DPP (1989) Crim L.R.365 where the conviction was quashed as there was no evidence that the air rifle could have been fired.

"component parts". R v Clarke (F), 82 Cr App R 308, CA states that the component part of a prohibited weapon is itself a prohibited weapon. Although there is no statutory definition, the Home Office Guidance to the Police at paragraph 13.70 states the following:

The term "component part" may be held to include (i) the barrel, chamber, cylinder, (ii) frame, body or receiver, (iii) breech, block, bolt or other mechanism for containing the charge at the rear of the chamber (iv), any other part of the firearm upon which the pressure caused by firing the weapon impinges directly. Magazines, sights and furniture are not considered component parts.

"Whether in fact this particular gas plug is a component part of a prohibited weapon, is a matter of fact for the court to decide the words have their ordinary natural meaning. as a matter of reasonable interpretation it means a part that is manufactured to the purpose screw or washer, would not be a component part for present purposes. Similarly, a component part must be a part that if it were removed, the Gun could not function without it."

Air Weapons

An air weapon is defined, under section 1(3)(b) and 57(4) of the Firearms Act 1968 as:

"an air rifle, air gun or air pistol which does not fall within section 5 (1) (a) and which is not of a type declared by rules made by the Secretary of State under section 53 of the Firearms Act to be especially dangerous".

Any air rifle, air gun or air pistol which uses or is designed or adapted for use with, a self-contained gas cartridge system is a prohibited weapon: section 5(1)(af) Firearms Act 1968 e.g. a Brocock

An air rifle is "especially dangerous" if it is capable of discharging a missile so that the missile has, on being discharged from the muzzle of the weapon, kinetic energy in excess in the case of a pistol of 6 ft lbs or, in the case of an air weapon other than an air pistol, 12 ft lbs: Firearms (Dangerous Air Weapons) Rules 1969 rr. 2, 3 (Archbold 24-8a.)

Paintball guns are a type of air weapon. The Home Office regard self-loading or pump action rifled airguns (including paintball guns) as outside the scope of the Firearms Act, unless they are sufficiently powerful to fall within the category of a "specially dangerous" air weapon (Archbold 24.8a). Paintball guns could be considered imitation firearms.

Unless an air weapon falls within one of the above exceptions, it is not subject to section 1 Firearms Act 1968.

Imitation Firearms

An imitation firearm means "anything which has the appearance of being a firearm (other than such a weapon as is mentioned in section 5(1) (b) of this Act), whether or not it is capable of discharging any shot, bullet or other missile." section 57(4). This means that an offence requiring "possession" or "having with him/her" a firearm or imitation firearm requires a "thing" which is separate and distinct from a person. Putting a hand inside a jacket and using fingers to force out the material to give the impression of a firearm falls outside the scope of such offences, as a person's bodily parts is not a "thing". (R v Bentham [2005] UKHL18.) R v Morris and King, 79 Cr App R 104, CA: when considering whether a thing has the appearance of being a firearm the jury should consider its appearance at the time of the offence and should also be assisted by the evidence of the witness who saw the thing at the time of the offence.

Unlike with "Realistic Imitation Firearms", it is not always necessary to obtain evidence from the FSP on whether the thing is an imitation firearm. Evidence of the Firearms Officer will usually be sufficient expert evidence.

Realistic Imitation Firearms

From 1 October 2007, section 36 Violent Crime Reduction Act 2006 created an offence to manufacture, bring into or cause to be brought into Great Britain, or sell realistic imitation firearms. It also made it an offence to modify an imitation firearm to make it realistic.

Section 37 relates to specific defences: this allows persons in the course of trade or business to import realistic imitation firearms for the purpose of modifying them to make them non-realistic. It also provides various defences if the realistic imitation firearm was available for:

a museum or gallery;

theatrical performances and rehearsals of such performances;

the production of films and television programmes;

the organisation and holding of historical re-enactments; or

crown servants.

Section 38 defines a "realistic imitation firearm" as "an imitation firearm which has an appearance that is so realistic as to make it indistinguishable, for all practical purposes, from a real firearm". As a result of "real firearm" (defined in section 38 (7)) imitations of pre-1870 firearms are not caught by the offence.

Whether an imitation firearm falls within the definition of a realistic imitation firearm should be judged from the perspective of how it looks at the point of manufacture, import or sale and not how it might be appearing if it were being misused. Section 38(3) provides that in determining whether an imitation firearm is distinguishable from a real firearm, its size, shape and principal colour must be taken into account.

It is worth understanding that the intention behind this measure is to stop the supply of imitations which look so realistic that they are being used by criminals to threaten and intimidate others. If it is not a realistic imitation firearm it may still be an imitation firearm.

Readily Convertible Imitations

If an imitation weapon, has the appearance of being a firearm to which section 1 of the 1968 Act applies and the imitation firearm is not capable of discharging a missile but can be readily converted into a firearm then section 1(1) Firearms Act 1982 states that the weapon is to be considered a firearm for the purposes of the Act. The Act defines "readily convertible" when "it can be so converted without any special skill on the part of the person converting it and the work involved in converting it does not require equipment or tools other than such as are in common use by persons carrying out works of construction and maintenance in their own homes." Section 1(6) Firearms Act 1982.

The Forensic Science Providers (FSP) will be required to test the weapon to ascertain whether it is readily convertible.

However, it shall be a defence for the accused to show that he did not know and had no reason to suspect that the imitation firearm was so constructed or adapted as to be readily convertible into a firearm, Section 1 (5) Firearms Act 1982.

De-activated Weapons and Antiques

If a weapon bears an approved house mark and has been certified in writing as de-activated, the item is presumed to be incapable of discharging bullets or shot. De-activated firearms are expressly excluded from the definition of realistic imitation firearm and are therefore not affected by the new realistic imitation offence: Section 8 Firearms (Amendment) Act 1988.

Antiques

Section 58(2) of the 1968 Act exempts from the provisions of the Act - including certificate controls under sections 1 and 2 and prohibition under section 5 - all antique firearms which are sold, transferred, purchased, acquired or possessed as curiosities or ornaments. The word "antique" is not defined in the Act but Home Office guidance on the subject can be summarised briefly as follows:

If modern ready-made ammunition can be bought and fired using the weapon it cannot be classed as an antique;

A muzzle loading firearm is antique;

A breech loading firearm using a rim-fire cartridge exceeding .23 (but not 9mm) is antique;

A breech loading firearm using an ignition system other than rim-fire or centre is antique;

A breech loading centre fire firearm originally chambered for cartridges which are now obsolete and retains that original chambering is antique.

However, each case should be dealt with on its merits and advice on individual weapons should be sought from the FSP. The case of R v Burke 67 Cr App R 220 dictates that it is for the Prosecution to prove that the firearm does not come within the ambit of section 58(2) and it is a matter for the jury to decide upon.

Transfer of Weapons

Section 3 of the 1968 Act creates an offence if, by way of trade or business without being registered as a firearms dealer he/she manufactures, sells, transfers, repairs, tests or proves any firearms or ammunition to which sections 1 and 2 applies; or a shotgun (Archbold 24.12).

Section 31 Violent Crime Reduction Act (VCRA) 2006: this offence is committed where on or after 6 April 2007, a person who is not a registered firearms dealer sells or transfers an air weapon or exposes an air weapon for sale or has in his possession for sale of transfer.

Section 32 of the VCRA 2006 requires that air weapons sold or transferred to an individual by way of trade or business must now be done in person. This provision is modelled on the arrangements which already exist in section 32 of the Firearms (Amendment) Act 1997 for other firearms. This is subject to exceptions.

Section 35 of the VCRA 2006 creates a summary offence on or after 6 April 2007 where a person sells, buys or attempts to sell or buy a primer or empty cartridge case incorporating a primer. There are a number of exceptions as expanded upon in section 35(3) VCRA 2006.

Section 40 of the VCRA 2006 creates an offence for anyone aged under 18 to purchase an imitation firearm and for anyone to sell an imitation firearm to someone aged under 18.

It is ultimately for the courts to decide whether any item falls within this definition but clearly it applies to the purchase and sale of realistic imitation firearms. However, it also applies to non-realistic imitations which nevertheless have "the appearance of being a firearm". This could include some children's toys. Where a toy is considered to be an imitation firearm, the purchase will have to be made by a parent or other person aged over 18. It is a defence if the seller can show that he had reasonable grounds for believing the purchaser to be 18 or over.

Conversions

Section 4 of the Firearms Act 1968 creates an offence of shortening or converting a firearm (Archbold, 24.16). This is committed when:

the barrel of a shotgun is shortened to a length less than 60.96 cm (24 inches) section 4 (1);

for a non-firearms dealer to convert into a firearm anything which had appearance of being a firearm, but originally was incapable of discharging any missile through its barrel section 4 (3).

Possession of Firearms by Adults

The Firearms Act 1968 creates offences of:

Section 1 - Possession of a firearm/especially dangerous air weapon and certain ammunition without a certificate, (Archbold, 24.3);

Section 2 - Possession of a "shotgun" without a certificate (Archbold, 24.9); NB: Shotguns can fall within various sections, see Evidence to Charge below.

Section 5 - Possession of a prohibited weapon (Archbold, 24.19).

The above offences are subject to certain exceptions (Archbold, 24.28 - 24.34)

Possession

Section 1(1) of the Firearms Act 1968 creates an absolute offence.

The prosecution only has to show that the defendant knew he had something in his possession. It is irrelevant what he knew or thought it was (R v Hussain (1981) 72 Cr. App. R. 143; R v Waller Crim. L.R. 1991, 381; Sullivan v Earl of Caithness [1976] 62 Cr. App. R 105). (Archbold 24-6).

Possession is both proprietary and custodial (Distinction from "have with him" in criminal use offences) (Hall v Cotton and Treadwell [1987] 83 Cr. App. R 257 DC).

Prohibited Weapons Defined by section 5 Firearms Act 1968 as Amended

The weapons below are subject to the mandatory minimum sentence see Mandatory Minimum Sentences section below.

Section 5(1)(a) any firearm which is so designed or adapted so that two or more missiles can be successively discharged without repeated pressure on the trigger, e.g. machine guns, burst fire weapons;

Section 5(1)(ab) any self-loading or pump-action rifled gun other than one which is chambered for .22 rim-fire, e.g. short barrelled rifles;

Section 5(1)(aba) any firearm which either has a barrel less than 30cm in length or is less than 60cm in length overall, other than an air weapon, a muzzle-loading gun or a firearm designed as signalling apparatus, e.g. handguns, revolvers;

Section 5(1)(ac) any self-loading or pump-action smooth-bore gun which is not an air weapon or chambered for .22 rim-fire cartridges and either has a barrel less than 24" in length or is less than 40" in length overall, e.g. self-loading shotguns;

Section 5(1)(ad) any smooth-bore revolver gun other than one which is chambered for 9mm rim-fire cartridges or a muzzle-loading gun, e.g. Dragon;

Section 5(1)(ae) any rocket launcher, or any mortar, for projecting a stabilised missile, other than a launcher or mortar designed for line-throwing or pyrotechnic purposes or as signalling apparatus;

Section 5(1)(af) any air rifle, air gun or air pistol which uses, or is designed or adapted for use with, a self-contained gas cartridge system, e.g. Brococks;

Section 5(1)(c) any cartridge with a bullet designed to explode on or immediately before impact, any ammunition containing or designed or adapted to contain any such noxious thing as mentioned in section 5(1)(b), and, if capable of being used with a firearm of any description, any grenade, bomb (or other like missile), or rocket or shell designed to explode as aforesaid, e.g. ammunition containing explosive in the bullets or missiles;

Section 5(1)(A)(a) any firearm which is disguised as another object, e.g. pen guns, key fob guns and phone guns.

In addition, the following are also prohibited but are not subject to mandatory minimum sentences:

Section 5(1)(b) any weapon of whatever description designed or adapted for the discharge of any noxious liquid gas or other thing. Generally, stun guns or electric shock devices, CS gas not usually cattle prods but depends on type. Note: Parliament has provided that disguised weapons fall within the provisions for a minimum sentence and so, an offence contrary to section 5(1A) should be charged rather than an offence contrary to section 5(1)(b) where a stun gun is disguised as another object and also meets the requirements of section 5(A1), (R v Brereton 2012 EWCA Crim2 85);

Section 5(1A)(b) any rocket or ammunition not falling within paragraph (c) of subsection (1) of this section which consists in or incorporates a missile designed to explode on or immediately before impact and is for military use;

Section 5(1A)(c) any launcher or other projecting apparatus not falling within paragraph (ae) of that subsection which is designed to be used with any rocket or ammunition falling within paragraph (b) above or with ammunition which would fall within that paragraph but for its being ammunition falling within paragraph (c) of that subsection;

Section 5(1A)(d) any ammunition for military use which consists in or incorporates a missile designed so that a substance contained in the missile will ignite on or immediately before impact, e.g. incendiary ammunition;

Section 5(1A)(e) any ammunition for military use which consists of, or incorporates, a missile designed, on account of its having a jacket and hard core, to penetrate armour plating, armour screening or body armour, e.g. armour piercing ammunition;

Section 5(1A)(f) any ammunition which incorporates a missile designed or adapted to expand on impact. For example, expanding ammo, e.g. soft-point or hollow-point ammo;

Section 5(1A)(g) anything which is designed to be projected as a missile from any weapon and is designed to be, or has been, incorporated in -

(i) any ammunition falling within any of the preceding paragraphs; or

(ii) Any ammunition which would fall within any of those paragraphs, but for its being specified in subsection (1) of this section.

Criminal Use of Firearms

The Firearms Act 1968 creates offences of:

Section 16 Possession of a firearm or ammunition with intent to endanger life (Archbold, 24.36);

Section 16 A Possession of a firearm or imitation with intent to cause fear of violence (Archbold, 24.39);

Section 17(1) Using a firearm or imitation to resist or prevent lawful arrest of himself or another (Archbold, 24.42);

Section 17(2) Possessing a firearm or imitation whilst committing certain offences (Archbold, 24.42) which are set out in Schedule 1 (Archbold, 24.43);

Section 18 Carrying a firearm or imitation with intent to commit an indictable offence or to resist arrest or prevent the arrest of another (Archbold, 24.51);

Section 19 Carrying a loaded shotgun, air weapon, (whether loaded or not), any other firearm (whether loaded or not) together with ammunition suitable for use in that firearm or an imitation firearm in a public place without lawful authority or reasonable excuse (Archbold 24.56). Possession of an air weapon or an imitation firearm in a public place (section 19 Firearms Act 1968) is triable summarily only (see Schedule 6) and carries a maximum sentence of 6 months' imprisonment prior to 1 October 2007. After that date section 41(1) Violent Crime Reduction Act 2006 increases the penalty for possession of an imitation firearm, but not an air weapon to 12 months and makes the offence triable either way.

Section 20 Entering a building or part of a building as a trespasser without reasonable excuse whilst having with him a firearm or imitation (Archbold, 24.62); Distinguish possession from "having with him" Section 21 Possession of a firearm by persons previously convicted of crime (Archbold, 24.65).

Prosecutors should check to see if a defendant commits an offence under section 21 Firearms Act 1968 whenever a firearm or ammunition is involved. A person commits such an offence if:

He has possession, of any class of Firearm (except imitations and deactivated weapons), or any ammunition, including shot gun and air weapon ammunition; and

At the time of possession has been previously convicted of any offence and was sentenced to a term of imprisonment (including detention in a Youth Offender Institute (YOI) and Detention and Training Order (DTO)).

If the sentence was 3 years or more the prohibition is for life.

If between 3 months and 3 years and is in possession within 5 years of release.

This section does not apply to those sentenced to a Hospital Order.

The release papers include an acknowledgement of this requirement. This offence should attract a consecutive sentence, although in practice it is usually concurrent and treated as an aggravating feature of the other offence. A memorandum of conviction or certificate of conviction and a signed copy of the release form should be obtained.

Section 28 of the Violent Crime Reduction Act 2006 creates an offence of using another person to mind a dangerous weapon on or after 6 April 2007. The offence is committed where a person uses another to look after, hide or transport a dangerous weapon for him and he does so under arrangements or in circumstances that facilitate or are intended to facilitate the weapon's being made available to that person for an unlawful purpose (section 28(1)).

A dangerous weapon is defined by section 28(3) as "a firearm other than an air weapon or a component part of or accessory to an air weapon or a weapon to which section 141 or 141A of the Criminal Justice Act 1998 applies (specified offensive weapons, knives and bladed weapons)".

Section 28(2) states that a weapon is to be regarded as being available for an unlawful purpose where the weapon is available for him to take possession of it at a time and place and his possession of the weapon at that time and place would constitute or be likely to involve or lead to the commission by him of an offence. This provision is intended to cover cases in which:

Mere possession would be an offence e.g. because the weapon is a prohibited weapon or is a firearm and the person taking possession is legally prohibited from possessing a firearm because he does not have a license as required by section 1 of the Firearms Act 1968 or because he is disqualified from possession under section 21 Firearms Act 1968 and;

The person was intending to commit an offence with the weapon in future;

This does not preclude other "arrangements or circumstances" from facilitating or intending to facilitate the availability of the weapon for an unlawful purpose.

Prosecutors should note that the evidential requirements of section 28 Violent Crime Reduction Act 2006 may be harder to satisfy than those of simple possession under sections 1, 2 or 5 Firearms Act 1968.

Sections 23(1) and (4) of the Firearms Act 1968 made it an offence to fire an air weapon beyond the boundary of premises. However, prior to 1 October 2007 the offences were limited to young persons and to the adults supervising them. Section 34 of the VCRA 2006 replaces the existing offences for young people with a new offence for anyone of any age to fire an air weapon beyond the boundary of premises. The offence relating to adults supervising young persons is preserved.

The Act also creates a number of offences in relation to the making and revocation of certificates, the controlling of transactions in firearms and in respect of police powers - sections 26, 29, 30, 38-42 and 47-49.

Acquisition and Possession of Firearms and Air Weapons by Minors

Sections 22 - 25 - Possession by and supply to minors and drunk/insane persons. (Stones, 8.10401).

Sections 22 and 24 were amended by section 33 of VCRA 2006 so as to increase age limits in a number of offences:

Section 22(1) - Purchase or hire of any firearm or ammunition by a person under 17. From 1 October 2007, the age limit is raised to 18.

Section 22(1A) - Use of a firearm by a person under 18 for a purpose not authorised by the European weapons directive.

Section 22(2) - Possession of any firearm or ammunition to which section 1 applies by a person under 14.

Section 22(3) - Person under 15 having an assembled shotgun except while under the supervision of a person aged 21 or over, or while the shotgun is so covered with a securely fastened gun cover that it cannot be fired.

Section 22(4) - Person under 17 having an air weapon or ammunition for an air weapon unless supervised by a person aged 21 or over. From 1 October 2007, the age limit is raised to 18.

Section 24(1) - Selling or hiring an air weapon to a young person. From 1 October 2007, the age limit is raised to 18.

Section 24(4) - Making a gift of an air weapon or parting with possession of an air weapon. From 1 October 2007, the age limit is raised to 18.

Section 24ZA - A person in possession of an air weapon failing to take reasonable precautions to prevent any person under the age of 18 having the weapon with him (from 10 February 2011).

Importation of Firearms

Section 170(1) of the Customs and Excise Management Act 1979 (CEMA) makes it an offence for any person to knowingly acquire possession of any of the following goods:

(i) goods which have been unlawfully removed from a warehouse or Queen's warehouse;

(ii) goods which are chargeable with a duty which has not been paid;

(iii) goods with respect to the importation or exportation of which any prohibition or restriction is for the time being in force under or by virtue of any enactment; or

(b) is in any way knowingly concerned in carrying, removing, depositing, harbouring, keeping or concealing or in any manner dealing with any such goods, and does so with intent to defraud Her Majesty of any duty payable on the goods or to evade any such prohibition or restriction with respect to the goods he shall be guilty of an offence under this section and may be detained.

Section 170(2) of CEMA 1979 covers the import "smuggling" offence in so far as a person knowingly concerned in the fraudulent evasion or attempted evasion relating to goods (namely firearms) that are subject to any "prohibition or restriction." The prohibition upon the importation of firearms is contained in Article 1 of the Import of Goods (Control) Order 1954 (SI 1954/23) which was made under section 1 of the Import, Export and Customs Powers (Defence) Act 1939.

Terrorism

Terrorism is not new, and even though it has been used since the beginning of recorded history, it can be relatively hard to define. Terrorism has been described variously as both a tactic and strategy; a crime and a holy duty; a justified reaction to oppression and an inexcusable abomination. Obviously, a lot depends on whose point of view is being represented. Terrorism has often been an effective tactic for the weaker side in a conflict. As an asymmetric form of conflict, it confers coercive power with many of the advantages of military force at a fraction of the cost. Due to the secretive nature and small size of terrorist organizations, they often offer opponents no clear organisation to defend against or to deter.

That is why pre-emption is being considered to be so important. In some cases, terrorism has been a means to carry on a conflict without the adversary realising the nature of the threat, mistaking terrorism for criminal activity. Because of these characteristics, terrorism has become increasingly common among those pursuing extreme goals throughout the world. But despite its popularity, terrorism can be a nebulous concept. Even within the U.S. Government, agencies responsible for different functions in the on-going fight against terrorism use different definitions.

The Terrorism Act 2000 is the first of a number of general Terrorism Acts passed by the Parliament. It superseded and repealed the Prevention of Terrorism (Temporary Provisions) Act 1989 and the Northern Ireland (Emergency Provisions) Act 1996.

As in previous Terrorism Acts, such as the Prevention of Terrorism (Temporary Provisions) Act 1989, the Home Secretary had the power to maintain a list of "proscribed groups" that they believe are "concerned in terrorism". The act of being a member of, or supporting such a group, or wearing an item of clothing such as "to arouse reasonable suspicion that they are a member or supporter of a proscribed organisation" is sufficient to be prosecuted for a terrorist offence.

A constable may arrest without warrant anyone they reasonably suspect to be a terrorist.

Terrorist is defined by someone who has committed an offence by being a member of a known terrorist organization under section 1, funding raising section 15, use and passion of terrorist material section 16, funding section 17, money laundering section 18, weapon training section 54, directing terror organisations section 56, possession of terrorist articles section 57, collection of terrorist information section 58, inciting overseas section 59, inciting Northern Ireland section 60, inciting Scotland section 61 , Bombing outside the UK section 62 or finance outside the UK section 63. Or they have been concerned in the commission, preparation or instigation of acts of terrorism.

Any powers under the terrorism act is additional to any other powers at common law or enactment, and will not affect those powers. A constable may use reasonable force if necessary in exercising the powers under the act.

Squatting in a Residential Building

This offence came into force on September 1 2012. Under existing legislation, squatting was a civil offence of trespass unless damage was caused or individuals refused to leave when the legitimate occupier arrived.

The new criminal offence has been brought in by Section 144 of the Legal Aid, Sentencing and Punishment of Offenders act 2012.

A person commits the offence if:

The person is in a residential building as a trespasser having entered as a trespasser.

The person knows or ought to know that he or she is a trespasser

The person living in the building or intends to live there for any period.

The offence is not committed by a person holding over after the end of a lease or licence, even if the person leaves and re-enters the building. For the purpose of this legislation "building" includes any structure or part of a structure, including temporary or moveable structures and a building is "residential" if it is designed or adapted, before the time of entry, for use as a place to live. The offence is triable summarily only and will carry a maximum penalty of six months' imprisonment, a fine or both.

Amended power to enter and search: Subsection (8) of section 144 – amends section 17 of the PACE to give uniformed officers the power to enter and search premises for the purpose of arresting a person for the offence of squatting in a residential building.

A-Z OF COMMON OFFENCES IN ENGLAND AND WALES

Here is a basic list of common offences along with their relevant acts. For a more definitive list of all criminal offences then go to the Appendix at the end of the book.

- Abstracting Electricity (Sec. 13 Theft act 1968)
- Actual Bodily Harm (Sec. 47 Offences Against the Person Act)
- Affray (Sec. 3 Public Order Act 1984)
- Aggravated Burglary (Sec. 10 (1) Theft act 1986)
- Arson (Sec. 1 (3) Criminal Damage act 1971)
- Assault (Sec. 39 Criminal Justice act 1998)
- Assault On Police (Sec. 89 (1) Police Act 1996)
- Assault With Intent To Resist Arrest (Sec. 38 Offences Against The Person Act 1861)
- Assault With Intent To Rob (Sec. 8 (2) Theft act 1968)
- Bail (Sec. 6 Bail act 1976)
- Bail To A Police Station – Fail To Appear (Sec. 46 (a) Police and Criminal Evidence Act 1984)
- Battery (Sec. 39 Criminal Justice act 1998)
- Begging (Sec. 3 Vagrancy act 1824)
- Breach Of The Peace (common law)
- Burglary (Sec 9 (1a) Theft act 1968)

- Burglary (Sec 9 (1b) Theft act 1968)
- Chanting (Sec. 3 Football act 1991)
- Criminal Attempts (Sec. 1 Criminal Attempts act 1988)
- Criminal Damage (Sec. 1 (1) Criminal Damage act 1971)
- Criminal Damage - Possession Of Articles With Intent To Commit (Sec. 3 Criminal Damage Act 1971)
- Criminal Damage With Intent To Endanger Life (Sec. 1 (2) Criminal Damage act 1971)
- Criminal Damage - Threatening To Commit (Sec. 2 Criminal Damage act 1971)
- Disorderly Conduct (Sec. 18 Public Order Act 1986)
- Drunk And Disorderly (Sec. 91 (1) Criminal Justice act 1967)
- Drunk And Incapable (Sec. 12 Licensing act 1872)
- Encouraging Another to Murder (Sec. 4 Offences Against The Person Act 1861)
- Fear Of Provocation Of Violence (Sec. 4 Public Order Act 1984)
- Going Equipped (Sec. 25 (1) Theft act 1968)
- Grievous Bodily Harm or Unlawful Wounding (Sec. 20 Offences Against The Person Act 1861)
- Grievous Bodily Harm With Intent (Sec. 18 Offences Against The Person Act 1861)
- Handling Stolen Goods (Sec. 22 Theft act 1968)
- Harassment, Alarm or Distress (Sec. 5 Public Order Act 1984)
- Impersonation of a Police officer (Sec. 90 Police Act 1996)
- Indecent Assault (Sec. 14 (1) & 15 (1) Sexual Offences act 1956)
- Indecent Exposure (Sec. 4 Vagrancy act 1824)
- Injury or Assault to a Child (Sec. 1 Children and Young Persons act 1933) (amended 1989)
- Intentional Harassment, Alarm or Distress (Sec. 4(a) Public Order Act 1984)
- Kerb Crawling (Sec. 1 Sexual Offences act 1985)
- Making Off Without Payment (Sec. 3 (4) Theft act 1978)
- Manslaughter (common law)

- Mobile Telephones (road Vehicles (Construction and Use) (Amendment) (No. 4) Regulations 2003)
- Murder (common law)
- Obstruct Police (Sec. 89 (2) Police Act 1996)
- Obtaining Property By Deception (Sec. 15 (1) Theft act 1968)
- Obtaining services By Deception (Sec. 1 (1) Theft act 1968)
- Offensive Weapons – Possession Of (Sec. 1 Prevention Of Crime act 1953)
- Possession Of A Controlled Drug (Sec. 5 (2) Misuse Of Drugs act 1971)
- Possession Of A Controlled Drug With Intent To Supply (Sec. 5 (3) Misuse Of Drugs act 1971)
- Racially Aggravated Assault (Sec. 29 (1c) Crime And Disorder act 1998)
- Racially Aggravated Actual Bodily Harm (Sec. 29 (1b) Crime And Disorder act 1998)
- Racially Aggravated Criminal Damage (Sec. 30 (1) Crime And Disorder act 1998)
- Racially Aggravated Grievously Bodily Harm (Sec. 29 (1a) Crime And Disorder act 1998)
- Racially Aggravated Harassment (Sec. 32 1(a) Crime And Disorder act 1998)
- Rape (Sec. 1 Sexual Offences act 1956)
- Riot (Sec. 1 Public Order Act 1986)
- Robbery (Sec. 8 Theft act 1968)
- Squatting in a residential building (sec 144 Punishment of offenders act 2012)
- Theft (Sec. 1 (1) Theft act 1968)
- Theft (Sec. 1 (1) Theft act 1968)
- Violent Disorder (Sec. 2 Public Order Act 1986)

Restorative Justice

Is something that is being used more and more by the Police for low-level crime, when it is felt using some form of restorative justice would be better than a criminal charge. Often it is the victim that agrees to restorative justice, and when there is no actual victim the police use their discretion.

Restorative justice is also a way of working that helps to deal with conflict. This could include victims and offenders meeting, allowing offenders to face up to the consequences of their crime or actions.

It is not a soft option as many offenders find it difficult to face up to the impact of their crimes. Some refuse to accept responsibility for their actions so it ends up being dealt with by the criminal justice system.

Benefits of restorative justice to the victim:

Make an offender realise how the crime has affected the victim's life.

Find out information to help put the crime behind them – for example, why the offender targeted them.

Ask for reparation, either financial or a verbal apology.

Reduces post-traumatic stress disorder.

Benefits of restorative justice to the offender:

Opportunity to offer explanation.

Opportunity to apologise.

Opportunity to repair the harm.

Often reduces re-offending.

Benefits of restorative justice generally:

Puts the needs of the victim first.

Gives victims a greater voice in the Criminal Justice system.

Finds positive solutions to crime.

Allows victims to receive an explanation and more meaningful reparation from offenders.

Makes offenders accountable for their actions.

Shows the community that offenders are facing up to their actions.

Can, in some cases, motivate offenders to stop their criminal behaviour.

How Restorative Justice Works

The use of restorative justice as a way to deliver cautions, reprimands and final warnings. It is also available for conditional cautions. How it is implemented is down to individual forces.

Often neighbourhood officers are also trained to use restorative justice to help them deal with neighbour disputes, minor crimes, community issues, and many other incidents they come across on a daily basis. The Police complaints department can use restorative justice to deal with complaints against police and internal grievances.

The more recently introduced Youth Restorative Disposals (YRDs) and Adult Restorative Disposals (ARDs) are delivered using restorative justice. These disposals- for low-level crime have been introduced to deal with offenders and keep them out of the criminal justice system and allow the victim to say what they would like the outcome of the incident to be. Often this is an acceptance by the offender of any wrongdoing and an apology. It can also include putting right and damage or clearing up any mess or even graffiti in some instances.

ROAD TRAFFIC POLICING

The first part about dealing with any form of road traffic policing is safety. If near to or on a road then you should be wearing a high visibility jacket that is fastened up, to increase your visibility. A police car also be used in a fend position with red or flashing lights to denote an accident or just a stop. The GOLDEN RULE of walking near or on a road is to NEVER have your back to oncoming traffic and ensure the safety of yourself, colleagues and the public.

Road Traffic Offences

Road traffic offences are quite varied in their type and are covered by the Road Traffic Act 1988. In the main most offences are non-enforceable, but they come under two types:

Endorsable which means penalty points as well as a fine. Non-endorsable, or summary offences, are for less serious offences that carry a £30 or more fixed penalty, such as parking on double yellow lines, or not wearing a seatbelt. No points are received on the offender's driving license.

Offence Code and Offence

GROUP 4 Offences involving negligent use of a motor vehicle

RC86321 Use a mobile phone while driving m/v

RC86325 Use mobile phone while supervising L driver drive a motor vehicle

RC86814 Driver not being in position to have proper control

RC86815 Drive not being in position to have full view

GROUP 7 Driving – Licence Related Offences

RT88334 Drive other than in accordance with licence (provisional licence conditions)

GROUP 15 Vehicle or Part in Dangerous or Defective Condition

RC86994 Use a wheeled mv/trailer with tyre unsuitable for use to which vehicle put

RC86037 Use a bus without mirrors fitted

RC86038 Use a goods vehicle without mirrors - maximum gross weight exceeding 3500 kg

RC86039 Use goods vehicle without mirrors - maximum gross weight exceeding 12000 kg

RC86251 Using Vehicle with Defective Brakes

RC86035 Using Vehicle with Defective Steering

RC86400 Tyre - over/under inflated

RC86024 Tyre - Different structure in same axle

RC86026 Tyre - Different types in different axles

RT88457 Danger of injury due to condition of mv/trailer/accessories/equipment

RT88503 Danger due to weight/position/ distribution /manner/ load carried/secured

RC86403 Use motor vehicle /trailer with tyre - Ply or cord exposed

RC86401 Use motor vehicle/trailer with tyre with cut in the fabric

RC86402 Use motor vehicle/trailer with tyre with lump/bulge/tear

RC86027 Use a small passenger vehicle with tyres with insufficient tread - less than 1.6mm (cars)

RC86393 Use a moped - original tread pattern of the tyre not clearly visible

RC86556 Use a motor cycle with tyre tread less than 1mm

GROUP 16 Speed limit offences-the following criteria are to be applied in all cases. All roads Inc Motorways

RR84071 Speeding - passenger mv/trailer exceed 60 mph - motorway – manned.

RR84130 Speeding - passenger mv/trailer exceed 50 mph - single carriageway - manned

RR84163 passenger mv and trailer exceeding 60 mph - dual carriageway - manned equipment

RR84061 Speeding - exceed 30 mph on restricted road -manned equip

RR84211 Speeding - exceed 40 mph - Local Order - manned equip

RR84019 Exceed 70mph Motorway Speed Limit-manned equip

SV77015 Exceed 50mph speed Limit (selected parts of the A60 road only)

RR84205 Speeding - exceed limit for type of vehicle (not goods / passenger) vehicle

RR84203 Exceed speed limit for goods vehicle - manned equipment (5/18/20/30/40/50/60mph)

RR84210 Speeding - exceed 20 mph - Local Order - manned equip

RR84213 Speeding - exceed 30 mph - local order - manned equipment

RC86056 Use motor vehicle - fastening not maintained - seat belt

SV77015 Exceed 60mph Single Carriage

SV77011 Exceeding speed limit-70mph dual carriage way

RR84214 Exceeding speed limit-60mph local order

RR84212 Exceeding speed limit-50mph local order

RR84207 Speeding - exceed limit for passenger vehicle

RR84160 Motorway-excess speed-temp restriction 60 mph

RR84217 Exceed Temp 30mph Speed Restriction - Roadworks

RR84218 Exceed Temp 40mph Speed Restriction - Roadworks manned equip

RR84219 Exceed Temp 50mph Speed Restriction - Roadworks manned equip

RR84215 Exceed Temp Limit of 40mph - Motorway (inc.roadworks) manned equipment

RR84216 Exceed Temp Limit of 50mph - Motorway (inc.roadworks) manned equipment

GROUP 17 Motorway Offences other than speeding

ME82002 Drive a vehicle the wrong way on a motorway slip road

RR84012 Excluded motor vehicle traffic using motorway

ME82006 Stopping motor vehicle on motorway carriageway

ME82007 Reversing on a Motorway

ME82003 Drive on central reservation/verge of a motorway

ME82009 Driving on the hard shoulder of a motorway

ME82017 Prohibited traffic in offside lane

ME82016 Drive passenger vehicle in right hand or offside lane of motorway
ME82015 Draw trailer in fast lane of motorway
ME82012 Provisional licence holder/drive on motorway
ME82004 Driving vehicle entering motorway at prohibited place
ME82001 Driving in wrong direction on motorway
ME82005 Making a U turn on motorway
ME82021 Animal - on motorway not on lead / escaped
TS02005 Motor vehicle fail comply with red/green arrow/lane closure flashing light signal
TS02007 Contravening STOP sign
TS02006 Motor vehicle fail to comply with solid white line road markings - manned equip

GROUP 18 Neglect of Traffic Directions
TS02005 Motor vehicle fail comply with red/green arrow/lane closure flashing light signal
TS02007 Contravening STOP sign
TS02006 Motor vehicle fail to comply with solid white line road markings - manned equip
RT88076 Failing to stop on signal of traffic constable (other than traffic survey)
TS02019 Contravening No entry sign
TS02018 Contravening automatic level crossing - drivers of large vehicles to phone
TS02008 Drive/propel vehicle fail to comply with height limit/toucan/equestrian sign
TS02014 Overtake moving/stationary vehicle in zig zag markings of toucan crossing

GROUP 19 Neglect of Pedestrian Rights
RR84081 Using vehicle in designated play street
ZP97001 Stopping within limits of zebra/pelican/puffin
ZP97006 Fail to accord precedence - zebra crossing
ZP97004 Fail to stop at Pelican/Puffin Crossing Red Light
ZP97007 Fail to accord precedence - pelican/puffin crossing

ZP97003 Stopping in zebra/pelican or puffin controlled area
ZP97005 Overtake stationary/moving vehicle on approach to zebra/pelican/puffin crossing
GROUP 20 Waiting offences
RT88508 Cause vehicle to be left so as to involve danger
GROUP 24 Offences Peculiar to Motorcycles
RT88506 Carrying more than 1 passenger on motorcycle
RT88505 Motorcycle passenger not sitting astride
GROUP 4 Offences involving negligent use of a motor vehicle
RC86143 Driver able to see television screen fitted in vehicle
RC86011 Unattended vehicle - engine running and/or brake not set
RC86140 Reversing unreasonable distance
RC86139 Opening door so as to cause injury/danger
GROUP 10 Vehicle Registration and Excise Licence Offences
VE94135 Registration mark not conforming to regulations
VE94128 Use an incorrectly registered vehicle
RV02038 Fail display vehicle licence in manner prescribed
VE94149 Keep motor vehicle fail to display front registration plate
VE94150 Drive mv/vehicle and trailer no rear registration plate
VE94151 Keep vehicle no rear registration plate
VE94148 Drive vehicle no front registration plate
VE94101 Keep works truck/road roller/agricultural machine on a road with no registration plate
VE94047 Keep a vehicle on which registration mark is obscured
VE94019 Keep a trailer - fail to fix display rear - registration mark
VE94102 Drive vehicle with trailer attached with no front registration plate - first registration pre 1/10/38
GV95002 Keep vehicle with trailer attached with no front registration plate - first registration pre 1/10/38
VE94099 Use vehicle while failing to display trade plates
VE94152 Registration mark not easily readable
Group 11 Drivers Hours Offences

TR68534 Use record sheet/drivers card for a period longer than authorised
TR68535 Fail to enter details on centre field of tachograph
TR68536 Use dirty/damaged record sheet/drivers card in tachograph
TR68537 Use tachograph with mode switch incorrectly set

GROUP 13 Vehicle test Offences

RC86238 Use a goods vehicle with no ministry plate fitted
RT88096 No test Certificate
RC86941 Ministry test date disc not displayed on motor vehicle/trailer

GROUP 15 Vehicle or Part in Dangerous or Defective Condition

RC86036 Use motor vehicle - driver's vision obscured
RC86049 Use motor vehicle with unlawful warning instrument/horn fitted
RC86980 Use mv - glass insufficient transmission of light
RC86025 Fail to equip mv or trailer with sufficient or suitable springs
RC86059 Use motor vehicle - material not maintained - seat belt
RC86060 Use motor vehicle - ends not secured - seat belt
RC86061 Use motor vehicle - disabled person seat belt not secured
RC86129 Use unbraked trailer gross weight not marked
RC86532 Use vehicle in dangerous condition by reason of parts of condition
RC86069 Vehicle emitting smoke/ vapour/ gases/oil
RC86307 Use motor vehicle - windscreen washers not conforming to regulations
RC86046 Use a motor vehicle with speedometer obscured
RC86305 Mirrors not conforming to requirements
RC86070 Use vehicle/trailer no wing/mudguard fitted
RC86045 Use motor vehicle - no speedometer/ speedometer not fitted
RC86047 Use motor vehicle - speedometer not maintained

RC86040 Use mv (other than bus/goods/agricultural) with mirrors not fitted
RC86041 Use vehicle with windscreen wipers not fitted
RC86306 Windscreen Wipers not conforming to Reg's
RC86042 Use mv with windscreen washers not fitted
RC86051 Use a vehicle with no seat belts fitted
RC86054 Use mv anchorages etc for seat belt not maintained affect restraint in accident
RC86294 Use motorcycle - side stand not conforming to regulation 38
RC86050 Vehicle fuel tank not secure or leak proof
RC86048 Use motor vehicle - no warning instrument/horn fitted
RC86107 Vehicle/ by construction/ Exceed Length
RC86283 Vehicle/ by construction/ Exceed Width
RC86304 Vehicle/ by construction/ Exceed Overhang
RC86124 Prescribed vehicle/ no unladen weight or Gross Vehicle Weight displayed

GROUP 17 Motorway Offences
ME82010 Stop vehicle on hard shoulder of motorway

GROUP 18 Neglect of Traffic Regulations
TS02024 Fail to comply with non endorsable traffic sign-
other than ACD including:
Give way, directional arrow, roundabout, vehicle
priority, bus/tram/cycle route, manually operated
stop, convoy/escort with no overtaking, stop
roadworks, mobile roadworks direction, give way
road stop road markings, road hatchings with
solid lines, box junction road markings, tramcar
light signal, weak bridge, police no waiting sign
RR84140 Fail to comply with max axle weight limit-outside G London
· RR84142 Fail comply max width limit - outside G London
RR84144 Fail comply max length limit - outside G London
RR84084 Vehicle contravene one way traffic on a trunk road

RR84146 motor vehicle fail to comply with an indication given by a traffic sign - local traffic order

RT88195/RT88578 Failing to stop for Police Constable

RR84171 Contravene Local Traffic Order outside G/London - other than parking

RR84087 Using a vehicle where prohibited

GROUP 19 Neglect of Pedestrian Rights

RT88469 Drive a vehicle on a road being a footpath / bridleway

HY35001 Ride/Drive a vehicle on the footway

GROUP 20 Obstruction, Waiting and Parking Offences

RC86430 Parking on offside at night

RT88036 Drive on cycle track

RC86705 Unnecessary Obstruction

HY80020 Wilful Obstruction

RR84138 Fail to comply with gross weight limit - outside London

RT88519 Park heavy commercial vehicle on a footway / verge

GROUP 21 Lighting Offences

RL89123 Use vehicle with unlit load overhanging front

RL89125 Use vehicle - additional side marker lamp - visibility

RL89126 Use a vehicle with additional side marker lamp of incorrect colour

RL89145 vehicle all warning beacons fitted not working

RL89208 Use a motor vehicle not fitted with an amber warning light

RL89001 Showing red light to front

RL89002 Showing other than red light to rear

RL89167 Lamp capable of being moved - vehicle in motion

RL89006 Use vehicle with flashing light

RL89175 "Filament lamp not ""E"" or ""e"" marked"

RL89168 Fitted with unauthorised warning beacon or special warning lamp

RL89075 Obligatory light not fitted

RL89160 Specified obligatory lamps not correctly fitted

RL89079 Optional lamps not complying with regulations

RL89124 Unlit projection/overhanging load
RL89159 No additional side marker lamps (long vehicle)
RL89171 Headlamp used to cause dazzle
RL89172 Rear fog lamp(s) not maintained to prevent dazzle
RL89177 Misuse of front fog lamps
RL89158 Use vehicle - reversing light lit when not reversing
RR84210 Use a vehicle / trailer - rear registration mark not lit during darkness
RL89076 Use vehicle with front / rear position lamps obscured
RL89077 Use vehicle with obligatory indicators obscured
RL89078 Use vehicle with obligatory rear reflector obscured
RL89166 Drive motor vehicle - No position lamps - poor visibility or dark
RL89142 Use Vehicle - No position lamps - stationary and dark
RL89165 Misuse of head lamps when vehicle parked
RL89162 Fail to use headlamps on unlit road at night or in poor visibility
RL89151 Misuse of hazard warning device
RL89161 Lamps/ reflector/ rear markings not maintained/clean
RL89178 Misuse of rear fog lamps

GROUP 22 Noise Offences

RC86066 Use motor vehicle with defective exhaust system / silencer
RC86095 Sound motor vehicle horn on restricted road at night
RC86097 Unauthorised sounding of audible warning instrument
RC86094 Sounding of horn when stationery
RC86094 Use vehicle to cause unnecessary noise
RC86065 Use vehicle without silencer being fitted
RC86068 Use vehicle with altered exhaust system/silencer
RC86093 Not stopping engine when stationery

GROUP 23 Load Offences

RC86996n Closet/urinal leaking onto the road - wheeled vehicle
RC86258 Exceeding permitted weight (closely spaced axles)
RC86958 Manufacturer's/DTP plate/ exceeding train weight

RC86561 Use motor vehicle load / passengers likely to cause danger
RC86362 Manufacturer's/DTP plate/ exceeding gross weight
RC86516 Use vehicle - axle weight shown on man plate exceeded by up to but no more than 10%
RC86390 Exceed vehicle max permitted laden weight by up to but no more than 10%
RC86504 Use loco with trailers weight exceed 44000 kg by up to but no more than 10%
RC86510 Use vehicle (not artic) max perm train weight exceeded by up to but not more than 10%
RC86519 Use vehicle exceed axle/gross/train weight on plating cert by up to 10%
RC86522 Use agricultural trailer exceed max gross plated weight by up to 10%
RC86527 Weights re compensating axles exceeded by up to 10%
RC86531 Use vehicle for unsuitable purpose as to cause/likely to cause danger/nuisance
RC86534 Use vehicle with insecure load - likely to cause danger
RV98022 Exceed max authorised vehicle weight by up to 10%
RV98026 Exceed max authorised vehicle combination weight by up to 10%
RV98030 Exceed max authorised vehicle axle weight by up to 10%
RC86132 Motorcycle - No foot rest when carrying pillion passenger
RC86092 Motorcycle - no protective headgear
RR84004 Contravening experimental traffic order
RC86091 Drawing more than permitted number of trailers
RC86269 Towing - distance between vehicles
RC86253 Motorcycle sidecar not properly maintained
RC86295 Wheeled goods vehicle not fitted with rear under-run guards

RC86997 Wheeled goods vehicle not fitted with side under-run guard
RC86297 Vehicle not equipped with spray suppression equip
RC86055 Carrying mascot etc on motor vehicle in position likely to cause injury
RC86296 Use a wheeled goods vehicle - rear under run guards not maintained
RC86298 Motor vehicle - fail to prevent movement of a trailer at rest on a road
RC86363 Use trailer for carriage of passengers for hire/reward
RC86514 Use wheeled goods vehicle spray suppression equipment not maintained
RC86364 Use living van for the carriage of passengers
RC86260 Lifting appliance not properly maintained
RC86259 No indication of travelling height to driver
RC86122 Use trailer - manufacturer's plate not displayed
RC86256 Use wheeled goods vehicle - side under run guards not maintained
RT88477 Driver Failing to wear seat belt
RT88478 Failing to wear seat belt - Adult front passenger
RT88353 Child under 14 in front passenger seat - no seat belt
RT88511 Drive m/v rear seat belt not fitted - child U.12 and not 150cm tall sat in rear
MP99001 Motorcycle Visor: Fail to conform with regulations
RC86441 Use mv - secondary coupling device on trailer not fitted
RT88514 Child under 3 failing to wear rear seat belt
RT88515 Child 3 or over but under 14 failing to wear rear seat belt
RT88516 Child in rear-facing restraining device on front seat air bag not deactivated
PV99005 Use vehicle in UK contra to Art 3(1)(a) EEC Reg's
RT88513 FAILING TO WEAR SEAT BELT - ADULT REAR PASSENGER

GROUP 37 Other Offences
RL89132 Use a pedal cycle with lights which were not clean

TS02002 Pedal Cycle - contravening traffic sign/road markings
RT88461 Fail to stop cycle when required by a constable
RL89133 Pedal Cycle - position lamps not illuminated at night
RL89074 Pedal Cycle - No specified obligatory lamps fitted
RL89131 Pedal Cycle - lamps reflectors not maintained/clean
HY35006 Cycling on footway

Drink Driving

The offence - it is an offence for you to drive - or even attempt to drive - a motor vehicle when you are unfit to do so as a result of consuming drink or drugs. Section 5 of the Road Traffic Act 1988 specifically provides that you will be guilty of an offence if you either:

Drive or attempt to drive a motor vehicle on a road or other public place, or are in charge of a motor vehicle on a road or other public place.

This is after consuming so much alcohol that the proportion of it in your breath, blood or urine exceeds the prescribed limit.

Maximum Penalty - a maximum penalty of six months' imprisonment, a fine of up to £5,000 and a minimum 12 month driving ban.

The penalty for refusing to provide a specimen of breath, blood or urine for analysis is a maximum six months' imprisonment, up to £5000 fine and a driving ban of at least 12 months.

The offence of driving whilst under the influence of alcohol is one to which there is no defence, as such. However, it may be possible to argue that special reasons exist which are such that you should not be disqualified from driving, despite having committed the offence.

The current limits are:
35 micrograms of alcohol in 100 ml of breath
80 milligrams of alcohol in 100 ml of blood
107 milligrams of alcohol in 100 ml of urine
Failing to Stop/Give Particulars after an accident (AC10) (AC20)

The offence - being the driver of a mechanically propelled vehicle, owing to the presence of which on a road an accident occurred whereby personal injury or damage was caused to another person or another vehicle or an animal not in the vehicle, or property on or near the road, then failed to stop or on being required by a person to give your name and address and the name and address of the owner and the identity mark of the vehicle, failed to do so.

Maximum Penalty - six months' imprisonment and/or a fine not exceeding £5000. Endorsement with 5 to 10 penalty points. Discretionary disqualification.

They only must stop and give particulars if someone or something (not in the other vehicle) is injured in the incident, or if they cause any damage to another vehicle or to anything else on or by the roadside (e.g. a lamp post, fence or wall).

The likelihood of being imprisoned increases with the severity of the accident, and if there is both a failure to stop and a failure to report the accident, if:

a) the Court believes that this was because you were trying to avoid a breath test, or

b) when serious injury is caused.

If you can satisfy the court that you were unaware that an accident had occurred this may be a defence to the charge.

Failing to Report an Accident

The offence - being the driver of a mechanically propelled vehicle, owing to the presence of which on a road an accident occurred whereby personal injury was caused to another person, and not having given your name and address to a person having reasonable grounds for requiring you to do so, failed to report the accident at a Police station or to a Constable as soon as reasonably practicable and in any case within 24 hours of the occurrence of the accident.

Maximum Penalty - six months' imprisonment and/or fine not exceeding £5000. Endorsement with 5 to 10 penalty points. Discretionary disqualification.

Speeding/Exceeding the speed limit (SP30)

Offence - driving on a road exceeding the prescribed speed limit.

Maximum penalty - fine not exceeding £1000. Endorsement with 3 to 6 penalty points. Discretionary disqualification.

If they are doing more than 30 mph over the limit they are very likely to be disqualified, depending on speed, road traffic conditions, weather, etc.

The fixed penalty option is often the best option and most drivers will take this option as their licence will be endorsed with the minimum number of penalty points and the fine is likely to be less than that imposed by the court. There will also be no court fees.

Possible defences are that they were not speeding, that it was not them driving, or that they were driving an exempted vehicle in an emergency.

The prosecution may obtain a conviction by producing in evidence, photographs taken from speed cameras. There is no requirement that such photos have any other evidence to back them up. If no photo is available then the evidence to convict must come from at least two different sources, although one of these may be mechanical, such as the Police car's speedometer/radar gun/VASCAR. Under s20 of the road Traffic Offenders act (as amended by s23 of the Road Traffic Act 1991), where a radar device is used the Police merely need to provide a record produced by the prescribed device AND (in the same or a separate document) a certificate as to the circumstances in which the record was produced, signed by Constable or authorised person.

Driving Without Insurance

The Offence - you will commit an offence if you use, or to let another person use, a motor vehicle on a road or public place which does not have in force in respect of it an insurance policy which at the very least insures against third party risks and which complies with section 143 of the Road Traffic Act 1988.

A maximum Penalty - fine not exceeding £5000. Endorsement with 6 to 8 penalty points. Discretionary disqualification.

Totting up - under the totting up provisions a driver can be disqualified when he/she accumulates a certain number of penalty points within a three-year period. The 'magic' number is 12.

If you reach 12 penalty points within the three-year period (and it is the date of the offences and NOT the date of the hearings that is relevant), then you will be disqualified for a minimum period of six months.

If you are then disqualified the slate is wiped clean of points on the date you get your licence back.

To avoid being banned for totting up, you will need to be able to convince the court that there are 'mitigating circumstances'. This means that you will have to show that a disqualification would cause exceptional hardship. The loss of your job could be considered to be exceptional hardship. This could extend to the loss of employment for others dependant on you, or hardship to members of your family.

A new driver only needs to gain six points within two years of passing their test to receive a ban and needing to retake their test.

Dangerous Driving

The main types of driving offences involving fatalities are more often than not 'dangerous driving' and 'careless or inconsiderate driving'. The driver's behaviour is what is important, not what the driver believes. Someone may be committing a dangerous driving offence, even though they believe they are driving safely. The offence is often based around other people's perceptions and any other evidence. For example the scene of the crash can yield evidence if the dangerous driving led to a RTC.

A person drives dangerously when:

The way they drive falls far below the minimum acceptable standard expected of a competent and careful driver; and it would be obvious to a competent and careful driver that driving in that way would be dangerous.

Some typical examples from court cases of dangerous driving are:

Racing, going too fast, or driving aggressively

Ignoring traffic lights, road signs or warnings from passengers

Overtaking dangerously

Driving under the influence of drink or drugs, including prescription drugs

Driving when unfit, including having an injury, being unable to see clearly, not taking prescribed drugs, or being sleepy

Knowing the vehicle has a dangerous fault or an unsafe load

The driver being avoidably and dangerously distracted, for example by:

Using a hand-held phone or other equipment

Reading, or looking at a map

Talking to and looking at a passenger

Lighting a cigarette, changing a CD or tape, tuning the radio.

Dangerous or Inconsiderate Driving

A person drives carelessly or inconsiderately when the way they drive falls below the minimum acceptable standard expected of a competent and careful driver.

Some examples of careless driving are:

Overtaking on the inside

Driving too close to another vehicle

Driving through a red light by mistake

Turning into the path of another vehicle

The driver being avoidably distracted by tuning the radio, lighting a cigarette etc.

Examples of inconsiderate driving include:

Flashing lights to force other drivers to give way

Misusing lanes to gain advantage over other drivers

Unnecessarily staying in an overtaking lane

Unnecessarily slow driving or braking

Dazzling other drivers with un-dipped headlights

Number Plate Offences

Number plate offences are quite common and sometimes they are done intentionally and sometimes by naivety. With the use of ANPR systems, the importance of having the correct type of number plate has been seen as even more important.

The basic rules for number plates:

You must display a number plate on the front and rear of your vehicle

Letters should be black on a white plate at the front

Letters should be black on a yellow plate at the rear

The background surface should be reflex-reflecting, but not the letters

Number plates should meet the British Standard

Rules on character dimensions differ slightly depending on whether your plates were fitted before or after 1st September 2001. Details are below.

Rules on character dimensions differ for traditional 'black and white' plates, which may be fitted on vehicles manufactured before 1st January 1973.

Any number plate made up after 1st September 2001 must meet the dimensions below:

Character Height 79 mm

Character Width (except the figure 1 or letter I) 50 mm

Character stroke 14 mm

Space between characters 11 mm

Space between groups 33 mm

Top, bottom, and side margins (minimum) 11 mm

Space between vertical lines 19 mm

Most offences are usually around not having the correct font or incorrect spacing. Other offences include using screws to alter a letter or number or the use of black or pressed plates.

Number plates that are incorrect can either be dealt with a Vehicle Defect Rectification Summons (VDRS) that will mean the vehicle owner will need to change the number plates and then get an MOT centre stamp a certificate. Which is then taken to their nearest police station, to verify that the plates are now correct. The other alternative is to issue a fixed penalty notice and request that the plates be changed to the correct format via a VDRS as well.

On private registrations, the DVLA have a form for the number plate infringement to be reported. If caught on a second occasion they can then have the registration taken off them.

Driving Offence Penalties

Causing death by dangerous driving

14 years- prison

Unlimited Fine

Obligatory driving ban. Min 2 years compulsory re–test.

3–11 points

Dangerous driving

2 years Prison

Unlimited fine

Obligatory driving ban Compulsory re–test.

Min 1 year

3–11 points

Causing death by careless driving under the influence of drink or drugs

Maximum 14 years prison sentence

Unlimited Fine

Obligatory driving ban Min 2 years

3–11 points

Careless driving, inconsiderate driving, driving without due care and attention

Maximum £5,000 fine

Discretionary driving ban

3–9 points

Driving while unfit through drink or drugs or with excess alcohol; or failing to provide a specimen for analysis

Maximum 6 months prison sentence

Maximum £5,000 fine

Obligatory driving ban

3–11 points

Failing to stop after an accident or failing to report an accident
Maximum 6 months prison sentence
Maximum £5,000 fine
Discretionary driving ban
5–10 points
Driving when disqualified
Maximum 6 months jail
Scotland: 12 months jail
Maximum £5,000 fine
Discretionary driving ban
6 points
Driving after refusal or revocation of licence on medical grounds
Maximum 6 months jail
Maximum £5,000 fine
Discretionary driving ban
3–6 points
Driving without insurance
Maximum £5,000 fine
FPN: £200
Discretionary driving ban
6–8 points
FPN: 6 points
Driving otherwise than in accordance with a licence
Maximum fine £1,000
Discretionary driving ban
3–6 points
Speeding
Maximum £1,000 fine
£2,500†
FPN: £60
Discretionary driving ban
3–6 points
FPN: 3 points
Traffic light offences

Maximum fine £1,000
FPN: £60
Discretionary driving ban
3 points

No MOT Certificate
Maximum £1,000 fine
FPN: £30
Seat belt offences
Maximum £500 fine
FPN: £60
Dangerous cycling
Maximum £2,500 fine
Careless cycling
Maximum £1,000 fine
Cycling on pavement
Maximum £500 fine
Failing to identify driver of vehicle
Maximum £1,000 fine
Discretionary driving ban
6 points
Use of hand–held mobile phone whilst in charge of a vehicle
Maximum £1,000 fine
FPN: £60
3 points

Driving Ban

For the vast majority of the public, the only time they are likely to come into contact with the criminal justice system is as a result of a motoring offence. On average, every year, up to a quarter of a million motorists receive a driving ban. There are 3 ways in which a driving licence can be revoked are.

Instant Driving Ban

Speeding Offences – when travelling far in excess of the speed limit, there is risk of an instant ban based on the speed recorded is way above the maximum and it is a court which will impose a driving ban.

Other Driving Offences – most offences are punishable with penalty points and a fine, some offences carry a discretionary or even a mandatory ban as listed above.

Totting Up Procedure

Should a driver reach 12 penalty points in a 3-year period, the Court guidelines are an automatic disqualification of 6 months should be imposed. The penalty points system was introduced in an attempt to provide the Courts with another method of punishing motorists apart from the original fine and driving ban option. In this way, the Court could endorse a person's driving licence with the number of points it felt appropriate, given the severity of the offence. It also allowed the introduction of a system that was able to monitor the effect the punishments were having, resulting in the potential to ban motorists who continued to commit driving offences on a regular basis.

New Drivers Act

A licence is revoked if a new driver amasses 6 penalty points within the first 2 years. The Road Traffic (New Drivers) Act 1995 applies to every motorist who passed their first full test after 1 June 1997.

The main effect of the Act is to impose a probationary period for the first 2 years after the test is passed. During this time, a new driver will be subject to immediate revocation of their licence, should they reach 6 or more penalty points. This is an automatic process which is triggered should any offence be committed in the first 2 years lead to a total of 6 points being endorsed on the licence. In theory, a new driver would therefore be given one chance by way of a Fixed Penalty but if two Fixed Penalties were accepted, or a more serious offence resulted in 6 points, the licence would be revoked.

It is important to note that points carried over from a provisional driving licence are still taken into account so any driver who transfers points from a provisional to a full licence would be revoked if any further offence were committed.

Likewise, it is the date of the offence that is relevant, not the date of conviction. Revocation will still take place even if the two-year probation period has elapsed before points are then imposed for an offence that occurred within the first 24 months.

RTC

RTC (Road Traffic Collision) can be anything from a minor bump to a major accident that involves fatalities. Any RTC will usually start with making sure everyone is all right and there are no injuries. If you are first on scene, you may need to alert any other emergency services that may also be required if they have not yet been alerted. With any injured persons dealt with the next priority will be any traffic, and deciding if any form of traffic management is required, or the road needs to be closed. Most simple bumps or shunts can be dealt with quite simply, and often disruption to other traffic is minimal. However, you need to be aware of your own safety as well as those involved in the RTC. Especially if the RTC occurred on a fast, or busy main road. Consider if the traffic needs to be stopped or re-directed for the safety of everyone.

As soon as you are called to an accident where there is either life changing injuries or a fatality, the scene of the accident becomes a crime scene and as such will require the road closing and a cordon putting in place. This is so that an accident investigator can assess the scene and collect vital evidence. In order to ascertain what has happened without further contamination of the scene.

All forces have their own collision investigators who will turn up to the scene of any serious or fatal collision. They will often be on scene for several hours taking pictures and measurements in order to ascertain what happened. They will also gather evidence from witnesses or get other officers to take witness statements to help build a picture of what happened. In some cases, it may be that charges on an individual or individuals involved need to be brought. With any collision, there will always be a reason for the accident, it could be mechanical failure, environmental conditions or the most likely cause of many collisions is driver error.

Any RTC usually requires some form of accident card being completed. Most are a simple tick sheet with an area to draw a diagram of the RTC. If there are injuries, these will also need to be recorded as well. As a rule of thumb from anyone involved in the RTC make sure you take:

Name, Address, Date of Birth and a contact number along with the vehicle registration. The vehicle and drivers details should be checked at the scene and any drivers involved needs to be breathalysed were possible. When a check on the vehicle is done, you will also be told if the car is insured or not, and who is able to drive the car on that policy. If any casualty is taken to hospital and it has not been possible to breathalyse the driver then a blood sample would have to be obtained for testing.

DOMESTIC VIOLENCE

Domestic violence is sadly a common occurrence and one that can have lasting physiological effects on families. Being able to read the warning signs and take positive action is essential for any police officer. Many forces now have robust domestic violence Polices in the light of tragic cases such as Casey Brittle, where Police missed opportunities to save the life of a young mother who was murdered by her violent ex-partner.

Casey was kicked and punched to death in front of her two-year-old daughter after suffering years of abuse. The little girl walked into the room where her father Sanchez Williams was carrying out the attack and afterwards stayed with her unconscious mother for two hours. Miss Brittle was so scared of her ex-partner, she 'played down' the incidents and was reluctant to press charges. As a result, Williams was never charged with a criminal offence in relation to her and the violence eventually escalated to murder. It is essential that a risk assessment is done with any domestic and that the relevant third parties are informed. Many forces have their own domestic violence units or will offer support and help to the victim. It is important to use you own perception as well. Does it feel right? Is there anything that seems not add up? If in doubt, seek advice from a supervisor or even the domestic violence unit itself. Even what seem like minor incidents can soon escalate and the abuse can be physical or mental. If children are involved, then there is an even greater concern for their safety and wellbeing as well as the victim.

A domestic incident can be between family members as well as current and ex-partners. The first action at any domestic is safeguarding the victim and any children involved. This may mean arresting the abuser or removing them from the property/locality. It could mean taking the victim and/or children to a place of safety. Second is to carry out a thorough investigation and involve partner agencies where necessary. To ensure no escalation of domestic violence occurs and robust measures are put in place to ensure safety and wellbeing of the victim. In the end it is your duty and responsibility to protect the victim and ensure their safety through using the policies and procedures put in place by a force.

Incidence and prevalence of domestic violence:

Domestic violence accounts for between 16% and one quarter of all recorded violent crime.

One incident is reported to the Police every minute.

45% women and 26% men had experienced at least one incident of interpersonal violence in their lifetimes. However, when there were more than 4 incidents (i.e. On-going domestic or sexual abuse) 89% of victims were women.

In any one year, there are 13 million separate incidents of physical violence or threats of violence against women from partners or former partners.

Women are much more likely than men to be the victim of multiple incidents of abuse, and of sexual violence: 32% of women who had ever experienced domestic violence did so four or five (or more) times, compared with 11% of the (smaller number) of men who had ever experienced domestic violence; and women constituted 89% of all those who had experienced 4 or more incidents of domestic violence.

Women are more likely than men to have experienced all types of intimate violence (partner abuse, family abuse, sexual assault and stalking) since the ages of 16. And nearly half the woman who had experienced intimate violence of any kind, were likely to have been victims of more than one kind of intimate abuse.

54% of UK rapes are committed by a woman's current or former partner.

On average two women a week are killed by a male partner or former partner: this constitutes around one-third of all female homicide victims.

All forms of domestic abuse have one purpose which is to gain and maintain control over the victim. Abusers use many tactics to exert power over their spouse or partner: dominance, humiliation, isolation, threats, intimidation, denial and blame.

Distinctions need to be made regarding types of violence, motives of perpetrators, and the social and cultural context. Violence by a person against their intimate partner is often done as a way for controlling "their partner", even if this kind of violence is not the most frequent. Other types of intimate partner violence also occur, including violence between gay and lesbian couples, and by women against their male partners.

Distinctions are not based on single incidents, but rather on patterns across numerous incidents and motives of the perpetrator.

Different Types of Abuse
Physical abuse

Physical abuse is abuse involving contact intended to cause feelings of intimidation, pain, injury, or other physical suffering or bodily harm.

Physical abuse includes hitting, slapping, punching, choking, pushing, and other types of contact that result in physical injury to the victim. Physical abuse can also include behaviours such as denying the victim of medical care when needed, depriving the victim of sleep or other functions necessary to live, or forcing the victim to engage in drug/alcohol use against his/her will.] It can also include inflicting physical injury onto other targets, such as children or pets, in order to cause psychological harm to the victim.

Sexual Abuse

Sexual abuse is any situation in which force or threat is used to obtain participation in unwanted sexual activity. Coercing a person to engage in sex, against their will, even if that person is a spouse or intimate partner with whom consensual sex has occurred, is an act of aggression and violence.

Sexual violence is defined by World Health Organization as: any sexual act, attempt to obtain a sexual act, unwanted sexual comments or advances, or acts to traffic, or otherwise directed, against a person's sexuality using coercion, by any person regardless of their relationship to the victim, in any setting, including but not limited to home and work.

Marital rape, also known as spousal rape, is non-consensual sex in which the perpetrator is the victim's spouse. As such, it is a form of partner rape, of domestic violence, and of sexual abuse.

Categories of sexual abuse include:

Use of physical force to compel a person to engage in a sexual act against his or her will, whether or not the act is completed;

Attempted or completed sex act involving a person who is unable to understand the nature or condition of the act, unable to decline participation, or unable to communicate unwillingness to engage in the sexual act, e.g., because of underage immaturity, illness, disability, or the influence of alcohol or other drugs, or because of intimidation or pressure.

Rape

1 in 4 women have experienced rape or attempted rape. 1 in 7 women have been coerced into sex rising to 1 in 3 in divorced or separated women. The most common perpetrators are husbands or partners.

Whatever happened, it is important the victim realises it was not their fault. The blame for a rape lies solely with the rapist. Sometimes a rapist will try to exert even more power by making the person who's been raped feel like it was actually his or her fault. A rapist may say stuff like, "You asked for it" or "You wanted it." This is just another way for the rapist to take control. The truth is that what a person wears, what a person says, or how a person acts is never a justification for rape.

Most people who are raped know their rapists. That can sometimes lead the person who's been raped to try to protect the perpetrator. Make protecting yourself, your priority. Don't worry about protecting the person who raped you. Encourage a victim to make a full report as it may help protect others from that person and may help you feel a little less like you were a victim.

But making a report to the police may be difficult for some people. If you don't feel comfortable reporting it, they don't have to. They may prefer to get advice about what to do from an experienced person who can be sympathetic to them. There are various charities such as the www.rapeandabuseline.co.uk or www.rapecrisis.org.uk that can offer initial support, many will want the police to become involved, but their main concern initially is to the victim and their feelings.

The first thing someone who has been raped needs to do is see a medical doctor. Most medical centres and hospital emergency departments have doctors and counsellors who have been trained to take care of someone who has been raped. It is important to get medical care because a doctor will need to check you for sexually transmitted diseases (STDs) and internal injuries.

They should get medical attention right away without changing your clothes, showering, douching, or washing. It can be hard not to clean up, of course — it is a natural human instinct to wash away all traces of a sexual assault. However, being examined right away is the best way to ensure you get proper medical treatment.

Immediate medical attention also helps when people decide to report the crime, providing evidence needed to prosecute the rapist if a criminal case is pursued. If you've been raped and think you don't want to report it, you could change your mind later — this often happens — and having the results of a medical exam can help you do this. (There are laws, known as statutes of limitations, that give a person only a certain amount of time to pursue legal action for a crime, though, so be sure you know how long you have to report the rape. A local rape crisis centre can advise you of the laws in your area.)

Even if they you don't get examined right away, it doesn't mean they cannot get a checkup later. It's always best to see a doctor immediately after a rape, of course. However, a person can still go to a doctor or local clinic to get checked out for STDs, pregnancy, or injuries any time after being raped. In some cases, doctors can even gather evidence several days after a rape has occurred.

A medical professional will test for STDs, including HIV/AIDS. These tests may involve taking blood or saliva samples. Although the thought of getting an STD after a rape is extremely scary, the quicker a person finds out about any infection, the more effectively he or she can be treated. Doctors can start you on immediate treatment courses for STDs, including HIV/AIDS, that will greatly increase your protection against developing these diseases.

A medical professional will examine them internally to check for any injury that might have been caused by the rape.

A medical professional or trained technician may look for and take samples of the rapist's hair, skin, nails, or bodily fluids from your clothes or body. If the victim thinks they have been given a rape drug, a doctor or technician can test for this, too.

Dealing with feelings

Rape isn't just physically damaging, it can be emotionally traumatic as well. The right emotional attention, care, and support can help a person begin the healing process and prevent lingering problems later.

Someone who has been raped might feel a lot of things: angry, degraded, frightened, numb, or confused. It's also normal for someone who has been raped to feel ashamed or embarrassed. Some people withdraw from friends and family. Others don't want to be alone. Some feel depressed, anxious, or nervous.

Sometimes the feelings surrounding rape may show up in physical ways, such as trouble sleeping or eating. It may be hard to concentrate in school or to participate in everyday activities. Sometimes it may feel like you'll never get over the trauma of the rape. Experts often refer to these emotions — and their physical side effects — as rape trauma syndrome. The best way to work through them is with professional help.

It can be hard to think or talk about a frightening experience, especially something as personal as rape. People who have been raped, sometimes avoid seeking help because they're afraid that talking about it will bring back memories or feelings that are too painful. But this can do more harm than good.

Talking about rape in a safe environment with the help and support of a trained professional is the best way to ensure long-term healing. Working through the pain sooner rather than later can help reduce symptoms like nightmares and flashbacks. It can also help people avoid potentially harmful behaviours and emotions, like major depression or self-injury.

Every rape survivor works through his or her feelings differently. Some people feel most comfortable talking one-on-one with a therapist. Others find that joining a support group where they can be with other survivors helps them to feel better, get their power back, and move on with their lives. In a support group, you can get help and support as well as give it. Your experiences and ideas may help others heal.

Emotional

Emotional abuse (also called psychological abuse or mental abuse) can include humiliating the victim privately or publicly, controlling what the victim can and cannot do, withholding information from the victim, deliberately doing something to make the victim feel diminished or embarrassed, isolating the victim from friends and family, implicitly blackmailing the victim by harming others when the victim expresses independence or happiness, or denying the victim access to money or other basic resources and necessities.

Emotional abuse can include verbal abuse and is defined as any behaviour that threatens, intimidates, undermines the victim's self-worth or self-esteem, or controls the victim's freedom. This can include threatening the victim with injury or harm, telling the victim that they will be killed if they ever leave the relationship, and public humiliation. Constant criticism, name-calling, and making statements that damage the victim's self-esteem are also common verbal forms of emotional abuse. Often perpetrators will use children to engage in emotional abuse by teaching them to harshly criticize the victim as well. Emotional abuse includes conflicting actions or statements which are designed to confuse and create insecurity in the victim. These behaviours also lead the victim to question themselves, causing them to believe that they are making up the abuse or that the abuse is their fault.

Emotional abuse includes forceful efforts to isolate the victim, keeping them from contacting friends or family. This is intended to eliminate those who might try to help the victim leave the relationship and to create a lack of resources for them to rely on if they were to leave. Isolation results in damaging the victim's sense of internal strength, leaving them feeling helpless and unable to escape from the situation.

People who are being emotionally abused often feel as if they do not own themselves; rather, they may feel that their significant other has nearly total control over them. Women or men undergoing emotional abuse often suffer from depression, which puts them at increased risk for suicide, eating disorders, and drug and alcohol abuse.

Verbal

Verbal abuse is a form of emotionally abusive behaviour involving the use of language. It may include profanity, but can occur with or without the use of expletives.

Verbal abuse may include aggressive actions such as name-calling, blaming, ridicule, disrespect, and criticism, but there are also less obvious aggressive forms of verbal abuse. Statements that may seem benign on the surface can be thinly veiled attempts to humiliate; falsely accuse; or manipulate others to submit to undesirable behaviour; make others feel unwanted and unloved; threaten others economically; or isolate victims from support systems.

Jekyll and Hyde behaviours, the abuser may fluctuate between sudden rages and false joviality toward the victim; or may simply show a very different "face" to the outside world than to the victim. While oral communication is the most common form of verbal abuse, it includes abusive communication in written form.

Economic

Economic abuse is a form of abuse when one intimate partner has control over the other partner's access to economic resources.

Economic abuse may involve preventing a spouse from resource acquisition, limiting the amount of resources to use by the victim, or by exploiting economic resources of the victim.

The motive behind preventing a spouse from acquiring resources is to diminish the victim's capacity to support himself/herself, thus forcing him/her to depend on the perpetrator financially, which includes preventing the victim from obtaining education, finding employment, maintaining or advancing their careers, and acquiring assets. In addition, the abuser may also put the victim on an allowance, closely monitor how the victim spends money, spend victim's money without his/her consent and creating debt, or completely spend victim's savings to limit available resources

Children

On children, there has been an increase in acknowledgment that a child who is exposed to domestic abuse during their upbringing will suffer in their developmental and psychological welfare. Due to the awareness of domestic violence that some children must face, it also generally impacts how the child develops emotionally, socially, behaviourally as well as cognitively. Some emotional and behavioural problems that can result due to domestic violence include increased aggressiveness, anxiety, and changes in how a child socializes with friends, family, and authorities. Depression, as well as self-esteem issues, can follow due to traumatic experiences. Problems with attitude and cognition in schools can start developing, along with a lack of skills such as problem-solving. Correlation has been found between the experience of abuse and neglect in childhood and perpetrating domestic violence and sexual abuse in adulthood. Additionally, in some cases the abuser will purposely abuse the mother in front of the child to cause a ripple effect, hurting not one but two of his victims. It has been found that children who witness mother-assault are more likely to exhibit symptoms of posttraumatic stress disorder (PTSD).

Long Term Effects

Physical Bruises, broken bones, head injuries, lacerations, and internal bleeding are some of the acute effects of a domestic violence incident that require medical attention and hospitalization. Some chronic health conditions that have been linked to victims of domestic violence are arthritis, irritable bowel syndrome, chronic pain, pelvic pain, ulcers, and migraines. Victims who are pregnant during a domestic violence relationship experience greater risk of miscarriage, pre-term labour, and injury to or death of the fetus. Psychological among victims who are still living with their perpetrators, high amounts of stress, fear, and anxiety are commonly reported. Depression is also common, as victims are made to feel guilty for 'provoking' the abuse and are constantly subjected to intense criticism. It is reported that 60% of victims meet the diagnostic criteria for depression, either during or after termination of the relationship, and have a greatly increased risk of suicidality. In addition to depression, victims of domestic violence also commonly experience long-term anxiety and panic, and are likely to meet the diagnostic criteria for Generalized Anxiety Disorder and Panic Disorder. The most commonly referenced psychological effect of domestic violence is PTSD. PTSD (as experienced by victims) is characterized by flashbacks, intrusive images, exaggerated startle response, nightmares, and avoidance of triggers that are associated with the abuse. These symptoms are generally experienced for a long span of time after the victim has left the dangerous situation. Many researchers state that PTSD is possibly the best diagnosis for those suffering from psychological effects of domestic violence, as it accounts for the variety of symptoms commonly experienced by victims of trauma.

Financial concerns are once victims leave their perpetrator, they can be stunned with the reality of the extent to which the abuse has taken away their autonomy. Due to economic abuse and isolation, the victim usually has very little money of their own and few people on whom they can rely when seeking help. This has been shown to be one of the greatest obstacles facing victims of domestic violence, and the strongest factor that can discourage them from leaving their perpetrators. In addition to lacking financial resources, victims of domestic violence often lack specialized skills, education, and training that are necessary to find gainful employment, and also may have several children to support. It has also been reported that one out of every three homeless women are homeless due to having left a domestic violence relationship. If a victim is able to secure rental housing, it is likely that her apartment complex will have "zero tolerance" policies for crime; these policies can cause them to face eviction even if they are the victim (not the perpetrator) of violence. While the number of shelters and community resources available to domestic violence victims has grown tremendously, these agencies often have few employees and hundreds of victims seeking assistance which causes many victims to remain without the assistance they need.

Clare's Law – Domestic Violence Disclosure Scheme

Clare Wood was murdered in 2009 by her partner after several domestic violence incidents were reported to the police. She was killed by her then ex-partner who had a history of violence against women. This new law initially a pilot run by three forces is based on the disclosure of domestic violence offender history to those at risk.

The information cannot just be disclosed to the public at will. It is only for those at risk or for someone who is safeguarding the victim. It then needs to be authorised usually by the Public Protection Inspector. If these circumstances do arise usually the checks can be made within 24 hours and then the victim will be contacted by a specialist team at a time, place and method that is safe and has been agreed. Common Law already allows for a disclosure to be made to safeguard people. So as such the law has not changed just a more specific application of it.

WITNESS STATEMENTS

A large proportion of Police time is taken up in writing statements. These may be for the IP or from a Police officer who has seized an item from a crime scene, made an arrest or even a witness themselves. In this chapter, we shall look at how to write a statement, go through what needs to be included and we'll look at some examples.

What is a Statement?

A statement is a pen picture of an incident or event. It needs to be detailed enough so that anyone reading it that was not at the scene can get a detailed picture of what went on: it also needs to meet the requirements of the CPS.

Witness statements are just one of the sources of information used by the Police and CPS to determine what actually happened in an incident, if there was a violation of the rules, and what penalty is appropriate.

The balance of a statement should record the version of the facts, what was heard and seen. Do not include any information from other people.

It is important that each witness write his/her statement, as it is unlikely that each witness saw every part of the incident or saw it from the same physical perspective and there will therefore be significant differences in the statements. Unfortunately, this does make for more paperwork, but it ensures that more facts are available to make the right decision.

Avoid deductions, conclusions, or opinions, as they are not facts. If you use words such as "I think" or "it appeared" or "probably", you are conveying to the statement reader that you did not observe, but are deducing, forming an opinion or concluding what you think you may have seen, and these statements could be given less consideration or discounted completely as not being factual. Present the details that you used to form an opinion, not the opinion itself. For example, you could say, "car A changed his line and suddenly moved left into the right side of car B" but not, "car A intentionally hit car B".

When writing statements for a third party which is a common occurrence for a police officer you may need to probe and ask questions to make sure you get a detailed statement. What a witness may feel insignificant can be very significant. Always include full descriptions of anyone involved and exactly what they did or said. Try to get statements as soon is practically possible for more serious incidents this is likely to be straight after it happened when all the detail is still fresh in the witness's mind. Writing statements is a skill that takes practice and time. The more statements you write, the more proficient you will become.

To aid in taking witness statements you can use the INSIDE model.

Introduction - introduction

Set the scene – any background information

Incident – describe the incident

Descriptions – Vehicles, nominals, ADVOKATE

Evaluation – Victim impact, points to prove, any costs, injuries

We will start with an acronym that needs to roll off the tongue. It will make life so much easier when writing statements that include a description of a suspect.

"ADVOKATE"

A Amount of time the incident was seen for.

D Distance from incident.

V Visibility - was it dark or sunny? Were street lights on? Was it night or day?

O Obstructions - did a tree or lampost, etc obstruct your/their view?

K Known or unknown - have you seen these people before and do you know them?

A Any reason to remember, e.g., unique points that make this memorable.

T Time Lapse - how much time has elapsed since the witness saw the incident/suspect.

E Error or material discrepancy - any differences between the description given by the witness and the actual appearance of the suspect.

When doing any witness statement to try to include all of the points if applicable. Below are two example, statements: the first is just an account and is too brief, the second is the same statement showing how it should be done.

One of the main issues, Police officers initially find in making statements is the level of detail that needs to be included. Practice is the key to writing good statements. If you are writing a witness statement for a third party start with name, date of birth and occupation. Then cover everything that has occurred start from just before the event and stop just after. Include descriptions of anyone involved and names if known. Next use ADVOKATE before finally finishing off with a witness impact statement, stating how they felt at the time and how they feel now. Will what has happened have any effects on them. Be it financial, physical or emotional it is an important aspect for the prosecution and defence to see if it goes to court.

I am Police Constable 1234 Rockitt of the Anytown Police, currently stationed at Any Station. I was on duty in full uniform with PC 8808 ANDERSON on 22nd May 2009 at 22:55.

When we were stationary at the traffic lights at the side of the Dog and Cat Pub Anytown we observed a group of white males pushing and attempting to punch each other. One Male I noticed punching and shoving was who I now know to be John Doe DOB 16/07/72 IC1 Male, shaved head, wearing a White Jumper and Blue Jeans about 6 feet tall. Once the lights had changed to green we went around to the front of the DOG AND CAT PUB and on leaving the Police Car I noticed DOE push another male who I could not see fully due to it being blocked by the building. Then on at 23:00 on that day (22/05/09) went over and attempted to arrest DOE for affray and said "I am arresting you for affray" CAUTIONED to which he said "I HAVE NOT DONE ANYTHING" then resisted arrest by trying to shake me loose and replied "I have not done anything fuck off" and continued to resist by pulling away even though I had my right hand on his left arm and left hand on his wrist. I noticed that he was heavily in drink and difficult to handle. At this point several of the males became hostile and tried to prevent me arresting DOE and his girlfriend Christine JONES DOB 03/02/72 IC1 Female with Blonde Hair White top and back skirt, black tights and black heeled boots tried to pull DOE away from me. On pulling away I was pulled to the ground and at this point fearing for my safety I pressed the panic button and requested backup. PC8808 ANDERSON tried to move the crowd away and regain control. At this point, DOE and JONES moved to the front of the DOG AND CAT PUB and continued to resist me arresting DOE at this point PC 999 ARREST arrived to give assistance and I drew my ASP to move the crowd away and told them to "Back off" at this point I noticed JONES kick PC 999 ARREST on the right leg to the knee. With further backup DOE was removed from JONES I arrested him still being abusive swearing and trying to resist arrest. DOE was then conveyed to the Custody.

This statement is for a large fight outside a pub but is far too short and lacks ADVOKATE fully, lacks detail as it is not a detailed pen picture. Setting the scene and describing the area and offenders is too brief.

Below is how the statement should have been written and the level of detail required.

I am Police Constable 1234 ROCKITT based at ANY STATION Police Station ANYTOWN for ANYTOWN POLICE. At 22:55 hours on Friday 6th March 2009 I was conducting uniformed patrol duties in company with SC 8088 ANDERSON in the ANYTOWN area. At this time, I was driving a fully liveried Police vehicle along LONG ROAD, ANYTOWN and was waiting to turn right onto SHORT ROAD at the traffic lights.

The DOG AND CAT PUB public house known locally as the DOG AND CAT PUB was located on my right-hand side. The property fronts onto LONG ROAD, one side is adjacent to SHORT ROAD and the rear of this public house backs onto END ROAD. To my right I noticed a large group of males, approximately 10 – 12 males, which were on the pavement between the side of the DOG AND CAT PUB and the safety railings. There looked to be two separate groups and I could see about four people jostling each other. The four were behaving aggressively towards each other and they looked like they were being abusive, their faces were contorted and confrontational to each other. I observed this group whilst waiting at the traffic lights for about two minutes and became concerned that a fight was breaking out, as the group continued to jostle each other and I feared things were going to escalate. I passed on what I had seen to Command and Control via my radio.

I would estimate the group were 20 feet away from me and I had a clear unobstructed view of the group. The weather was clear and the street lighting illuminated the streets to a good degree. I saw a male in a grey top throw a punch at a male in a white top. From now on I will refer to the male in the grey top as male 1. The male in the white top I now know to be John DOE DOB 16/09/1973. I would describe DOE as a white male with a shaved head and approximately 6 feet tall. Doe was a medium build and spoke with a local accent, aged in his early thirties. DOE was wearing a knitted white polo neck jumper and plain dark blue jeans.

Male 1 I would describe as white and of medium build, he was between 5'08" and 5'10" tall. Aged in his early thirties, he had short cropped dark hair and he was wearing a short sleeved grey t-shirt with white piping around the neck area. I have not seen this male before, nor do I know him, but I would recognise him again.

DOE then shoved male 1 away, causing him to stumble backwards. Male one, then came forward again and tried to throw another punch at DOE. DOE then lunged forward towards male 1 and at this point the traffic lights changed and I moved off to park the Police vehicle on LONG ROAD. I lost visual contact with the group for about one minute whilst parking the vehicle in a safe place.

I then got out of the Police vehicle by the railings on LONG ROAD opposite the entrance to the public house. I saw the same group of people standing on the pavement by SHORT ROAD, however, I could only see three people at this stage. I could see DOE, he was about 30 feet away from where I was standing with no obstructions. I saw DOE use both his arms to push another male, hard. DOE appeared to push the male deliberately with significant force.

At 23:00 hours I ran over to DOE and said "I am arresting you for affray" CAUTION to which he said "I'VE NOT DONE ANYTHING, WE'RE JUST MESSING AROUND!" I put my right hand on DOE's left shoulder and my left hand on DOE's right wrist in a prisoner escort technique to lead DOE away from the scene to diffuse the situation. DOE immediately resisted my attempt to lead him away from the scene by standing still and tensing his body. DOE was heavily into drink, I could smell intoxicating liquor on his breath and his eyes were watery. DOE was very aggressive in both his manner and tone. DOE had an aggressive look in his eyes as if he had just been involved in a fight or heated argument with another person.

At this point I became surrounded by a number of males who began to shout at me "HE HASN'T DONE ANYTHING!" At least two males got within 15 centimetres of my face and repeatedly shouted ""HE HASN'T DONE ANYTHING!". I immediately began to be concerned for the safety of SC ANDERSON and myself at this point. The males had closed down my reactionary gap and were becoming increasingly hostile. I still had DOE in an escort hold.

At this point a white female approached, who I now know to be Christine JONES DOB 03/02/1972 who I would describe as having shoulder length or longer blonde hair, of slim build aged in her thirties, around 5'04" – 5'06" tall. JONES was wearing a white t-shirt type top, black skirt, and black tights with black heeled boots and came to the left side of me and threw her arms around DOE's waist in order to prevent me from taking DOE away. JONES who appeared quite emotional continued to violently pull at DOE's waist causing him to fall backwards, onto the pavement. JONES also fell onto her back and DOE fell onto JONES. I kept hold of DOE to try and prevent him from falling over with JONES. This pulled me off balance and dragged me down to the point where I was down on one knee. I immediately let go of DOE as I was now very concerned and felt both PC 8088 ANDERSON and myself were in grave danger. I immediately pressed my emergency button on the Airwave radio to summon assistance.

I managed to get back to my feet and I saw SC ANDERSON shout loudly at the crowd. "WILL YOU GET BACK! The crowd then moved around towards the front door of the DOG AND CAT PUB, JONES was still holding onto DOE and they were resting up against the side of the DOG AND CAT PUB.

I would estimate there were now about 12 – 14 people out on the pavement in front of the DOG AND CAT PUB. PC 999 ARREST arrived and he was standing less than two feet in front of JONES and DOE. He attempted to split up JONES and DOE, JONES reacted and kicked PC 999 ARREST in a toe poke frontward kick to PC 999 ARREST's right knee to make him back off.

PC ARREST backed away so as to prevent further assault. As he did this the crowd began to shout angrily and aggressively "DON'T TOUCH HER SHE IS A WOMAN!" Both PC 999 ARREST and myself were totally surrounded by the crowd who were increasingly hostile towards Police. I became fearful for my safety so I withdrew my Police issue ASP baton and placed the baton over my right shoulder and shouted at the crowd "BACK OFF! BACK OFF! BACK OFF! BACK OFF!" I felt the situation was escalating and getting out of control.

Other officers arrived very quickly and began to disperse the crowd. I located DOE shortly after the initial crowd had been dispersed and reminded DOE he was under arrest for affray. I handcuffed DOE to the rear and double locked the handcuffs and checked for tightness. C division officers then conveyed DOE to the CUSTODY suite in a marked Police van.

At this time, there was still a large crowd with parts of the crowd still hostile. I was advised that there was already a prisoner in our Police vehicle. Then in company with PC ANDERSON I conveyed a male I now know to be Antony WOOD into CUSTODY where the custody sergeant authorised his detention.

Later I returned to the DOG AND CAT PUB with PC 8088 ANDERSON who seized CCTV footage from the premises.

I shall now outline some key points from the statement. You will notice all surnames are in capitals as are any quotes so that they stand out, the description of the offender is written first by physical description, then by clothes.

"John DOE DOB 16/09/1973. I would describe DOE as a white male with a shaved head and approximately 6 feet tall. Doe was a medium build and spoke with a local accent, aged in his early thirties. DOE was wearing a knitted white polo neck jumper and plain dark blue jeans."

Seizure Statement

Here is an example of a seizure statement. Whenever you seize anything that is part of a crime or investigation a statement must be written.

I am a Police Constable 1234 ROCKITT of ANYTOWN Police currently stationed at ANYSTATION.

I was on duty in full uniform on 7th September 2008 at 20:00 when I attended 124 ACACIA road, ANYTOWN to assist other officers in the execution of a search warrant as part of an ongoing investigation. Whilst at the address I seized the following items.

Seized four mobile phones and I refer to these as Police item JR/1 Nokia mobile phone, JR/2 Sony Ericson mobile phone, JR/3

Samsung mobile phone, JR/3 Blackberry mobile phone from the front left bedroom under a pile of clothes in the left-hand corner next to the bed.

I subsequently handed these exhibits to PC999 ARREST, the exhibits officer.

Basic Arrest Statement

I am a Police Constable 1234 ROCKITT of ANYTOWN Police currently stationed at ANYSTATION.

I was on duty in full uniform on (date) at 19:45 I was on duty with PC 8088 ANDERSON.

At 19:45 on that day (date) I attended the address of Jane DOE born 18/12/68 of 53 COLLEGE Street, ANYTOWN.

As a result of two witness statements gathered earlier the same day, I said to DOE "I am arresting you on suspicion of criminal damage at 55a COLLEGE Street, ANYTOWN.

CAUTIONED.

DOE made no reply to the caution.

DOE was then conveyed to custody where her detention was authorised.

At 21:38 hours that day I commenced a tape-recorded interview with DOE.

Present was PC ANDERSON.

At 21:45 that day the interview was concluded. The master tape was signed and sealed and I referred to it as Police item JR/1.

CAREER DEVELOPMENT

One of the reasons people join the police service is for the career progression and opportunities they can get as their career progresses. Many are happy to be a PC for their entire career, enjoying being at the sharp end more than moving into management. Very similar in many ways, to a teacher in a school or college who prefers to be in the classroom teaching rather than moving into management and away from the classroom. Many though do want to progress and aspire to become a leader moving up the ranks.

After a few years of service, you may decide that you want to change what you do within the Police service. The options are wide and varied even for Special Constables

A Special Constable may decide to do extra training to specialise in an area or even work with CID. Some Specials aspire to become Special Sergeants or Inspectors which usually means attending a selection board. More recently special management are attending a weekend management course

For the full-time officer who want to progress within the management structure, then you must pass your OSPRE® exams

OSPRE

The Objective Structured Performance-Related Examination (OSPRE®) was introduced nationally in 1991, as the primary means through which Police officers in England and Wales are selected for promotion to the ranks of sergeant and Inspector. It is designed to test knowledge and understanding of the law and procedure of future sergeants and inspectors.

The examination involves 150 multiple-choice questions over a three-hour period. Questions used in the examination are prepared by trained writers who have extensive policing experience and knowledge of the relevant legislation. During the development period, all questions are extensively quality assured by a team of internal and independent experts. Any full-time police officer can apply to undertake the first examination after successful completion of their two-year probation period. The exams are needed to be able to be promoted from PC to Sergeant or Sergeant to Inspector. Along with the exam pass you will also need to fulfil your forces requirement for promotion and attend some form of selection board or interview as well as possibly up to six months on the job assessment.

Rules for OSPRE®

Admission to the qualifying examination for promotion to the rank of

Sergeant is currently restricted to regular constables (those appointed to office of regular Constable) who, by 30 November of the calendar year in which they take the OSPRE®

Part I, will have: completed not less than two years' service; and been confirmed in their appointment; and not previously obtained a pass to the rank of sergeant in a recognised Police promotion process.

Admission to the qualifying examination for promotion to the rank of Inspector is currently restricted to sergeants who, on 01 July of the calendar year in which they take the OSPRE®

Part I, will have: attained the substantive rank of sergeant 1; and not previously obtained a pass to the rank of Inspector in a recognised Police promotion process.

High Potential Development Scheme: An officer who is a member of the national High Potential Development Scheme (HPDS) may undertake OSPRE®

Part I before completing the above admission requirements. HPDS officers are subject to specific provisions made by the Police (Promotion) (Amendment) Regulations. The HPDS scheme is open to Officers with at least a 2:1 or greater degree. Officers have to go through a separate selection procedure to be accepted on the scheme. Which sees a successful candidate reach Inspector in five years.

Structure

Pass/Fail criteria

Part I The pass requirement in the Sergeants' and Inspectors' OSPRE®

Part I is an absolute standard (set pass mark). Those candidates who achieve a score equal to or above the set pass mark will be awarded a pass.

Further details in relation to the pass mark and the 'low band fail' and 'exceptional' cut scores will be communicated in the Instructions to Candidates document, which candidates receive prior to the examination.

Details of candidates attaining the 'exceptional' and 'low band fail' scores will be notified to their Chief Officer.

Was the part I exam has been passed an officer is eligible to an acting post. To be eligible for a substantive Sgt position there is a six-month period of on the job continuous assessment, with this assessment phase passed the individual can apply for a substantive post.

Example Questions
Crime

John has had a falling out with a business colleague over their business deals. His partner has refused to sell his share of the business. Knowing that on the death of his partner, he would have full control he arranges a contract killing. Unknown to John, the person he speaks to is an undercover Police officer. What is the most appropriate offence committed by John?

Answer The offence 'Solicitation of murder' is against The Offences Against the Person Act 1861: Section 4 "Whosoever shall solicit, encourage, persuade or endeavour to persuade or shall propose to any person to murder any other person, whether he be a subject of Her Majesty or not. Shall be guilty". Triable Either way Offence (Indictment only - life imprisonment)

Brian knows his neighbour is away and so, in a cunning plan, decides to make use of his absence to power his concrete mixer and other tools while Brian builds a patio in his own garden. Brian uses a coat hanger to pull the latch on the back door and open it. Inside he plugs in five extension cables running them into his back garden. Brian uses the cables to power a number of tools whilst he works. With regard to Brian's actions, which of the following statements is true?

Answer Under 9(1)(a) and (b) "stealing" means "an intention to commit theft". However, this does not include abstracting electricity. The property which is intended to be stolen must be in the building or part of a building (Low v Blease (1975)).

Evidence and Procedure

Sergeant Fisher the custody officer is considering bailing conditions for Godfrey, who is presently in custody for an offence. Which is NOT a condition that a custody officer can impose?

Answer A custody officer may only refuse to grant bail on the grounds of further offences if that offence relates to an imprisonable offence not any offence. In making the decision the custody officer should consider if the person has committed offences whilst previously on bail.

Section 16 of the Crime and Disorder Act 1998 deals with the removal of truants and in the section, makes reference to a designated premises. What is a designated place?

Answer Although a designated place is not defined in the act however they are a matter for the local authority.

General Police Duties

An Anti-Social Behaviour Order is an order to prevent an individual acting in an anti-social manner. Which does form part of the definition of anti-social?

Answer Anti-Social Behaviour is defined as a manner that caused or was likely to cause harassment, alarm or distress to one or more persons and not of the same household as himself.

In order to apply for an Anti-Social Behaviour Order, it must appear to the relevant authority that a person acted in a manner that caused or was likely to cause, harassment, alarm or distress. Who, or what is the relevant authority that can apply for such an order?

Answer The relevant authority is BOTH the Local Authority and the Chief Officer of Police, any part of whose area lies within the area of the local authority. Housing action trusts and social landlords are also included.

Road Policing

Section 148(1) of the Road Traffic Act 1988 (requirements for insurance) makes the effects of some restrictions in a policy void. If a policy purports to restrict the extent of its cover by reference to certain features, breaches of them by the insured person will not affect the validity of that policy for the purpose of section 143. Which, if any of the following would NOT be covered by this section?

Answer The list covered by S.148 is far reaching, previous driving convictions however is not included.

With regard to the penalty for causing death by dangerous driving, which of the following statements are true?

Answer Causing Death by Dangerous Driving carries an obligatory 2-year minimum disqualification and a compulsory re-test. It is an indictable offence. The re-test and disqualification applies regardless of what sentence the defendant receives.

Police Associations and Agencies

College of Policing

The College of Policing has replaced the NPIA in the learning and development capacity. They are responsible for the recruitment, assessment, leadership development, specialist training and also offer training to overseas officers.

National Crime Agency

The National Crime Agency is the proposed national law enforcement agency in the United Kingdom, serving as a replacement for the existing Serious Organised Crime Agency. This has taken on some of the functions of the NPIA.

The new agency will also include the Child Exploitation and Online Protection Centre and parts of the National Policing Improvement Agency. Some of the responsibilities of the UK Border Agency will also fall to the new Agency.

Police Federation

The Police Federation of England and Wales is a staff association for all police constables, sergeants and inspectors (including chief inspectors). It was created by the Police Act 1919, passed a year after a crippling strike by the unrecognised National Union of Police and Prison Officers (NUPPO).

The Police Federation of England and Wales is still a staff association that represents all 140,000 police officers up to and including the rank of Chief Inspector. They ensure that their views on all aspects of policing, including welfare and efficiency, are accurately relayed to government, opinion formers and key stakeholders. They are there to support all police officers in all aspects of the job and also give legal advice and support to police officers undergoing any form of disciplinary or criminal investigation.

The Federation has evolved from being a voluntary, unfunded organisation in its early years, to a modern, professional staff association that covers all subjects and issues that affect the police service, including all aspects of pay, allowances, hours of duty, annual leave and pensions, ensuring the views of its members are heard.

On behalf of its members, the Federation is also consulted when police regulations are set and when issues such as training, promotion, discipline and professional standards are discussed at both national and force level.

The Federation is based at its headquarters in Leatherhead. It currently employs approximately 80 people, with extensive Communications, HR, Printing, ICT and Research departments, as well as support and administrative staff for all members of the Joint Central Committee and sub-committees.

APPENDIX – FULL LIST OF CRIMINAL OFFENCES

Class A: Homicide and related grave offences

Murder - Common law

Manslaughter - Common law

Soliciting to commit murder - Offences against the Person Act 1861 s.4

Child destruction - Infant Life (Preservation) Act 1929 s.1(1) 1861 c. 100 1929 c. 34

Infanticide - Infanticide Act 1938 s.1(1) 1938 c. 36

Causing explosion likely to endanger life or property - Explosive Substances Act 1883 s.2

Attempt to cause explosion, making or keeping explosive etc. - Explosive Substances Act 1883 s.3

Class B: Offences involving serious violence or damage, and serious drugs offences

Endangering the safety of an aircraft - Aviation Security Act 1982 s. 2(1)(b) 1982 c. 36

Racially-aggravated arson (not endangering life) - Crime and Disorder Act 1998 s. 30(1) 1998 c. 37

Kidnapping - Common law

False imprisonment - Common law

Aggravated criminal damage - Criminal Damage Act 1971 s.1(2) 1971 c. 48

Aggravated arson - Criminal Damage Act 1971 s.1(2), (3) 1971 c. 48

Arson (where value exceeds £30,000)- Criminal Damage Act 1971 s.1(3) 1971 c. 48

Possession of firearm with intent to endanger life -Firearms Act 1968 s.16

Use of firearm to resist arrest - Firearms Act 1968 s.17 1968 c. 27

Possession of firearm with criminal intent - Firearms Act 1968 s.18

Possession or acquisition of certain prohibited weapons, etc. - Firearms Act 1968 s. 5

Aggravated burglary - Theft Act 1968 s.10 1968 c. 60

Armed robbery - Theft Act 1968 s.8(1) 1968 c. 60

Assault with a weapon with intent to rob - Theft Act 1968 s. 8 (2) 1968 c. 60

Blackmail - Theft Act 1968 s.21 1968 c. 60

Riot - Public Order Act 1986 s.1 1986 c. 64 1986 c. 64

Violent disorder - Public Order Act 1986 s.2 1986 c. 64

Contamination of goods with intent - Public Order Act 1986 s.38 1986 c. 64

Causing death by dangerous driving - Road Traffic Act 1988 s.1 1988 c. 52

Causing death by careless driving while under the influence of drink or drugs - Road Traffic Act 1988 s.3A

Aggravated vehicle taking resulting in death - Theft Act 1968 s.12A 1968 c. 60

Causing danger to road users - Road Traffic Act 1988 s.22A

Attempting to choke, suffocate, strangle etc. - Offences against the Person Act 1861 s.21 1861 c. 100

Causing miscarriage by poison, instrument - Offences against the Person Act 1861 s.58 1861 c. 100

Making threats to kill - Offences against the Person Act 1861 s.16 1988 c. 52 1861 c. 100

Wounding or grievous bodily harm with intent to cause grievous bodily harm, etc. - Offences against the Person Act 1861 s. 18 1861 c. 100

Endangering the safety of railway passengers - Offences against the Person Act 1861 ss.32, 33,
34 1861 c. 100

Impeding persons endeavouring to escape wrecks - Offences against the Person Act 1861 s.17 1861 c. 100

Administering chloroform, laudanum etc. - Offences against the Person Act 1861 s.22 1861 c. 100

Administering poison, etc. so as to endanger life - Offences against the Person Act 1861 s.23 1861 c. 100

Cruelty to persons under 16 - Children and Young Persons Act 1933 s.1 1933 c. 12

Aiding and abetting suicide - Suicide Act 1961 s.2 1961 c. 60

Prison mutiny - Prison Security Act 1992 s.1 1992 c. 25

Assaulting prison officer whilst possessing firearm, etc. - Criminal Justice Act 1991 s. 90 1991 c. 53

Producing or supplying a Class A or B drug - Misuse of Drugs Act 1971 s.4 1971 c. 38

Possession of a Class A or B drug with intent to supply - Misuse of Drugs Act 1971 s.5(3) 1971 c. 38

Manufacture and supply of scheduled substances - Criminal Justice (International Co-operation) Act 1990 s.12 1990 c. 5

Fraudulent evasion of controls on Class A and B drugs - Customs and Excise Management Act 1979 s.170(2)(b), (c) 1979 c. 2

Illegal importation of Class A and B drugs -Customs and Excise Management Act 1979 s.50 1979 c. 2

Offences in relation to proceeds of drug trafficking - Drug Trafficking Act 1994 ss.49, 50 and 51 1994 c. 37

Offences in relation to money laundering investigations - Drug Trafficking Act 1994 ss.52 and 53

Practitioner contravening drug supply regulations - Misuse of Drugs Act 1971 ss.12 and 13

Cultivation of cannabis plant - Misuse of Drugs Act 1971 s.6

Occupier knowingly permitting drugs offences etc. - Misuse of Drugs Act 1971 s.8

Activities relating to opium - Misuse of Drugs Act 1971 s.9

Drug trafficking offences at sea - Criminal Justice (International Co-operation) Act 1990 s.18 1990 c. 5

Firing on Revenue vessel - Customs and Excise Management Act 1979 s.85 1971 c. 38 1979 c. 2

Making or possession of explosive in suspicious circumstances - Explosive Substances Act 1883 s.4(1) 1883 c. 3

Causing bodily injury by explosives - Offences against the Person Act 1861 s.28 1861 c. 100

Using explosive or corrosives with intent to cause grievous bodily harm - Offences against the Person Act 1861 s.29

Hostage taking - Taking of Hostages Act 1982 s.1 1982 c. 28

Offences against international protection of nuclear material - **Nuclear Material** (Offences) Act 1983 1983 c. 18 Placing explosives with intent to cause bodily injury s.2 Offences against the Person Act 1861 s.30 1861 c. 100

Membership of proscribed organisations - Terrorism Act 2000 s.11 2000 c. 11

Support or meeting of proscribed organisations - Terrorism Act 2000 s.12 2000 c. 11

Uniform of proscribed organisations - Terrorism Act 2000 s.13 2000 c. 11

Fund-raising for terrorism - Terrorism Act 2000 s.15 2000 c. 11

Other offences involving money or property to be used for terrorism - Terrorism Act 2000 ss.16-18 2000 c. 11

Disclosure prejudicing, or interference of material relevant to, investigation of terrorism - Terrorism Act 2000 s.39 2000 c. 11

Weapons training - Terrorism Act 2000 s.54 2000 c. 11

Directing terrorist organization Terrorism Act 2000 s.56 2000 c. 11

Possession of articles for terrorist purposes - Terrorism Act 2000 s.57 2000 c. 11

Unlawful collection of information for terrorist purposes - Terrorism Act 2000 s.58 2000 c. 11

Incitement of terrorism overseas - Terrorism Act 2000 s.59 2000 c. 11

Concealing criminal property - Proceeds of Crime Act 2002 s.327 2002 c.29

Involvement in arrangements facilitating the acquisition, retention, use or control of criminal property - Proceeds of Crime Act 2002 s.328 2002 c.29

Acquisition, use or possession of criminal property - Proceeds of Crime Act 2002 s.329 2002 c.29

Failure to disclose knowledge or suspicion of money laundering - regulated sector - Proceeds of Crime Act 2002 s.331

Failure to disclose knowledge or suspicion of money laundering - nominated officers in the regulated sector - Proceeds of Crime Act 2002 s.330

Failure to disclose knowledge or suspicion of money laundering - other nominated officers - Proceeds of Crime Act 2002 s.331

Tipping off -Proceeds of Crime Act 2002 s.333

Disclosure under sections 330, 331, 332 or 333 of the Proceeds of Crime Act 2002 otherwise than in the form and manner prescribed - Proceeds of Crime Act 2002 s.339(1A)

Causing or allowing the death of a child - Domestic Violence, Crime and Victims Act 2004 s.5

Class C: Lesser offences involving violence or damage, and less serious drugs offences

Racially-aggravated assault - Crime and Disorder Act 1998 s. 29(1) 1998 c.37

Racially-aggravated criminal damage - Crime and Disorder Act 1998 s. 30(1) 1998 c.37

Robbery (other than armed robbery) - Theft Act 1968 s.8(1) 1968 c. 60

Unlawful wounding - Offences against the Person Act 1861 s.20 1861 c. 100

Assault occasioning actual bodily harm - Offences against the Person Act 1861 s.47 1861 c. 100

Concealment of birth - Offences against the Person Act 1861 s.60 1861 c. 100

Abandonment of children under two - Offences against the Person Act 1861 s.27 1861 c. 100

Arson (other than aggravated arson) where value does not exceed £30,000 - Criminal Damage Act 1971 s.1(1) 1971 c. 48

Criminal damage (other than aggravated criminal damage) - **Criminal Damage** Act 1971 s.1(3) 1971 c. 48

Possession of firearm without certificate - Firearms Act 1968 s.1 1968 c. 27

Carrying loaded firearm in a public place - Firearms Act 1968 s. 19 1968 c. 27

Trespassing with a firearm - Firearms Act 1968 s.20 1968 c. 27

Shortening of shotgun or possession of shortened shotgun - Firearms Act 1968 s.4 1968 c. 27

Shortening of smooth bore gun - Firearms Amendment Act 1988 c. 45 1988 s.6(1) 1968 c. 27

Possession or acquisition of shotgun without licence - Firearms Act 1968 s.2 1968 c. 27 certificate

Possession of firearms by person convicted of crime - Firearms Act 1968 s.21(4)

Acquisition by or supply of firearms to person denied them - Firearms Act 1968 s.21(5)

Dealing in firearms - Firearms Act 1968 s.3

Failure to comply with certificate when transferring - Firearms Act 1968 s.42

Permitting an escape Common law

Rescue - Common law

Escaping from lawful custody without force - Common law

Breach of prison - Common law

Harbouring escaped prisoners - Criminal Justice Act 1961 s.22 1961 c. 39

Assisting prisoners to escape - Prison Act 1952 s.39 1952 c. 52

Fraudulent evasion of agricultural levy - Customs and Excise

Management Act 1979 s.68A(1) and (2) 1979 c. 2

Offender armed or disguised - Customs and Excise Management Act 1979 s.86

Making threats to destroy or damage property - Criminal Damage Act 1971 s.2 1971 c. 48

Possessing anything with intent to destroy or damage property- Criminal Damage Act 1971 s.3

Child abduction by connected person - Child Abduction Act 1984 s.1 1984 c. 37

Child abduction by other person - Child Abduction Act 1984 s.2

Bomb hoax - Criminal Law Act 1977 s.51 1977 c. 45

Producing or supplying Class C drug - Misuse of Drugs Act 1971 s.4 1971 c. 38

Possession of a Class C drug with intent to supply - Misuse of Drugs Act 1971 s.5(3) 1971 c. 38

Fraudulent evasion of controls on Class C drugs - Customs and Excise Management Act 1979 s.170(2)(b), (c) 1979 c. 2

Illegal importation of Class C drugs - Customs and Excise Management Act 1979 s.50 1979 c. 2

Possession of Class A drug - Misuse of Drugs Act 1971 s.5(2) 1971 c. 38

Failure to disclose knowledge or suspicion of money laundering - Drug Trafficking Offences
Act 1986 s.26B 1986 c. 32

Tipping-off in relation to money laundering investigations - Drug Trafficking Offences Act 1986 s.26C 1986 c. 32

Assaults on officers saving wrecks - Offences against the Person Act 1861 s.37 1861 c. 100

Attempting to injure or alarm the Sovereign - Treason Act 1842 s.2 1842 c. 51

Assisting illegal entry or harbouring persons - Immigration Act 1971 s.25 1971 c. 77

Administering poison with intent to injure, etc. - Offences against the Person Act 1861 s. 24 1861 c. 100

Neglecting to provide food for or assaulting servants, etc. Offences against the Person Act 1861 s.31

Setting spring guns with intent to inflict grievous bodily harm Offences against the Person Act 1861 s.26

Supplying instrument, etc. to cause miscarriage - Offences against the Person Act 1861 s.59

Failure to disclose information about terrorism - Terrorism Act 2000 s.19 2000 c. 11

Circumcision of females -Prohibition of Female Circumcision Act 1985 s.1 1985 c. 38

Breaking or injuring submarine telegraph cables - Submarine Telegraph Act 1885 s.3 1885 c. 49

Failing to keep dogs under proper control resulting in injury - Dangerous Dogs Act 1991 s.3 1991 c. 65

Making gunpowder etc. to commit offences - Offences against the Person Act 1861 s.64

Stirring up racial hatred - Public Order Act 1986 ss.18-23 1986 c. 64

Class D: Sexual offences and offences against children

Administering drugs to obtain intercourse - Sexual Offences Act 1956 s.4 1956 c.69

Gross indecency between male of 21 or over and male under 16 - Sexual Offences Act 1956 s.13 1956 c.69

Indecent assault on a woman - Sexual Offences Act 1956 s.14 1956 c.69

Indecent assault on a man - Sexual Offences Act 1956 s.15 1956 c.69

Abuse of position of trust - Sexual Offences (Amendment) Act 2000 s.3 2000 c. 44

Man living on earnings of prostitution - Sexual Offences Act 1956 s.30 1956 c.69

Woman exercising control over prostitute - Sexual Offences Act 1956 s.31 1956 c.69

Living on earnings of male prostitution - Sexual Offences Act 1967 s.51967 c. 60

Incitement to commit incest - Criminal Law Act 1977 s.54 1977 c. 45

Ill-treatment of persons of unsound mind - Mental Health Act 1983 s.127

Abduction of unmarried girl under 18 from parent -Sexual Offences Act 1956 s.19

Abduction of defective from parent - Sexual Offences Act 1956 s.21

Procuration of girl under 21 - Sexual Offences Act 1956 s.23

Procurement of a defective to use premises for intercourse - Sexual Offences Act 1956 s.9 1956 c.69

Incest other than by man with a girl under 13 - Sexual Offences Act 1956 ss.10 and 11 1861 c. 100 1956 c.69

Gross indecency between male of 21 or over and male under 16 - Sexual Offences Act 1956 s.13

Incitement to commit incest - Criminal Law Act 1977 s.54 1977 c. 45

Ill-treatment of persons of unsound mind - Mental Health Act 1983 s.127 1983 c. 20

Abduction of defective from parent - Sexual Offences Act 1956 s.21 1956 c. 69

Causing or encouraging prostitution of defective - Sexual Offences Act 1956 s.29

Sexual assault - Sexual Offences Act 2003 s.3 2003 c. 42

Causing sexual activity without penetration - Sexual Offences Act 2003 s. 4 2003 c. 42

Engaging in sexual activity in the presence of a child - Sexual Offences Act 2003 s. 11 2003 c. 42

Causing a child to watch a sexual act - Sexual Offences Act 2003 s. 12 2003 c. 42

Child sex offence committed by person under 18 - Sexual Offences Act 2003 s. 13 2003 c. 42

Meeting child following sexual grooming - Sexual Offences Act 2003 s. 15 2003 c. 42

Abuse of trust: sexual activity with a child - Sexual Offences Act 2003 s. 16 2003 c. 42

Abuse of position of trust: causing a child to engage in sexual activity - Sexual Offences Act 2003 s. 17 2003 c. 42

Abuse of trust: sexual activity in the presence of a child - Sexual Offences Act 2003 s. 18 2003 c. 42

Abuse of position of trust: causing a child to watch sexual activity - Sexual Offences Act 2003 s. 19 2003 c. 42

Engaging in sexual activity in the presence of a person with a mental disorder- Sexual Offences Act 2003 s. 32 2003 c. 42

Causing a person with a mental disorder to watch a sexual act - Sexual Offences Act 2003 s. 33

Engaging in sexual activity in the presence of a person with a mental disorder - Sexual Offences Act 2003 s. 36 2003 c. 42

Causing a person with a mental disorder to watch a sexual act - Sexual Offences Act 2003 s. 37

Care workers: sexual activity in presence of a person with a mental disorder - Sexual Offences Act 2003 s. 40 2003 c. 42

Care workers: causing a person with a mental disorder to watch a sexual act - Sexual Offences Act 2003 s. 41 2003 c. 42

Causing or inciting prostitution for gain - Sexual Offences Act 2003 s. 52 2003 c. 42

Controlling prostitution for gain - Sexual Offences Act 2003 s. 53 2003 c. 42

Administering a substance with intent - Sexual Offences Act 2003 s. 61 2003 c. 42

Committing an offence with intent to commit a sexual offence - Sexual Offences Act 2003 s. 62 2003 c. 42

Trespass with intent to commit sexual offence Sexual Offences Act 2003 s. 632003 c. 42

Sex with adult relative - Sexual Offences Act 2003 s. 64, 65 2003 c. 42

Exposure - Sexual Offences Act 2003 s. 66 2003 c. 42

Voyeurism - Sexual Offences Act 2003 s. 67 2003 c. 42

Intercourse with an animal - Sexual Offences Act 2003 s. 69 2003 c. 42

Sexual penetration of a corpse - Sexual Offences Act 2003 s. 70 2003 c. 42

Class E: Burglary etc

Burglary (domestic) - Theft Act 1968 s.9(3)(a) 1968 c. 60

Going equipped to steal - Theft Act 1968 s.25 1968 c. 60

Burglary (non-domestic) - Theft Act 1968 s.9(3)(b) 1968 c. 60

Classes F, G and K: Other offences of dishonesty

The following offences are always in class F

Destruction of registers of births, etc. - Forgery Act 1861 s. 36 1861 c. 98

Making false entries in copies of registers sent to register - Forgery Act 1861 s.37 1861 c. 98

Possession (with intention) of false identity documents - Identity Cards Act 2006 c.15 s.25(1)

Possession (with intention) of apparatus or material for making false identity documents - Identity Cards Act 2006 s.25

Possession (without reasonable excuse) of false identity documents or apparatus or material for making false identity documents - Identity Cards Act 2006 s.25(5)

The following offences are always in class G

Undischarged bankrupt being concerned in a company - Insolvency Act 1986 s. 360 1986 c.45

Counterfeiting notes and coins - Forgery and Counterfeiting Act 1981 s.14 1981 c. 45

Passing counterfeit notes and coins - Forgery and Counterfeiting Act 1981 s.15 1981 c. 45

Offences involving custody or control of counterfeit notes and coins - Forgery and Counterfeiting Act 1981 s.16 1981 c. 45

Making, custody or control of counterfeiting materials, etc. - Forgery and Counterfeiting Act 1981 s. 175 1981 c. 45

Illegal importation: counterfeit notes or coins - Customs and Excise Management Act 1979 s.50

1979 c. 2

Fraudulent evasion: counterfeit notes or coins - Customs and Excise Management Act 1979 s.170(2)(b), (c) 1979 c. 2

The following offences are in class G if the value involved exceeds £30,000, class K if the value exceeds £100,000 and in class F otherwise

VAT offences - Value Added Tax Act 1994 1994 c.23 s. 72(1-8)

Fraudulent evasion of duty - Customs and Excise Management Act 1979 s. 1979 c. 2

170(1)(b)

Theft - Theft Act 1968 s.1 1968 c. 60

Removal of articles from places open to the public - Theft Act 1968 s.11 1968 c. 60

Abstraction of electricity - Theft Act 1968 s.13 1968 c. 60

Obtaining property by deception - Theft Act 1968 s.15 1968 c. 60

Obtaining pecuniary advantage by deception - Theft Act 1968 s.1 1968 c. 60

False accounting - Theft Act 1968 s.17 1968 c. 60

Handling stolen goods - Theft Act 1968 s.22 1968 c. 60

Obtaining services by deception - Theft Act 1978 s.1 1978 c. 31

Evasion of liability by deception - Theft Act 1978 s.2 1978 c. 31

Illegal importation: not elsewhere specified - Customs and Excise Management Act 1979 s.50

Counterfeiting Customs documents - Customs and Excise Management Act 1979 s.168

Fraudulent evasion: not elsewhere specified - Customs and Excise Management Act 1979 s.170(2)(b), (c) 1979 c. 2

Forgery - Forgery and Counterfeiting Act 1981 s.1 1981 c. 45

Copying false instrument with intent - Forgery and Counterfeiting Act 1981 s.2 1981 c. 45

Using a false instrument - Forgery and Counterfeiting Act 1981 s.3 1981 c. 45

Using a copy of a false instrument - Forgery and Counterfeiting Act 1981 s.4 1981 c. 45

Custody or control of false instruments etc. - Forgery and Counterfeiting Act 1981 s.5 1981 c. 45

Offences in relation to dies or stamps - Stamp Duties Management Act 1891 s.13 1891 c. 38

Counterfeiting of dies or marks - Hallmarking Act 1973 s.6 1973 c. 43

Fraud by false representation - Fraud Act 2006 s.2 2006 c.35 2006 c.35

Fraud by failing to disclose information - Fraud Act 2006 s.3 2006 c.35

Fraud by abuse of position - Fraud Act 2006 s.4 - As above 2006 c.35

Possession, etc. of articles for use in frauds - Fraud Act 2006 s.6 2006 c.35

Making or supplying articles for use in frauds - Fraud Act 2006 s.7 2006 c.35

Participating in fraudulent business carried on by sole trader etc. - Fraud Act 2006 s.9 Obtaining services dishonestly - Fraud Act 2006 s.11 2006 c.35

Class H: miscellaneous other offences

Breach of anti-social behaviour order - Crime and Disorder Act 1998 s. 1(10) 1998 c. 37

Breach of sex offender order - Crime and Disorder Act 1998 s. 2(8) 1998 c. 37

Racially-aggravated public order offence - Crime and Disorder Act 1998 s. 31(1) 1998 c. 37

Racially aggravated harassment/putting another in fear of violence - Crime and Disorder 1998 s. 32(1)

Having an article with a blade or point in a public - Criminal Justice Act 1988 s. 1988 c. 33 place 139

Breach of harassment injunction - Protection from Harassment 1997 c. 40 Act 1997 s. 3(6)

Putting people in fear of violence - Protection from Harassment Act 1997 s. 4(1)

Breach of restraining order - Protection from Harassment As above Act 1997 s. 5(5)

Being drunk on an aircraft - Air Navigation Order 2005,S.I. article 75 2005/1970

Possession of offensive weapon - Prevention of Crime Act 1953 c. 14 1953 s.1

Affray - Public Order Act 1986 s.3 1986 c. 64

Assault with intent to resist arrest - Offences against the Person Act 1861 s.38 1861 c. 100

Unlawful eviction and harassment of occupier - Protection from Eviction Act 1977 c. 43 1977 s.1

Obscene articles intended for publication for gain - Obscene Publications Act 1964 c. 74 1964 s.1

Gross indecency between males (other than Sexual Offences Act 1956 1956 c. 69 where one is 21 or over and the other is under 16) s.13

Solicitation for immoral purposes - Sexual Offences Act 1956 s.32 1956 c. 69

Buggery of males of 16 or over otherwise than in private - Sexual Offences Act 1956 s.12 as above

Acts outraging public decency - Common law

Offences of publication of obscene matter - Obscene Publications Act 1959 s.2 1959 c. 66

Keeping a disorderly house - Common law; Disorderly Houses Act 1751 s.8 1751 c. 36

Indecent display - Indecent Displays (Control) Act 1981 s.1 1981 c. 42

Presentation of obscene performance - Theatres Act 1968 s.2 1968 c. 54

Procurement of intercourse by threats, etc. - Sexual Offences Act 1956 s. 2 1956 c. 69

Causing prostitution of women - Sexual Offences Act 1956 s.22 1956 c. 69

Detention of woman in brothel or other premises - Sexual Offences Act 1956 s.24

Procurement of a woman by false pretences - Sexual Offences Act 1956 s.3

Procuring others to commit homosexual acts - Sexual Offences Act 1967 s.41967 c. 60

Trade description offences (9 offences) - Trade Descriptions Act 1968 ss.1, 8, 9, 12, 13, 14 1968 c. 29

Misconduct endangering ship or persons on board ship - Merchant Shipping Act 1970 s.27 1970 c. 36

Obstructing engine or carriage on railway - Malicious Damage Act 1861 s.36 1861 c. 97

Offences relating to the safe custody of controlled drugs - Misuse of Drugs Act 1971 s.11 1971 c. 38

Possession of Class B or C drug - Misuse of Drugs Act 1971 s.5(2) 1971 c. 38

Wanton or furious driving - Offences against the Person Act 1861 s.35 1861 c. 100

Dangerous driving - Road Traffic Act 1988 s.2 1988 c. 52

Forgery and misuse of driving documents - Public Passenger Vehicles Act 1981 s.65 1981 c. 14

Forgery of driving documents - Road Traffic Act 1960 s.233 1960 c. 16

Forgery etc. of licences and other documents - Road Traffic Act 1988 s.173 1988 c. 52

Mishandling or falsifying parking documents, etc. - Road Traffic Regulation Act 1984 s. 115 1984 c. 27

Aggravated vehicle taking - Theft Act 1968 s.12A 1968 c. 60

Forgery, alteration, fraud of licences etc. - Vehicle Excise and Registration Act 1994 s.44 1994 c.22

Making off without payment - Theft Act 1978 s 3 1978 c. 31

Agreeing to indemnify sureties - Bail Act 1976 s.9(1) - 1976 c. 63

Sending prohibited articles by post - Post Office Act 1953 s.11 1953 c. 36

Impersonating Customs officer - Customs and Excise Management Act 1979 s.13 1979 c. 2

Obstructing a Customs officer - Customs and Excise Management Act 1979 s. 16 1979 c. 2

Class I: Offences against public justice and similar offences

Conspiring to commit offences outside the United Kingdom - Criminal Justice (Terrorism and Conspiracy) Act 1998 s. 5 1998 c.40

Perverting the course of public justice - Common law

Perjuries (7 offences) - Perjury Act 1911 ss.1-7(2) 1911 c. 6

Corrupt transactions with agents - Prevention of Corruption Act 1906 s.1 1906 c. 34

Corruption in public office - Public Bodies Corrupt Practices Act 1889 s.1 1889 c. 69

Embracery - Common law

Fabrication of evidence with intent to mislead a tribunal - Common law

Personation of jurors - Common law

Concealing an arrestable offence - Criminal Law Act 1967 s.5 1967 c. 58

Assisting offenders - Criminal Law Act 1967 s.4(1)

False evidence before European Court - European Communities Act 1972 s.11 1972 c. 68

Personating for purposes of bail, etc. - Forgery Act 1861 s. 34 1861 c. 98

Intimidating a witness, juror, etc. - Criminal Justice and Public Order Act 1994 s.51(1)

Harming, threatening to harm a witness, juror, etc. - Criminal Justice and Public Order Act 1994 s.51(2)

Prejudicing a drug trafficking investigation - Drug Trafficking Act 1994 s.58(1) 1994 c. 33 1994 c. 37

Giving false statements to procure cremation - Cremation Act 1902 s.8(2) 1902 c. 8

False statement tendered -under section 9 - Criminal Justice Act 1967

Making a false statement to obtain interim possession order - Criminal Justice Act 1967 s.89 1967 c. 80

Making false statement to resist making of interim possession order - Criminal Justice and Public

Order Act 1994 s.75(1)Criminal Justice and Public Order Act 1994 s.75(2) 1994 c. 33

False statement tendered under section 5B of the Magistrates' Courts Act 1980 - Magistrates' Courts Act 1980 s.106 1980 c. 43

Making false statement to authorised officer - Trade Descriptions Act 1968 s.29(2) 1968 c. 29

Class J: Serious Sexual Offences

Rape - Sexual Offences Act 1956 s.1(1) 1956 c. 69

Sexual intercourse with girl under 13 - Sexual Offences Act 1956 s.5 1956 c. 69

Sexual intercourse with girl under 16 - Sexual Offences Act 1956 s.6 1956 c. 69

Sexual intercourse with defective - Sexual Offences Act 1956 s.7 1956 c. 69

Incest by man with a girl under 13 - Sexual Offences Act 1956 s. 10 1956 c. 69

Buggery of person under 16 - Sexual Offences Act 1956 s.12 1956 c. 69

Indecency with children under 14 -Indecency with Children Act 1960 s.1(1) 1960 c. 33

Taking, having etc. indecent photographs of children - Protection of Children Act 1978 s.1 1978 c. 37

Assault with intent to commit buggery - Sexual Offences Act 1956 s.1 1956 c. 69

Abduction of woman by force - Sexual Offences Act 1956 s.17 1956 c. 69

Permitting girl under 13 to use premises for sexual intercourse - Sexual Offences Act 1956 s.25 1956 c. 69

Allowing or procuring child under 16 to go abroad to perform - Children and Young Persons Act 1933 ss.25, 26 1933 c. 12

Sexual intercourse with patients - Mental Health Act 1959 s.128 1959 c. 72

Abduction of unmarried girl under 16 from parent - Sexual Offences Act 1956 s.20 1956 c.69

Permitting girl under 16 to use premises for intercourse - Sexual Offences Act 1956 s.26

Causing or encouraging prostitution of girl under 16 - Sexual Offences Act 1956 s.28

Rape - Sexual Offences Act 2003 s. 1 2003 c. 42

Assault by penetration - Sexual Offences Act 2003 s. 2 2003 c. 42

Causing sexual activity with penetration - Sexual Offences Act 2003 s. 4 2003 c. 42

Rape of child under 13 - Sexual Offences Act 2003 s. 5 2003 c. 42

Assault of child under 13 by penetration - Sexual Offences Act 2003 s. 6 2003 c. 42

Sexual assault of child under 13 - Sexual Offences Act 2003 s. 7 2003 c. 42

Causing a child under 13 to engage in sexual activity - Sexual Offences Act 2003 s. 8 2003 c. 42

Sexual activity with a child - Sexual Offences Act 2003 s. 9

Causing a child to engage in sexual activity - Sexual Offences Act 2003 s. 10

Arranging child sex offence - Sexual Offences Act 2003 s. 14

Sexual activity with a child, family member, with penetration - Sexual Offences Act 2003s. 25

Inciting a child, family member to engage in sexual activity - Sexual Offences Act 2003 s. 26

Sexual activity with a person with a mental disorder - Sexual Offences Act 2003 s. 30

Causing or inciting a person with a mental disorder to engage in sexual activity - Sexual Offences Act 2003 s. 31

Offering inducement to procure sexual activity with a person with a mental disorder - Sexual Offences Act 2003 s. 34

Inducing person with mental disorder to engage in sexual activity Sexual Offences Act 2003 s. 35

Care workers: sexual activity with a person with a mental disorder - Sexual Offences Act 2003 s. 38

Care workers: inciting person with mental disorder to engage in sexual act - Sexual Offences Act 2003 s. 39

Paying for sexual services of a child - Sexual Offences Act 2003 s. 47

Causing or inciting child prostitution or pornography - Sexual Offences Act 2003 s. 48

Controlling a child prostitute - Sexual Offences Act 2003 s. 49

Facilitating child prostitution - Sexual Offences Act 2003 s. 50

Trafficking into UK for sexual exploitation - Sexual Offences Act 2003 s. 57

Trafficking within UK for sexual exploitation - Sexual Offences Act 2003 s. 58

Trafficking out of UK for sexual exploitation - Sexual Offences Act 2003 s. 59

Class K: Other offences of dishonesty (high value)

Class K offences are listed under Class F and G.

Printed in Great Britain
by Amazon